WITHDRAWN

Cadres, Commanders, and Commissars

Studies of the East Asian Institute
Columbia University

Westview Special Studies on China and East Asia

Women in Changing Japan
Edited by Joyce Lebra, Joy Paulson, and Elizabeth Powers

Cadres, Commanders, and Commissars: The Training of the Chinese Communist Leadership, 1920-45
Jane L. Price

This important study traces the evolution of the Chinese Communist educational system for higher-level leadership cadres, contending that it was this leadership education that gave the Communists an edge over the Nationalists and enabled them to engineer their revolutionary movement.Examining in detail the training programs at the Peasant Movement Training Institute, the Red Army Academy and Red Army School in Juichin, the Anti-Japanese Military and Political University, the Central Party School, and Yenan University, the author explores the relationship between careful preparation of elites and the Chinese Communists' strategy for revolution and nation-building that led to their takeover and reunification of China in 1949. The institutions discussed in the book produced many of China's ranking military and political leaders and developed the basic leadership models and styles of Chinese Communism that became a source of intra-elite tension. Thus, the molding of Chinese Communist cadres through education has had a major impact on the leadership structure and remains a prominent feature of Chinese political life.

Jane L. Price received her Ph.D. in East Asian History from Columbia University in 1974. She has taught at Columbia University, Barnard College, and the City University of New York and is currently a Research Associate.at the East Asian Institute of Columbia University.

Jane L. Price

Cadres, Commanders, and Commissars

The Training of the Chinese Communist
Leadership, 1920-45

Westview Press
Boulder, Colorado

for Annette Spear Price

Copyright 1976 by Westview Press, Inc.

Published 1976 in the United States of America by

Westview Press, Inc.
1898 Flatiron Court
Boulder, Colorado 80301
Frederick A. Praeger, Publisher and Editorial Director

Library of Congress Cataloging in Publication Data

Price, Jane L.   1945—
  Cadres, commanders, and commissars.

  Bibliography: p.
  1. Communism—China. 2. Communist education. 3. Leadership.
I. Title.
HX388.5.P74 1975   335.43'4'071151   75-25612
ISBN 0-89158-001-8

Printed in the United States of America.

The East Asian Institute of Columbia University was established
in 1949 to prepare graduate students for careers dealing with East
Asia, and to aid research and publication on East Asia during the
modern period. The faculty of the Institute are grateful to the
Ford Foundation and the Rockefeller Foundation for their
financial assistance.

The Studies of the East Asian Institute were inaugurated in 1962
to bring to a wider public the results of significant new research
on modern and contemporary East Asia.

Acknowledgments

This book began as a doctoral dissertation at Columbia University. I am deeply indebted to Professors C. Martin Wilbur and James P. Harrison, who were my principal readers and critics. Their interest, concern, and commitment sustained me throughout all phases of the project. Professors Michel Oksenberg, C. T. Hu, and Loren Graham provided many stimulating comments and suggestions. Professors Andrew Nathan and Donald Zagoria gave many hours of time and effort to reviewing the study at the book stage, and I am especially grateful for their scholarly advice. The book could not have been completed without contributions from Professors Peter Seybolt, Ilpyong Kim, William Dorrill, Roy Hofheinz, Robert Burton, Donald Klein, and Lynda Shaffer as well as Phyllis Andors, Kathy Bloomgarden, David Tseng, C. P. Ch'en, John S. Service, and Richard Sorich. I would also like to thank the Woodrow Wilson Foundation for its financial support during the early stages of the project and the East Asian Institute of Columbia University, the Center for Chinese Studies of the University of California at Berkeley, and the East Asia Collection of the Hoover Institution on War, Revolution and Peace, for granting me research privileges.

Jane L. Price
New York, N.Y.
August 1975

229096

Contents

1 Introduction

A distinctive feature of Chinese Communism has been its continuing concern with leadership questions. Periodic rectification campaigns and mass movements directed against alleged abuses of the Party vanguard highlight Chinese political life. The Chinese Communists have created an extensive literature on the principles and methods of leadership, especially for the leadership cadres that link state and society. Along with traditional habits and customs, conflicts among interest groups, and the limits of technology and human nature, the quality of leadership determines the management and transformation of Chinese civilization.[1]

Chinese Communism develops much of its leadership talent through *hsüeh-hsi* or formal study. Communist cadres at all levels spend considerable time in training programs that range from small study groups to high-level Party schools. Leadership talent, as developed through education, is thought to have a close relationship to political effectiveness.

This approach to education and leadership doctrine took form during the Chinese Communists' struggle for power before 1949. The Chinese Communists took seriously Stalin's dictum that "cadres decide everything" and found their leadership resources perhaps their most valuable asset. Throughout their history they allocated a large portion of their human and material reserves to programs that fashioned men and women into political instruments. The question of how Chinese Communism

1

trained its leadership is thus fundamental to understanding its evolution and prospects for the future.

Unlike the Bolsheviks, the Chinese Communists did not come to power through a coup d'état unleashed by spontaneous mass uprisings they could not control. Their victory in 1949 represented an achievement in social engineering—a multiclass, multi-issue movement that balanced nationalism with social revolution.[2] The Party's ability to orchestrate multiple interest groups, issues, and activities within one political movement depended heavily on its leadership and organizational skills.

The rural setting in which Chinese Communism took root placed severe strains on its organizational capacity. Relative to the urban proletariat, the Chinese peasantry proved much more difficult to mobilize on a long-term basis. The Chinese Communists' first recorded encounter with peasant organizing illustrates the magnitude of the problem:

> A peasant some thirty years of age in the village saw me coming and said to me while shoveling manure in front of the village: "Sir! Please sit down and have a smoke. Did you come to collect taxes? We do not have any entertainment here." I replied, "I didn't come to collect entertainment taxes. I have come to make friends with you. Because you are suffering, I came here to talk with you." The peasant replied, "Ah! Life is suffering. Sir, please have some tea. Please forgive me but we haven't the time to talk with you." Having spoken these words, he ran away.[3]

Other times, as Mao Tse-tung observed, the peasants could erupt spontaneously "like a mighty storm, like a hurricane, a force so swift and violent that no power, however great, will be able to hold it back."[4]

Further limiting the potential for rural revolution were a host of counterrevolutionary pressures. They ranged from armed militia on the local level, to warlord forces on the regional level, to the army of the National Government on the transregional level, and between 1937 and 1945 the army of Japan was added to these groups. In confronting the challenges of these counterrevolutionary pressures, the Chinese Communists developed their own armed forces and allocated a large portion of their meager material and manpower reserves to military activities.

Heavy reliance on the military during more than twenty years of struggle generated its own set of problems. Militarization had been a growing trend in Chinese political life since the mid-nineteenth century, a trend which other political movements—to varying degrees—found difficult to control. Could the Chinese Communists keep their military operations in line with their general political objectives? Or would their armies fall back into "warlord" patterns, carving out regional "kingdoms" impervious to outside constraints?

Militarization did not mean that the Chinese Communists were victorious by wresting power from another group. The erosion of traditional Chinese civilization through imperialism, war, and partial modernization had left an institutional vacuum that other political forces could not fill. Any political movement seeking to reunify China had "to make power, to mobilize groups into politics and organize their participation in politics."[5]

The Chinese Communists outpaced their rivals by creating new political and economic forms that tapped the grass roots level for the first time in Chinese history. The institutional framework through which they built power became the basis of national reconstruction from a "heap of loose sand." To supply skills for nation-building, the Communists recruited the educated elite, especially "intellectuals" from China's urban areas. Nonpeasant elites spearheaded the Communists' mobilization and modernization drives in their rural base areas.[6]

Many among the educated who joined the Communists occupied a pivotal position in Chinese political life. They could have swung toward the National Government or other political contenders. Most—including the founders of the Chinese Communist Party themselves—were first attracted to the nationalist, anti-imperialist content of Communism. To absorb this critical elite the Chinese Communist Party had to reconcile this group's outlook with the demands of peasant revolution.

The Chinese Communists' victory in 1949 represents more than a small group's rise to rule one-fourth of humanity. It is also the story of how one set of dedicated individuals succeeded where all others failed in building a viable and cohesive organization. The Communists as well as their adversaries started out with odds weighing heavily against them. After the 1911 revolution—under the Republican political culture characterized by strong tendencies toward factionalism, militarism, official inertia, and mass apathy—most political groups were quickly fragmented and paralyzed. The National Government was unable to eliminate regional militarists or take hold of the Chinese countryside. Its leadership was caught up in intricate maneuvers among competing factions. Most of the National Government's resources were spent on conserving what little power it had. Preoccupied with self-preservation, it could neither reunify nor rebuild Chinese civilization.[7]

The Chinese Communists were never monolithic, but they were able to overcome these problems. They brought unity to China for the first time since the T'ai-p'ing Rebellion (1850-1864). And they achieved, in rapid measure, a degree of centralization that even the imperial system at its peak could not match. They have not limited their role to that of guardians of stability and order, and they have continued to launch dramatic changes to give China a modern form.

For many years scholars of modern China have debated the factors behind the "success story" of Chinese Communism.[8] My approach to this question draws attention to organizational issues. It attempts to explain the relationship between the manner in which the Chinese Communists prepared their leadership and their ability to weld diverse interest groups, issues, and activities into a cohesive political force.

Other factors besides formal training have governed the formation of Chinese Communist leadership. The Chinese Communists had more cautious recruitment policies than those of their adversaries.[9] They generally made leaders of individuals who had a high degree of commitment even before joining the Party. Ideological correctness, class background, and the will to struggle and sacrifice have all—in changing proportions—been important criteria for leadership selection. The Chinese Communists have periodically shaped their elites through purges and mass campaigns. Revolutionary life itself, with the "steeling" effect of trials such as the Long March, has also bolstered the Chinese Communist leaders' discipline and solidarity.

Nevertheless, without leadership training the Chinese Communists' growth as a political movement would have been severely retarded. Tasks such as the management of class struggle, institution-building, and the exercise of arms were too far-ranging and complex for manpower without special skills. Also, Chinese Communism drew a number of social types with varying degrees of commitment to Communism and varying interpretations of Communist beliefs: the outlook of a peasant Communist was not the same as that of a Communist intellectual or soldier. Further transformation had to take place to give all Communists a common set of goals and values. Leadership training programs helped the Chinese Communists to creatively reconcile diversity with unity. The programs defined the relationship between the Party's general objectives and specific military, administrative, and mobilization activities. They have also provided centers to recharge and sustain commitment.

This book traces the growing political effectiveness of Chinese Communism, as seen through its study programs that prepared predominantly higher-level leaders, from just before the founding of the Party to the end of the Sino-Japanese War. During this time a small coterie of alienated intellectuals mushroomed into a vanguard of over one million that controlled one-third of China. Facilities to train Communist leaders began as exclusive study groups imparting radical rhetoric and grew into a vast network of training programs for proletarian and peasant organizers, Party functionaires, educators, theorists, bureaucrats, technicians, military commanders, and political commissars for all levels of Communist operations. Procedures developed in training programs before 1945 still govern the preparation of Chinese Communist leaders today.

LEADERSHIP AND EDUCATION IN TRADITIONAL AND TRANSITIONAL CHINA

Behind the Chinese Communists' approach to leadership issues is the heritage of traditional Chinese political life. Many observers have commented upon the durability and sophistication of the imperial machinery of state that commanded one of the world's largest premodern empires. However, the Chinese bureaucracy was still a traditional one, without access to modern technology or communications. Its effectiveness depended not only on its design but on the quality of its leadership.

The input of leadership into traditional institutions was very much like the relationship described by Chalmers Johnson:

> Karl Popper once said, "Institutions are like fortresses. They must be well designed and properly manned." In practice, a well designed set of institutions can go a long way toward compensating for poor elite role performances and conversely, a high order of political

leadership will occasionally make the most rickety of institutions function extraordinarily well.[10]

That the Chinese placed much of the responsibility for ordering human affairs with leadership itself can be seen in Confucian pronouncements favoring "men of ability"[11] over formal techniques or organizational structures.

The primary means of preparing elites in traditional China for government service was through education. One's ability to master a corpus of specified materials—the Confucian classics— was thought to develop the appropriate ethical qualities for governing others. Omnicompetence took precedence over practical skills, nurtured by the belief that right thought bred right conduct. Elites were recruited and selected through a series of civil service examinations that were all based on the same texts. The whole educational and testing system was designed to unify officials' behavior and outlook, to add cultural cement to a centralized state.

Preparation for civil service examinations took place in a variety of learning institutions—family schools, clan schools, village schools, charitable schools, and academies. The educational experience at these schools affected the nature of the leadership they produced. Other than at the academies, which functioned as high-level centers of scholarship and research, instruction took the form of rote memorization under the guidance of an authoritarian teacher.[12] The elite produced under these conditions was geared for a traditional society that idealized stability, models from the past, and a course of moderation. There was no glorification of vigorous martial qualities or skills that could press for far-reaching change.

A carefully chosen and cultivated elite helps to account for the longevity of traditional Chinese civilization. But what worked well for the Middle Kingdom for over two thousand years could not withstand the impact of the West in the nineteenth and twentieth centuries. After the Opium War the system that had molded leaders in the imperial period became a major obstacle to modernization.

From the T'ai-p'ing Rebellion onward, revolutionary momentum built up for a total overhaul of traditional Chinese civilization. It marked a radical departure from pre-nineteenth century forms of opposition. Neither the conventional protests of scholarly and bureaucratic cliques nor the antiestablishment activities of popular heroes, bandit gangs, secret societies, and peasant rebels had previously sought more than to correct imbalances in the standing political and social framework.

Like the imperial state, successful forms of opposition, too, depended upon effective leadership. Well-disciplined and far-sighted leaders could turn a local uprising into a major peasant rebellion. The first peasant movement to pose an alternative to the traditional order, the T'ai-p'ing Rebellion, failed in part because it lacked reliable leadership cadres.[13] Secret societies, sustained for centuries by strict disciplinary codes and initiation rites, furnished early organizational models for the revolutionaries of 1911 and 1949.[14]

The radicals of 1911 had called for eliminating foreign influence in China along with the traditional political and social system. In pursuit of these ends they drew on both the tradition of scholarly protest and the romantic images of knights errant, self-sacrificing Bodhisattvas, and popular heroes. Without a coherent ideology and organization, their vehement personal protests often became ends in themselves.

The radicals did instill some discipline and solidarity through education. Many Chinese educational centers were points of contact and preparation for 1911 leaders. They provided settings for informal "student circles" that exchanged new ideas. Occasionally, potential revolutionaries were prepared at specific schools, the most notable being the Patriotic School set up by the Chinese Educational Association in Shanghai in 1903.[15] However, formal education itself was not an important instrument of radical politics at this time.

The 1911 milieu and traditional styles of leadership and protest formed the backdrop for Chinese Communist leadership policy. The Chinese Communist Party started out as a product of radical elite activity stimulated by 1911 and the May Fourth Movement. One will find the first Chinese Communists nurtured in learning centers, employing education to sharpen their political skills.

However, the evolution of Chinese Communism reflected important qualitative changes in the Chinese revolutionary environment. From the May Fourth period onward, revolutionary goals became much more explicit. They made clearcut targets out of foreign imperialism, residual tradition, and the prevailing system of economic and social relationships. Most significant, in comparison to the anarchists, 1911 revolutionaries, and premodern forms of protests, May Fourth radicals adopted a distinct model for opposition politics—the strategy of class conflict and the Leninist revolutionary party.   These were the means and ends that inspired the Chinese Communists' approach to leadership and political life.

NOTES

[1]My own research on Chinese Communist agrarian policy in 1947-48 and the study by Thomas Bernstein on collectivization in China and the USSR have shown that the quality of leadership was decisive in furthering very ambitious social, economic, and political goals.   See Jane L. Price, "Chinese Communist Land Reform and Peasant Mobilization, 1947-48" (unpublished East Asian Institute Essay, Columbia University, 1970) and Thomas P. Bernstein, "Leadership and Mass Mobilization in the Soviet and Chinese Collectivisation Campaigns of 1929-30 and 1955-56: A Comparison," *China Quarterly*, no. 31 (July-September 1967), pp. 9-12, 20-26.

[2]On contrasts between the Bolshevik and Chinese Communist revolutionary strategy see Seweryn Bialer, "Leninism and the Peasantry in the Russian Revolutions," SEADAG Rural Development Seminar, Savannah, Georgia, June 2-5, 1974. See also Stephen F. Cohen, *Bukharin and the Bolshevik Revolution: A Political Biography 1888-1938* (New York: Alfred A. Knopf, 1973), pp. 46-54.

[3]My translation of P'eng P'ai's account of his first rural organizing experience in May 1922. P'eng P'ai, "Hai-feng-nung-min yün-tung" [The Hai-feng Peasant Movement], *Ti-i-tz'u kuo-nei chan-cheng shih-ch'i ti nung-min yun-tung* [The Peasant Movement During the First Revolutionary Civil War] (Peking: Jen-min ch'u-pan she, 1953), p. 52.

[4]Mao Tse-tung, "Report on an Investigation of the Peasant Movement in Hunan," *Selected Works*, vol. 1 (Peking: Foreign Language Press, 1965), p. 23.

[5]Samuel P. Huntington, *Political Order in Changing Societies* (New Haven: Yale University Press, 1968), pp. 144-145.

[6]For Ying-mao Kao's discussion of the role of cities and towns in providing the Chinese Communist movement's top and middle-level leadership, see "Urban and Rural Strategies in the Chinese Communist Revolution," *Peasant Rebellion and Communist Revolution in Asia* (Stanford, Calif.: Stanford University Press, 1974), pp. 254-270.

[7]This discussion is based on the analysis of the National Government and the Republican period of Chinese history in Lloyd Eastman, *The Abortive Revolution: China under Nationalist Rule 1927-1937* (Cambridge, Mass.: Harvard University Press, 1974).

[8]The studies that have shaped the "debate" on the sources of Chinese Communist victory are Chalmers Johnson, *Peasant Nationalism and Communist Power: The Emergence of Revolutionary China 1937-1945* (Stanford, Calif.: Stanford University Press, 1962); Donald Gillin, " 'Peasant Nationalism' in the History of Chinese Communism," *Journal of Asian Studies*, 23, no. 2 (February 1964); Roy Hofheinz Jr., "The Ecology of Chinese Communist Success: Rural Influence Patterns, 1923-45," in *Chinese Communist Politics in Action*, ed. A. Doak Barnett (Seattle: University of Washington Press, 1969), pp. 3-77; and Tetsuya Kataoka, *Resistance and Revolution in China: The Communists and the Second United Front* (Berkeley and Los Angeles: University of California Press, 1974). Johnson and Gillin pit nationalism against the land revolution as the main issue by which the Communists mobilized their peasant base of support. Hofheinz's examination of the contribution of ecological factors, such as tenancy, political and cultural backwardness, and Western impact, to Communist strength questions simple monocausal factors. Kataoka suggests the importance of the united front in neutralizing the power of Nationalist forces and local counterrevolutionary groups in North China threatening to suppress Communist expansion.

[9]The National Government also did not make use of formal training to prepare most of its leaders. See Eastman, especially pp. 3-14, on leadership recruitment in the National Government.

10Quoted in Chalmers Johnson, *Revolutionary Change* (Boston: Little, Brown and Co., 1966), p. 88.

11See Mary C. Wright, *The Last Stand of Chinese Conservatism* (New York: Atheneum, 1966), especially pp. 68-69.

12Academy students were generally of much higher calibre than those preparing for examinations in conventional channels. Students were often accomplished scholars before matriculation. They spent most of their time studying on their own, with the role of their teacher confined to dispensing advice or criticism. On occasion scholars would lecture on a selected topic. On academies and traditional Chinese education see C.T. Hu, *Chinese Education Under Communism* (New York: Columbia University, Teachers College, 1962), pp. 12-13, and William Ayers, *Chang Chih-tung and Educational Reform in China* (Cambridge, Mass.: Harvard University Press, 1971), pp. 16, 54-61.

13Philip Kuhn, *Rebellion and Its Enemies in Late Imperial China* (Cambridge, Mass.: Harvard University Press, 1970), p. 195.

14On organizational features and initiation practices of secret societies, see Charlton M. Lewis, "Some Notes on the Ko-lao Hui in Late Ch'ing China," pp. 102-106, and Mark Mancall and Georges Jidkoff, "The Hung Hu-tzu of Northeast China," in *Popular Movements and Secret Societies in China 1840-1850*, ed. Jean Chesneaux (Stanford, Calif.: Stanford University Press, 1972), p. 128. Chu Te traced the use of cells in the Chinese Communist Party to *T'ung-meng hui* practices which emulated secret societies. Agnes Smedley, *The Great Road: The Life and Times of Chu Teh* (New York: Monthly Review Press, 1956), p. 87.

15This discussion of the 1911 revolutionaries and education is based on Mary Backus Rankin, *Early Chinese Revolutionaries: Radical Intellectuals in Shanghai and Chekiang, 1902-1911* (Cambridge, Mass.: Harvard University Press, 1971), pp. 1-39, 64-79. The Patriotic School taught conventional courses such as mathematics, science, history, philosophy, and literature. But the students it attracted were primarily radical youth whose exposure to modern subjects reinforced antitraditional attitudes. Students devoted most of their time to political discussions among themselves and to military drill. The Patriotic School became a model for other educational institutions for revolutionary intellectuals.

2   The Road to Revolution

Now let us consider those students who graduate and leave their
schools where they have been completely isolated from the practical
activities of society. In what position do they find themselves?[1]

Mao Tse-tung's indictment of ivory-tower intellectuals could well
have applied to the earliest leaders of the Chinese Communist
Party. They were primarily young middle-school and college
students with a deep hostility to the existing social order. They
were fascinated by Marxism's dramatic rhetoric and utopian
claims but had no idea of how to initiate revolutionary change.
Their first taste of revolution came through books and magazine
articles and they had little understanding of the workings of a
Communist party.

Yet the early Chinese Communists did not wait long to plunge
into revolutionary work. Well before the founding of the Party
they had taken to the streets to develop ties to the common
people. Through experiments in consciousness-raising, popular
education, and work and study abroad they acquired a rudi-
mentary organizational strategy and sense of political identity
that guided their first steps toward revolution.

MAY FOURTH STUDY SOCIETIES

Experiences growing out of the May Fourth Movement facilitated the Chinese Communists' transition from a bookish study
group to practitioners of radical politics. Stimulated by the

11

provocative melange of ideas in *New Youth (Hsin ch'ing-nien)* magazine, study groups dedicated to national regeneration sprung up in many Chinese urban centers. A number of these study societies became radicalized while exploring various ideologies, methods, and "isms" to set China on her feet. Their consciousness-raising activities were an early form of preparation for Chinese Communists.

One of the most famous of the May Fourth study societies was the New People's Study Society (*Hsin min hsüeh-hui*) organized by Mao Tse-tung and Ts'ai Ho-sen in Changsha. It held its first formal meeting on April 18, 1918, at Ts'ai's home, attended mainly by students from the First Normal School or other institutions in the Changsha vicinity.[2]

Society members were expected to adhere to a strict code of discipline that forbade gambling, frequenting prostitutes, and indolence. Those seeking admission to the society had to demonstrate high standards of learning and a desire to transform themselves to serve the nation. Meetings took place every one or two weeks. Each participant reported on individual work and study plans, and the group debated and criticized the ideas raised during the session. The society's concern with collective discussion and criticism, group discipline, and character development foreshadowed later Chinese Communist organizational trends.

Having grown to between eighty and ninety members by the May Fourth Incident, the New People's Study Society began to polarize politically in the beginning of 1920. After purging the rightists, those who remained active in the society, such as Kuo Liang, Hsia Hsi, and Hsiao Shu-fan, became the first members of the Hunan Socialist Youth League. This group in turn was absorbed into the Hunan branch of the Chinese Communist Party toward the end of 1921.

The New People's Study Society was but one of a number of *New Youth*-inspired radical study societies that nurtured future Chinese Communist leaders. Activists from the Tientsin Student Union and the Tientsin Association of Women Patriotic Comrades founded an Awakening Society (*Chüeh-wu she*) on September 16, 1919. Its leading members included Chou En-lai, Ma Chün, Teng Ying-ch'ao, Sun Hsiao-ching (later secretary of the Kuomintang Canton Committee), Kuo Lung-chen and Kuan Hsi-pin. The society began publishing its own magazine, *Awakenings (Chüeh-wu)*, in early 1920. A portion of the group later formed a Marxist Research Society, but the Awakening Society itself remained primarily anarchist.

Also in Tientsin, Chang T'ai-lei founded a Society for Socialist Reconstruction in February 1919 that led to the formation of a branch of the Socialist Youth League in October 1920. In Wuhan, Yün Tai-ying, Lin Piao, and his cousin Chang Hao organized in the fall of 1919 the Social Welfare Society (*She-hui fu-li hui*) and the Social Benefit Bookstore (*Li ch'ün shu-she*). Juan Hsiao-hsien in Hangchow set up a New Students' Society (*Hsin hsüeh-sheng she*) that issued the periodical *New Student* (*Hsin hsüeh-sheng*). Peking produced the Resurgence Society (*Fu she*) and similar groups operated in Shanghai and Hankow. Concentrating on the study of socialism, Li Ta-chao organized in Peking in the fall of 1918 a Marxist Research Society. It was superseded in December 1919 by the Society for the Study of Socialism and in March 1920 by the Marxist Theory Research Society.

Although the activities of the May Fourth study societies were primarily intellectual, their members had strong activist inclinations. Populist sentiment was high at this time among Chinese intellectuals, who could not identify with a traditional agrarian society in transition.[3] The desire to identify with the toiling masses found expression in numerous proposals to strengthen the nation by uplifting the common people. Striving to forge ties with the masses while rebuilding China, intellectuals initiated numerous popular-education projects.

Experiments in popular education had begun during World War I when several Chinese schools and universities opened night schools. After the May Fourth Incident many schools followed suit, offering evening sessions for workers and poor children.[4] Wall newspapers and public libraries proliferated at the same time to spread knowledge to the poor.

Li Ta-chao had been among the first Chinese Communists to propose that intellectuals "go to the people." Taking up the banner, Teng Chung-hsia, Chang Kuo-t'ao, Lo Chia-lun, Liao Shu-ts'ang, K'ang Pai-ch'ing, Yi K'e-ni, Chou Ping-lin, Hsü Te-heng, and Wang Kuang-ch'i organized a Mass Education Speech Corps in March of 1919.[5] The corps set up four lecture halls in the working class sections of Peking, printed speeches, and sponsored Sunday lectures on national salvation, the sufferings of the common man, popular culture, socialism, patriotism, the new ethics, scientific knowledge, the theory of mutual aid, Japanese aggression, the significance of reading, eliminating superstition, and Labor Day. In early 1920 the Mass Education Speech Corps moved into villages outside of Peking. Following the May Fourth Incident students throughout China launched similar drives to organize the masses.

The range of May Fourth activities—protests, demonstrations, and boycotts involving student alliances with merchants and workers— made a case for united action that had profound implications for Chinese political life. Armed with Marxist-Leninist theory and organizational models, the Chinese Communists transformed a loose association of education, self-transformation, national regeneration, and collective activity into a new style of Chinese politics.

THE IMPACT OF MARXIST THEORY

Much of the early Chinese Communist leadership emerged from the May Fourth intellectual circles that had become attracted to Marxism. Unlike European and Russian Marxists, these Chinese radicals did not brood for years over theory before stepping into political life.[6] Their rapid plunge into revolutionary work can be attributed to the strength of their activist tendencies and the nature of their first exposure to Marxist theory.

Before the May Fourth period Chinese discussions of socialism had taken place within a gradualist framework. Most works on socialist thought available in China before the Bolshevik Revolution treated socialism as a preventive against the "social problem" of capitalism—the unequal distribution of wealth which threatened social harmony. Early Chinese writings on socialism[7] did little to inspire political forms that used the forces of discontent as agents of rapid change.

Chinese interest in revolutionary socialism was stimulated by the Bolshevik Revolution and the May Fourth climate. After 1919 there appeared a flurry of translations of Marx, Engels,[8] and Lenin[9] along with Chinese discussions of Marxism in leading newspapers and journals. These translations represented only a fraction of the Marxist canon. However, the pieces available to the Chinese did set forth the concepts of historical materialism and class conflict, showing social change as not confined to gradual parliamentary means. They also accentuated the voluntarist strain of Marxism and left the question of material preconditions for revolution in the background.

Marxism furnished a comprehensive intellectual system that could interpret Chinese problems in historical and economic terms. It was an "ism" (*chu-i*) that could guide action, and it defined ideas as instruments to transform man's surroundings. The early Marxist translations in China did not contain a complete exposition of Marxist epistemology. However, they did touch on features of a theory of knowledge[10] that was to influence the Chinese Communists' approach to politics and education.

Dialectical materialism, a term first employed by G. V. Plekhanov, attempted to explain the workings of material and social forces and man's capacity to understand them. It saw human knowledge as derived from a material world constantly in flux and existing independent of the mind itself. Change was governed by laws termed "dialectical" because they described patterns of motion as transformations of quantity into quality and the clash and synthesis of opposites.

Despite skepticism about man's ability to comprehend the material world in totality, Marxism-Leninism viewed human beings as capable of finding truth by acting purposefully on their surroundings. Its doctrine of the "unity of theory and practice" appreciated ideas in terms of their capacity to change reality rather than as abstract concepts. Unless applied to changing material and social conditions, education for a Marxist had no value. Radical activists could find in the Marxist view of learning further justification for leaving their books.

Whether the first Chinese Communists derived a clearcut guide to action from early translations of Marxist writings is unclear. The Chinese Communist leadership did not attain a firm grasp of Marxist theory until years later.[11] However, exposure to Marxist thought helped channel Chinese Communist dynamics toward social revolution and toward the urban proletariat. The limited number of Marxist translations available during the early twenties furnished little fuel for prolonged study sessions that could slow down political momentum.

The Marxist-Leninist works read in China before the founding of the Chinese Communist Party dealt little with the design and operation of a revolutionary party. Most of the Chinse Communist Party's early organizational knowledge came from contacts with representatives of the Soviet Union. Grigory

Voitinsky, an emissary of the Far Eastern Secretariat of the Comintern, arrived in North China in April 1920 with his wife, I. K. Mamaev, and the Chinese interpreter Yang Ming-chai. Voitinsky and other Comintern representatives were critical of the Marxist study groups' academic orientation and encouraged them to set up a Communist Party. In the course of discussions with Chinese Communist leaders, Voitinsky dispensed advice on propaganda and organizational work.[12]

Sergei Polevoy, Voitinsky's first contact in Peking, also worked with the early Chinese Communists. While teaching Russian at Peking University he supplied Li Ta-chao with Communist literature, including an English translation of *The ABC of Communism*. He may also have given Li some organizational guidance. Some Korean Communists working for the Comintern were active in Shanghai, but little is known about their relationship to early Chinese Communist activities.

WORKERS' SUPPLEMENTARY SCHOOLS

After a Provisional Central Committee was set up in Shanghai in May 1920, small Communist groups were formed in a number of Chinese cities. By the end of 1920 Communist Party cells and in some cases branches of the Socialist Youth League were functioning in Peking, Shanghai, Wuhan, Changsha, Canton, and Tsinan. To make contact with the urban working class, these groups issued periodicals addressed to labor issues and set up workers' supplementary schools.

The first of the workers' supplementary schools was formed by members of the Peking Communist group at Ch'ang-hsin-tien,[13] a station at the northern end of the Peking-Hankow Railroad that housed a large train repair shop with over a thousand workers. Students from Peking University had agitated at Ch'ang-hsin-tien during the May Fourth Movement, and the Mass Education Speech Corps had set up one of its lecture halls in the area.

The workers' positive response to these activities had encouraged the Peking group to select Ch'ang-hsin-tien for its first venture in labor organizing. The group made preparations for the workers' school during the autumn of 1920 and opened the school officially on January 1, 1921, offering a day class for workers' children and an evening session for the workers themselves. Contributions from students and the Peking Communist group financed school activities.

There was one resident instructor, who was assisted by student activists Chang K'un-ti, Ho Meng-hsiung, Chu Wu-hsi, and Ch'en Wei-jen. From Peking, Teng Chung-hsia came to give lectures twice each week and Yang Jen-ch'i and Chang Kuo-t'ao lectured weekly. Li Ta-chao periodically visited the school to observe his students' progress.

Subjects of instruction included the national language, arithmetic, and "common knowledge," which presented elementarty scientific and political concepts in terms of factory and railroad issues. Since most of the workers were illiterate, the bulk of class time was devoted to basic reading and writing. Lessons dealt primarily with familiar aspects of the workers' own lives and tried to convey a political message.

For example, in the first class the instructor wrote on the blackboard the characters for "work" (*tso-kung*) and "labor" (*lao-tung*). He then explained the terms:

> To work is the most glorious [thing] and to labor is the greatest [thing]. Therefore, it is said that 'to labor is sacred'. . . . Who built the railroad? Who operates the locomotives? Who makes the machines? If we workers did not build houses there would be no place for anyone to live. If workers did not weave cloth, no one could wear clothes. If there were no workers we could not live. Then is this not to say that to work is great?

In another lesson the instructor inquired "Does everyone understand why we are poor?" The workers replied that it was "because of bad fortune." The instructor then told the class its misery came from exploitation by the wealthy. When he introduced the character for "railroad," he blamed the financing and operation of the railroads by imperialist powers for China's weakness and her people's impoverishment. The remedy for these ills was introduced through the characters for "unity" and a "political party" representing the workers' own interests. It is evident from this description that the level of political education in these workers' classes was very elementary.

Four months after the Ch'ang-hsin-tien school opened, the adult student body had doubled to forty or fifty. A number of workers-students, such as Yang Pao-k'un, Wang Chun, and Shih Wen-pin, were among the first proletarians to join the Chinese Communist Party. The Ch'ang-hsin-tien workers' supplementary school led to the formation of the Peking-Hankow Railroad Workers' Union in 1921.

The results of the Ch'ang-hsin-tien experiment inspired other workers' supplementary schools in the Hsiao-sha-tu cotton mills

of Shanghai, on the Canton-Hankow Railroad, in the Anyüan
mines near the Hunan-Kiangsi border, and in Changsha,
Shuikoushan, Canton, and selected sites in Chekiang. Workers'
supplementary schools became the model for organizational
contact with the proletariat and a means of developing communications skills to reach the masses.

REVOLUTIONARY EXPERIENCES ABROAD

The molding of early Chinese Communist leaders also took
place abroad. As the "first socialist nation," the Soviet Union
was the young Chinese radicals' first choice for a revolutionary
training ground. However, before 1921 it was difficult for
most Chinese to study there or in other countries, like Germany,
Austria, and Czechoslovakia, with active proletarian movements.
The two foreign countries that furnished revolutionary classrooms before the founding of the Chinese Communist Party were
France and Japan.

An advanced industrial nation with a sizable working class movement, France was a natural choice. Its democratic and liberal
thinkers had influenced twentieth century Chinese intellectuals.
French utopian socialism and anarchism had also inspired the
activities of radical Chinese students during World War I. For
those who joined the Chinese Communist Party, France was
an avenue for new ideas and radicalizing experiences.

To alleviate acute manpower shortages during World War I,
France had imported thousands of Chinese workers. By 1919
about 200,000 Chinese were employed by the French, British,
and American governments in France, the Middle East, and
French colonies. Among them were 28,000 literates—former
teachers, students, and student interpreters. Educated Chinese
learned how to relate to workers by toiling alongside them,
and Chinese workers in turn learned to read and write. From
fellow European laborers Chinese workers also gained knowledge
of the European labor movement and elevated their class
consciousness. The French experience facilitated alliances between students and workers when they returned to China.

Some of the Chinese students who had gone abroad for work
and study moved progressively toward the left.[14] Between
1919 and 1921 there were over forty radical groups of
Chinese students distributed among Paris, Lyon, Montargis,
Grenoble, and Charleroi (in Belgium). Almost one-fourth of

the Chinese Communist Party Central Committee of the 1950s was in France during this period.

Most of the radical Chinese students earned their expenses by working in French factories. Hsiang Ching-yü worked in rubber and textile plants; Ts'ai Ch'ang worked part-time in a machine factory. Ho Ch'ang-kung undertook a series of menial jobs before working four months in a Renault plant outside Paris. Hsü T'e-li earned his stay in France through tutoring and metal work. Nieh Jung-chen supported himself in France and Belgium working in the Schneider-Creusot arms factories, the Renault Auto Works, and the Thomson Electric Company.

While not on the job Chinese leftists studied Marxist-Leninist theory. Both the headmaster and assistant of the church-sponsored school on the Normandy coast where Ho Ch'ang-kung studied mechanical engineering were Communists. They encouraged him to read Marxist texts instead of attending chapel. Most of the Chinese students from Changsha were enrolled at the Collège de Montargis south of Paris, and they organized their own branch of the New People's Study Society. Marxism was the leading subject of discussion at society meetings. Such experiences inspired the Hunanese group to organize the Work and Study Cooperative Society (*Kung-hsüeh hu-chu she*) that evolved into the Socialist Youth League in 1921. The league in turn became the French branch of the Chinese Communist Party in July 1922.

Japan, which had been the principal seedbed of Chinese radicalism before 1911, remained a source of revolutionary influence throughout the May Fourth period. It is likely that the Chinese Communist leaders who had studied in Japan[15] were exposed to ideas and experiences that heightened their interest in Communism.

Left-wing political groups were organized in Japan after World War I, responding to a growing proletariat and painful modernization. The *Shinjinkai* (New Men's Society), founded at Tokyo Imperial University in December 1918, was oriented toward the Japanese labor movement. The *Kensetsusha Dōmei* (Reformers' Alliance), founded at Waseda University on September 18, 1919, set its sights on the radical agrarian movement.[16]

Both groups encouraged contacts with student radicals from other countries, including China. The *Kensetsusha Dōmei* had several Chinese members. Japanese student activities at this time had much in common with those in China during the May Fourth period—study groups of intellectuals experimenting with various "isms," campus meetings, provincial speaking tours, and the populist call to "go to the people."

Some of the early Chinese Communists had their first serious exposure to Marxist thinkers while studying in Japan. Those involved with the Japanese student movement may have also sampled their first taste of revolutionary life. There is no documentation of Chinese participation in the *Shinjinkai*, but the *Kensetsusha Dōmei* may have influenced Chinese Communist experiments with rural revolution.

P'eng P'ai, the first Chinese Communist to organize the Chinese peasants, joined the *Kensetsusha Dōmei* after registering at the Waseda University College of Political Science and Economics in September 1918.[17] In ideology the *Kensetsusha Dōmei* had blended anarcho-syndicalism, Soviet Communism, and English social democracy. Its leading faction, dominated by Asanuma Inejirō, Wada Iwao, and Kitazawa Shinjirō, espoused a moderate brand of social democracy centered on the labor or peasant union. The *Kensetsusha Dōmei* began to work in the Japanese agrarian movement after the 1918 rice riots and started organizing peasants in the Kantō area in 1920.

P'eng P'ai was said to have been a close associate of *Kensetsusha Dōmei* member Takatsu Masamichi and to have been peripherally involved in the group. It is unclear if he participated in peasant organizing while in Japan, and his early failure to win peasant followers after his return to China in July 1921 suggests he had little rural experience. However, the *Kensetsusha Dōmei*'s concern with peasant problems may have inspired P'eng to choose the countryside over the city when he became a Communist in China. P'eng's strategy for organizing peasant unions was similar to the ideas of Kitazawa Shinjirō and helped guide early Chinese Communist rural activities.

THE SELF-EDUCATION COLLEGE

Both foreign and indigenous experiences fashioned committed revolutionaries out of young radicals. During the early years of Chinese Communism, the preparation of Party leadership was unsystematic and did not take place in formal institutional settings. One experiment, however, prefigured later Chinese

Communist training programs. This was the Self-Education College, founded in August 1921 by Mao Tse-tung and other members of the New People's Study Society on the site of the Ch'uan-shan Academy[18] in Changsha.

The college recruited radical youth for instruction in Marxism-Leninism. Although it cannot qualify as the first real Party school in China, it strengthened the case for preparing Chinese Communist leadership in special learning centers. A more literal translation of the Chinese characters for "Self-Education College" (*Tzu-hsiu ta-hsüeh*) would be "Self-Cultivation College." "Cultivation" in later Chinese Communist usage came to denote the development of leadership qualities through education.

The Self-Education College[19] selected its students on the basis of their personal qualities and desire to learn. The questionnaire for prospective students inquired:

1. What school did you attend before? What did you do and what was the economic status of your family and yourself?
2. What subjects would you like to study and why?
3. What subjects did you study before?
4. How many semesters have you studied previously? What did you do afterward?
5. What is your world-view (philosophical outlook)?
6. What are your criticisms of society?

The college was designed to incorporate the best features of traditional Chinese private academies and modern schools. Students chose their own subjects of study and kept daily records of the books they read. Their progress was measured by essays submitted to the head of the school. The best of the daily compositions were published in the school's monthly magazine. Professors limited their role to raising questions and correcting students' essays and notes.

Although students were permitted to read what they themselves chose, the college encouraged the study of Marxism-Leninism. Organized group study sessions and "sit and talk" meetings were heavily Marxist in content. In 1922 the college sponsored a series of lectures on Marxist theory. An instructional staff of ten included Communists Li Wei-han, Hsia Hsi, Hsia Ming-han, Chiang Meng-chou, Ho Shu-heng, and Meng Hsüeh-tsan. Ho Shu-heng also managed daily school affairs.

The Self-Education College did not focus on specifically preparing Chinese Communist Party members until its second year. In September 1922 the college opened a preparatory class, followed by a junior-middle class, that openly recruited and trained Party leaders. The subjects of study—national language, English, mathematics, history, and geography—resembled those of conventional schools but contained large doses of Marxist analysis. For example, one of the essays on national language discussed the condition of the Hunan peasantry. It analyzed the social and economic differences among the Hunan peasants and the causes of unequal land distribution. The piece concluded that revolution was the only solution to this problem. Chinese Communist Party and Socialist Youth League organs *Hsiang-tao (the Guide)* and *Chung-kuo ch'ing-nien (Chinese Youth)* were required reading for the preparatory and junior-middle classes.

Most students trained at the college to be Chinese Communists were activist intellectuals or workers. At its peak, enrollment totalled over two hundred, furnishing many promising recruits for the Socialist Youth League and Chinese Communist Party. The Self-Education College also issued Chinese Communist propaganda materials. On April 15, 1923, Mao Tse-tung helped launch *Hsin shih-tai (the New Age),* a mass circulation periodical devoted to Marxist theory and problems of the Chinese revolution. The first issue included an article on imperialism, a summary of Marx's *Critique of the Gotha Programme*, and Mao's essay on "Foreign Influence, Warlords and Revolution." In the second and fourth issues there were articles on "Marxist Theory and China," "Critique of Historical Idealism," and "Communism and Economic Development."

In November 1923 Chao Heng-t'i, the governor of Hunan, tried to close down the Self-Education College. Fearing arrest, Mao Tse-tung had fled to Shanghai in April or May and maintained only indirect ties with the college and *Hsin shih-tai.* Chao's orders had little effect and the junior-middle and preparatory classes merely moved to the quarters of a conventional middle school.

The Hsiang River School opened shortly thereafter. Its head was Meng Tsung-han, a scholar who had been an early member of the New People's Study Society. Communist Chiang Meng-chou actually managed school affairs. The Hsiang River School had two divisions—a middle school and a village normal school with curricula comparable to other institutions.

Until closing in 1927, part of the Hsiang River School continued to train Chinese Communists, as illustrated by the diary of student Ho Erh-k'ang:

April 28, 1924: Two hours of civics on Lenin's National Revolution. Received instructions to organize a speech corps to speak on "May Day" in the town and suburbs.

May 5, 1924: Today is the celebration of the 107th birthday of Marx, the founder of Communism.

May 7, 1924: Big demonstration shouting all the way, "Down with Japanese imperialism, British and American imperialism! Repudiate the Twenty-one Demands!"

May 29, 1924: Discuss the second chapter of *Introduction to Political Economy*: "Class Struggle and Political Parties."[20]

Both the Hsiang River School and the Self-Education College thus contributed to the radicalization of Chinese youth and their recruitment into the Chinese Communist Party. Like the workers' supplementary schools they brought together intellectuals and proletarians, encouraging both to shed their old images. They pioneered in learning practices that later influenced Chinese Communist leadership training programs.

Chinese Communist leaders shaped by the Self-Education College or by contact with the proletariat at home or abroad still bore little resemblance to iron-willed masters of revolutionary change. They remained an elite vanguard without a large mass following until mid-1925. It would be many years before they attained a thorough comprehension of the social forces at work in China or the dynamics of class conflict.

Yet they had begun to change from radical intellectuals to revolutionaries. Few continued, as charged by Karl Radek in 1922, to "close themselves in their rooms to study Marx and Engels as they formerly studied Confucius."[21] The experiences that developed their commitment to Chinese Communism taught them to live by action rather than words. Intellectuals caught up in the clash of ideas have traditionally had difficulty forming cohesive political movements.[22] The early Chinese Communists did not become unified in thought and action overnight. But participation in actual revolutionary work curbed some of their unruly tendencies.

At work in the making of the first Chinese Communists were the key ideas of the founders of the Party. Ch'en Tu-hsiu, a leading "tradition-smasher" among the May Fourth intelligentsia, advocated new ideas to assault the stagnant traditions that inhibited national rejuvenation. Li Ta-chao sought a form of consciousness that would enable human beings to transform

their lives.   He encouraged intellectuals to "go to the people."[23]
"Tradition-smashing" and developing a movement that could
"go to the people" remained major priorities for Chinese Communism for many years.

NOTES

[1]Mao Tse-tung, "Reform in Learning, the Party and Literature" (February 1, 1942),
in Boyd Compton, *Mao's China: Party Reform Documents, 1942-44* (Seattle:
University of Washington Press, 1966), p. 15.

[2]Among the original members of the New People's Study Society were Ho Shu-heng,
Ch'an Ch'ang, Chang K'un-t'i, Lo Hsüeh-tsan, Kuo Liang, Hsiang Ching-yü, Hsia Hsi,
Li Wei-han, Hsiao Yü, Hsiao San, and Ts'ai Ch'ang. This discussion of May Fourth
study societies is based on Li Jui, *Mao Tse-tung t'ung-chih ti ch'u-ch'i ko-ming huo-tung*
[The Early Revolutionary Activities of Comrade Mao Tse-tung] (Peking: Chung-kuo
ch'ing-nien ch'u-pan she, 1957), pp. 72-74, 149; *Shih-yüeh ko-ming tui Chung-kuo
ko-ming ti ying-hsiang* [The Influence of the October Revolution on the Chinese
Revolution], ed. Ting Shou-ho et al. (Peking: Jen-min ch'u-pan she, 1957), pp. 65-68;
Chow Tse-tsung, *The May Fourth Movement* (Cambridge, Mass.: Harvard University
Press, 1960), pp. 75, 189, 251; James P. Harrison, *The Long March to Power: A
History of the Chinese Communist Party, 1921-72*(New York: Praeger Publishers,
1972), pp. 21-22; and Hsiao San, *Mao Tse-tung t'ung-chih ti ch'ing-nien shih-tai*
[Comrade Mao Tse-tung's Youth] (n.p., Hsin Hua shu-tien, 1949), p. 82.

[3]On populism in China see Maurice Meisner, "Leninism and Maoism: Some Perspectives
on Marxism-Leninism in China," *China Quarterly,* no. 45 (January-March 1971), p. 32,
and his study of *Li Ta-chao and the Origins of Chinese Marxism* (Cambridge, Mass.:
Harvard University Press, 1967).

[4]On popular education projects see Chow Tse-tsung, pp. 187-194; Li Jui, pp. 59-63;
and Hu-nan sheng-chih pien-tsuan wei-yuan-hui, *Hu-nan sheng-chih, vol. 1, Hu-nan
chin-pai-nien ta shih-shu* [Chronicle of Hunan Province, vol. 1, Historical Annals of
Hunan for the Past Hundred Years] (Changsha, 1958), p. 434.

[5]Discussions of the Mass Education Speech Corps can be found in Chow Tse-tsung,
pp. 193-194; Harrison, *March,* pp. 21-22; and Chang Kuo-t'ao, *The Rise of the
Chinese Communist Party, 1921-1927* (Lawrence, Kansas: The University Press of
Kansas, 1971), pp. 50-51.

[6]On conditions affecting the absorption of Marxism in China see Meisner, *Li Ta-chao,*
pp. 24-27, 46, 56-57, 69.

[7]The most extensive scholarly treatment of early socialism in China is the study by
Li Yu-ning, *The Introduction of Socialism into China* (New York: Columbia
University Press, 1971). See also Martin Bernal, "The Triumph of Anarchism over
Marxism, 1906-1907, in *China in Revolution: The First Phase 1900-1913,*
ed. Mary Clabaugh Wright (New Haven: Yale University Press, 1968), pp. 98-112.

[8]Prior to the May Fourth period the only known translations of Marx and Engels
were of portions of *The Communist Manifesto* (translated in 1906 and 1908 by
Chu Chih-hsin in *Min-pao* and Min Ming in *T'ien-i pao*). The year 1919 witnessed
the publication of "Labor and Capital," a translation by Shih Li of Marx's *Wage-
Labor and Capital* in *Ch'en-pao* [Morning Post] from May 9-June 1; chapter two
of the last section of *The Communist Manifesto* on proletarian revolution and
dictatorship in the April 6 issue of the *Weekly Review*; the first chapter of
The Communist Manifesto on "The Bourgeoisie and the Proletariat" in the
November 1 issue of *Kuo-min* [the Citizens] magazine; and an entire issue of
New Youth (vol. 6, no. 5) devoted to Marxism. Li Ta-chao's article on "My
Views on Marxism" included a general introduction to Marx's concepts of materi-
alism, class struggle, and political economy and excerpts on historical material-
ism from *Poverty of Philosophy, The Communist Manifesto,* and *Critique of
Political Economy.*

In 1920 a translation by Feng Chüeh-t'ien of Marx's preface to *Das Kapital* in the *Citizens* and a translation of the latter half of Engels' *Socialism: Scientific and Utopian* by Cheng Tz'u-ch'uan was issued in Shanghai. The December issue of *Construction* (Chien-she) featured a translation of section 3 of Engels' *Anti-Duhring*. The same year saw the first complete translation of *The Communist Manifesto* by Ch'en Wang-tao. In 1921 the People's Publishing Company in Canton issued a translation by Yüan Jang of *Wage-Labor and Capital* and the January issue of the *Eastern Miscellany* (Tung-fang tsa-chih) printed the portions of *The Critique of Political Economy* concerned with historical materialism. The New Youth Publishing House also issued an eight-volume *New Youth Library* consisting mainly of works explaining Marxism, such as Merciere's *Elementary Guide to Marxism;* Kirkup's *History of Socialism;* and Kautsky's *Class Struggle.* Among other works of Kautsky available to the Chinese were a full translation of *The Economic Theory of Karl Marx* in *Ch'en-pao* between June 2 and November l, 1919; a piece with the Chinese title of "The Study of Socialist Ethics"; and an essay entitled in Chinese "The Cultural Marx." Frederic Wakeman, in *History and Will: Philosophic Perspectives on Mao Tse-tung's Thought* (Berkeley and Los Angeles: University of California Press, 1973), points out that both Kautsky and Kirkup would have been supportive of early Chinese Communists' voluntaristic and activist tendencies and their desire to transcend rigid blueprints for revolution unsuited to China; see especially pp. 212-219. This list of Marxist translations is extracted from Wei Li, "Introduction to the Classical Works of Marxism-Leninism About the Time of the May 4 Movement," translated from *Jen-min jih-pao* [People's Daily], May 5, 1959, *Survey of China Mainland Press*, no. 2021, pp. 7-9. For a list of other works on socialism available in Chinese after 1919 see Li Yün-han, *Ts'ung jung-kung tao ch'ing-tang* [From Admission of the Communists to Party Purification] (Taipei, 1966), pp. 82-86.

9Works of Lenin in translation before the First Chinese Communist Party (CCP) Congress included part of Lenin's "Report on the Party Program to the Eighth Congress of the Soviet Communist Party" in the November 1, 1920, issue of *New Youth;* part of Lenin's "Report in the Name of the Central Committee to the Ninth Congress of the Soviet Communist Party" in the November 7, 1920, issue of *Communist Party* (Kung-ch'an-tang) monthly; "From the Destruction of the Established Old Order to the Creation of the New Order" in the sixth issue of *Dawn*(Shu-kuang) magazine in 1920; "Lenin's Views on the Emancipation of Russian Women," part of an article called "The Great Innovation," translated in *Juvenile World* 1, no. 7, 1920; "Economy and Politics in the Period of the Proletarian Dictatorship," in the December 1, 1920 issue of *New Youth* and the first 1920 issue of *Dawn;* a portion of the first chapter of *State and Revolution* in the May 7, 1921, issue of *Communist Party;* and Lenin's "Address to the Third Congress of the All-Soviet National Economic Committee" in the first 1920 issue of *Dawn.* The third issue of *Communist Party* was devoted to the founding of the Comintern and its member Communist parties. It included a biography of Lenin, a list of Lenin's works, and "Conditions for Participation in the Communist International" drafted by Lenin at the Second Comintern Congress. In Canton the People's Publishing Company issued a translation by Li Li of Lenin's "Present Tasks of the Soviet Government" under the title of "Construction of Workers' and Peasants' Unions." See Wei Li, p. 9, and Chang Ching-lu, *Chung-kuo ch'u-pan shih-liao pu-pien* [Expanded Edition of Historical Materials of Chinese Publishing] (Peking: Chung-hua shu-chü, 1957), pp. 452-453.

10This discussion of dialectical materialism is based on: Loren R Graham, *Science and Philosophy in the Soviet Union* (New York: Alfred A. Knopf, 1972), pp. 25-64; Raymond A. Bauer, *The New Man in Soviet Psychology* (Cambridge, Mass.: Harvard University Press, 1952), pp. 100-103, 135, 176; Vsevolod Holubnychy, "Mao Tse-tung's Materialistic Dialectics," *China Quarterly*, no. 19 (July-September 1964), pp. 3-37; Zev Katz, "Party-Political Education in Soviet Russia" (Ph.D. dissertation, University of London, 1957), pp. 494-496; and Meisner, *Li Ta-chao*, pp. 157-161, 197-199. The term "dialectical materialism" was first employed by G. V. Plekhanov to designate Marx and Engels' theory of knowledge. Marx and Engels themselves used terms like "modern materialism" or the "new materialism" to distinguish their orientation from that of other philosophers. See Graham, pp. 25-26.

11On the Chinese Communists' theoretical immaturity, see Chang Kuo-t'ao, *Rise*, p. 101, and James P. Harrison, *The Communists and Chinese Peasant Rebellions* (New York: Atheneum, 1969), pp. 25-26. A number of early Chinese Communist leaders during the twenties read Bukharin and Preobrazhensky's *ABC of Communism*, an "elementary textbook of Communist knowledge" used widely by Communist parties until both authors fell into political disgrace in the late twenties. See the "Editor's Introduction" to Bukharin and Preobrazhensky, *The ABC of Communism,* ed. E. H. Carr (London: Penguin Books, 1969), pp. 17-18, 57.

12Chang Kuo-t'ao recalled that at his first meeting with Voitinsky in January 1921 he discussed Communist beliefs, principles of organization, the founding of the Comintern and the Russian Revolution. See *Rise,* pp. 93, 122-126, and Harrison, *March,* pp. 27-28, n. 29-30.

13This discussion of workers' supplementary schools is based on *Chōshinten tetsudō monogatari* [Story of the Ch'ang-hsin-tien Railroad], ed. Chōshinten kikanryō kōba shi hensan iinkai (n.p., Shin-Nippon shuppansha, 1963), pp. 24-53; Chang Kuo-t'ao, *Rise,* pp. 114-120; *Shih-yüeh ko-ming,* pp. 158-161; Li Jui, pp. 166-168; and Ho Ch'ang-kung, *Ch'in-kung chien-hsüeh sheng-huo hui-i* [Recollections of Diligent Work and Frugal Study Life](Peking: Kung-jen ch'u-pan she, 1958), pp. 13-17. These sources name the resident instructor at Ch'ang-hsin-tien and Wu Ju-ming, Wu Jung-ts'ang, or Wu Yü-tso. Treatment of the workers' supplementary schools and the Chinese labor movement can also be found in Jean Chesneaux, *Le Mouvement Ouvrier Chinois de 1919 a 1927* [The Chinese Labor Movement from 1919 to 1927] (Paris: Mouton and Co., 1962), p. 249, and Lynda Norene Womack, "Anyüan: The Cradle of the Chinese Workers' Revolutionary Movement, 1921-1922" (unpublished East Asian Institute Essay, Columbia University, 1970).

14On Chinese leftists in France, see Chow Tse-tsung, pp. 35-40; Harrison, *March,* pp. 22-23; Ho Ch'ang-kung, pp. 42-52; and Conrad Brandt, "The French-Returned Elite in the Chinese Communist Party," *Symposium on Economic and Social Problems of the Far East,* ed. E. F. Szczepanik (Hong Kong: Hong Kong University Press, 1962), p. 234. Among the early Chinese Communist leaders in France were Ho Ch'ang-kung, Hsiang Ching-yü, Hsü T'e-li, Li Fu-ch'un, Li Li-san, Li Wei-han, Ts'ai Ch'ang, Nieh Jung-chen, Chao Shih-yen, Ch'en I, Ch'en Yen-nien, Ch'en Ch'iao-nien, Chou En-lai, Teng Hsiao-p'ing, Ts'ai Ho-sen, Wang Jo-fei, and Wu Yü-chang. Chou En-lai, Ho Ch'ang-kung, Hsü T'e-li, and Nieh Jung-chen also went to Belgium, and Chou En-Lai and Hsü T'e-li also travelled to Germany. See their biographies in Donald W. Klein and Anne B. Clark, *Biographic Dictionary of Chinese Communism* (Cambridge, Mass.: Harvard University Press, 1971).

15Among the early Chinese Communists that studied in Japan were Ch'en Tu-hsiu, Lin Po-ch'ü, Wu Yü-chang, Li Ta-chao, Li Han-chün, Wang Jo-fei, Tung Pi-wu, Chou En-lai, P'eng P'ai, and Wang Wei-chou. Ch'en, Lin, and Wu completed their studies there before the 1911 Revolution. While in Japan Chou En-lai was influenced by the writings of the Japanese socialist Kawakami Hajime, and Li Han-chün became acquainted with Marxist ideas while studying in the engineering department of Tokyo Imperial University. See the biographies of these figures in Klein and Clark.

16On Japanese left-wing movements see George Oakley Totten III, *The Social Democratic Movement in Prewar Japan* (New Haven: Yale University Press, 1966), p. 31, and Henry DeWitt Smith II, *Japan's First Student Radicals* (Cambridge, Mass.: Harvard University Press, 1972), pp. 54-79. It is unlikely that either Japanese or Chinese students were radicalized from their learning experience at Japanese universities. Curriculum and teaching methods were modelled on the German system, with little interplay between student and teacher. Most politicization took place outside of formal classes. The *Shinjinkai* employed study groups with an "anti-curriculum" similar to May Fourth study societies in China to indoctrinate its members and transform their "bourgeois class character" into "true proletarian consciousness." See Smith, especially pp. 6-12, 61-62, 131-133.

17The influence of study in Japan upon P'eng P'ai is treated in Yung Ying-yue, "P'eng P'ai and the *Kensetsusha-dōmei:* A Case Study of Sino-Japanese Relations Among Left-wing Intellectuals in the Early Twentieth Century" (Masters essay, Columbia University, 1971), pp. 31-66), pp. 31-66. See also part 1 of Eto Shinkichi, "Hai-lu-feng—The First Chinese Soviet Government," *China Quarterly,* no. 8 (October-December 1961), p. 167.

18The Ch'uan-shan Academy had been established in 1913 by Hunan literati to study the thought of Wang Fu-chih (Wang Ch'uan-shan). Chinese Communist Party member Ho Shu-heng was an academy member and obtained consent to use the school grounds and four hundred *yüan* of academy funds per month to run the Self-Education College. According to Jerome Ch'en, *Mao and the Chinese Revolution* (London: Oxford

University Press, 1965), p. 83, Mao Tse-tung himself "took a very small part" in the operation of the academy.

[19]On the Self-Education College, see Li Jui, pp. 154-159, and Jerome Ch'en, pp. 83, 87.

[20]Ho Erh-k'ang was a Chinese Communist from Hsiang-t'an in Hunan. After attending the Hsiang River School he was sent by the CCP to work among Hunanese peasants and took charge of the Hsiang-t'an Peasant Association. He was imprisoned in 1927 and executed in April 1928.

[21]Cited in Harrison, *March,* p. 18.

[22]See the discussion of intellectuals and political movements in T. B. Bottomore, *Elites and Society* (Great Britain: Penguin Books, 1966), pp. 75-77.

[23]On Ch'en Tu-hsiu and Li Ta-chao see Meisner, *Li Ta-chao,* pp. 24-25, 82-88, 118, 159-161, 170, and Chow Tse-tsung, pp. 46-48.

3 Party Schools in the Soviet Union and China

In 1925 the Chinese Communist Party made the critical transition from an elite to a mass-based political movement. Its membership mushroomed from under 1,000 before the May Thirtieth Movement to 10,000 six months later and peaked at close to 58,000 by the spring of 1927. Many of those who joined the Party at this time were working class leaders representing a constituency of three million in the Chinese labor movement.[1]

The Party itself matured as a complex organization. Its network spanned the major Chinese cities and could exert leverage over hundreds of labor unions and the lives of millions. The Party center coordinated the activities of tens of thousands of operatives in the labor, women's, and youth movements. These responsibilities required specialized leadership skills and a much higher degree of organizational cohesion than was needed before 1925.

To handle increasingly ambitious functions, the Chinese Communist Party systematically applied Leninist principles and tightened its discipline. It developed distinct leadership types to operate its multilevel internal apparatus and communications system and to direct mass mobilization work. One can attribute the Chinese Communists' growing political expertise to accumulated experience "in the field," continued contacts with Soviet advisers in China, and yearly additions to Marxist-Leninist works in Chinese.[2] However, the Chinese Communists' rise to political prominence in the twenties also owes a large debt to programs that cultivated Chinese Communist leadership in the Soviet Union.

29

Graduates of Soviet leadership training schools were able to steer Chinese Communist activities more closely towards those of the model Leninist party. "Returned students" from Moscow infused the Chinese Communist Party with improved understanding of both theoretical and organizational aspects of Marxism-Leninism. They acquired a working knowledge of democratic centralism, Party building, and revolutionary strategy. With these skills, "Russian-returned" students were elevated to the top directing positions in the Chinese Communist Party. They were also instrumental in establishing the first system of Party schools in China that provided the leadership for Chinese Communist expansion during the twenties.

VISITS TO THE SOVIET UNION

By the First Party Congress in July 1921, the Soviet Union had become the principal foreign training ground for Chinese revolutionaries.[3] Once civil war had subsided, Soviet attention turned to its nationality areas and to revolutionary movements outside its borders. Both the Communist Party of the Soviet Union and the Far Eastern Secretariat of the Comintern[4] brought Asian radicals to the Soviet Union for training.

Headed by Chang T'ai-lei, the first formal delegation of Chinese Communists to the Soviet Union represented the Chinese Communist Party at the Third Comintern Congress in June and July of 1921. Forty-three Chinese Communist Party and Socialist Youth League members attended the Congress of the Toilers of the Far East in Moscow between January 21 and February 1, 1922.[5] Chinese Communists participated in various Comintern meetings throughout the twenties, and during these trips to the Soviet Union they often received instructions from Comintern authorities on revolutionary work in China. For example, Karl Radek rebuked Ch'en Tu-hsiu for his "utopian optimism" concerning the imminence of socialist revolution in China and for "excessive emphasis" on "theoretical study."[6]

A number of Chinese Communist visitors to the Soviet Union stayed on for formal leadership training. The major Soviet institution that prepared Chinese Communist leaders before 1925 was the Communist University of the Toilers of the East. The university was part of the Soviet educational complex devoted to Asian affairs and the training of activists and Party functionaries for the Asiatic Soviet Union. Other schools with Asian programs included the Sverdlov Communist University in Moscow, the Eastern Faculty of the Workers'

and Peasants' Red Army Military Academy, the Narimanov or
Moscow Institute of Eastern Studies, the Lenin School, and East-
ern Institutes in Baku, Tashkent, Kazan, Samarkand, and
Vladivostok.[7]

THE FOREIGN LANGUAGE SCHOOL

To recruit and prepare young Chinese activists for study in the
Soviet Union, the Shanghai Communist group had founded in
the autumn of 1920 the Foreign Language School. The school
gave Russian language instruction to future Chinese Communist
Party leaders to enable them to attend the Communist University of the Toilers of the East in Moscow, and it also provided
a measure of training for political work within China. An informal center for the discussion of Marxism-Leninism among
Shanghai activists, the Foreign Language School became a major
base of operation for the Socialist Youth Corps.[8]

The Foreign Language School was situated on Hsia Fei Lu, Six
Yu Yang Lane, in the French concession of Shanghai. Although
the school constitution listed English and French as subjects of
study, they were never taught; the study of the Russian language
—spiced with numerous discussions of all matters related to
Marxism—constituted the sole course offering. Yang Ming-chai,
guide and interpreter for the Voitinsky and Mamaev Comintern
delegation to China in 1920, directed the school. He was assisted
in his teaching by Mme. Voitinsky and a Korean surnamed Bu.

A total of sixty students attended the Foreign Language School.
For each class in Russian, enrollment fluctuated between one
and two dozen, reaching a peak in the spring of 1921. According
to former student P'eng Shu-chih, the students at the Foreign
Language School were unable to learn much Russian. They
nevertheless began departing for the Soviet Union in early
1921,[9] travelling secretly from Shanghai to Vladivostok and on
to Moscow by rail.

THE COMMUNIST UNIVERSITY OF THE TOILERS OF THE EAST

Facilities in the Soviet Union for the training of revolutionaries
were part of the postrevolutionary system of Soviet Party-political
education. A complex of formal Party schools was set up after

the civil war to prepare Communist Party functionaries for leadership positions in the new Soviet state.

Among the high-level institutions established in the early twenties, Communist universities specialized in the preparation of Party officials. Other high-level schools in operation at that time, such as the Socialist (Communist) Academy (founded in 1918), the Marx-Engels Institute (founded in 1920), the Commission (Institute) for Party History (founded in 1920), and the Institute of Red Professors (founded in 1921), were primarily research centers.

Besides general Communist universities such as Sverdlov and Zinoviev universities (founded in 1919 and 1921, respectively, in Moscow and Leningrad), special Communist universities were set up to train Party officials for minority areas and the Soviet national republics.[10] The two most famous national Communist universities, both founded in 1921, were the Communist University of the Toilers of the East in Moscow and the Communist University of the National Minorities of the West[11] in Moscow and Leningrad.

The Communist University of the Toilers of the East, which trained Chinese Communist Party members, had been originally designed for Communist Party technical or business cadres from eastern areas of the Soviet Union such as Georgia, Uzbekistan, Kazakhstan, Azerbaidjan, Kirghizia, Tadjikistan, Armenia, and Turkmenistan. However, as Comintern policy turned eastward, the university looked beyond Soviet borders to the cultivation of revolutionaries from China, Japan, Korea, India, Mongolia, Arabia, Indochina, and the Philippines.

A decree on April 21, 1921, from the All-Russian Central Executive Committee of the Communist Party of the Soviet Union marked the official opening of the university.[12] The school, operating under the jurisdiction of the Far Eastern Department of the Executive Committee of the Comintern, was located in a five-story structure on Tverskaya Avenue. Until he was replaced by B. F. Shumiatsky in 1927, Grigory Broido served as university rector.

Enrollment initially totalled three to four hundred students but mounted to over eight hundred by the end of one year. At its height the student body reached fifteen hundred to two thousand, about five hundred of whom were women. Approximately forty Chinese students (including the transfers from the Shanghai Foreign Language School) were enrolled in the first class. Their ranks swelled to around one hundred by late 1924, after absorbing an influx in 1923 of Chinese Communist Party members from Europe.[13]

Interpreters enabled all students to attend large lectures and meetings. Ch'ü Ch'iu-pai, Li Tseng-wu, Wu Ho-chün, and Wang Hung-tung were translators for the Chinese students. Nevertheless, language difficulties slowed the learning process, which was compared to asking "a toothless old man to chew iron and steel."[14] Students consumed a great deal of time in Russian language study. Most had to start from scratch, often without benefit of adequate texts or study aids.

During its first year of operation, the university's course of training lasted only seven months. The matriculation period was lengthened to three years in early 1923 to offer students a wider range of courses and a thorough grounding in Party work, and all students were expected to take foundation courses in the areas of administration, economics, and political knowledge.[15]

Those considered well qualified were permitted to attend seminars. Owing to language difficulties the students were divided into separate classes for each of the nationalities represented. Where students of one nationality proved numerous the class was again split into subsections. Chinese students were arranged in two or three classes, one for intellectuals, another for illiterate workers and peasants, and a special military class for lower-level military cadres. An instructor who belonged to the Communist Party of the Soviet Union (CPSU) was assigned to each student group to direct political activities.[16]

Academic standards at the university were also tempered by considerations of expediency. Because of the immediate need for qualified leaders for foreign revolutionary movements, the curriculum eliminated "preparatory" courses. Soviet and foreign students of over fifty national and ethnic origins, of worker, peasant, and intelligentsia backgrounds, of varying degrees of literacy and ideological and practical training, were lumped together in essentially the same program of study. Placement into study groups was based only on a simple examination involving a physical checkup and several questions answered in the presence of the rector, the head of the Department of School Affairs, and a Communist Party representative.[17]

The instructional program tried to build commitment to Marxism-Leninism while depicting the dynamics of revolutionary movements. Besides Russian language study there were courses in dialectical materialism, Marxist-Leninist theory, world history,

history of the labor movement, history of the Russian revolutionary movement and the CPSU (with emphasis on the distinction between Narodniks, Social Democratic Labor Party, Bolsheviks, and Mensheviks), political economy (Marxian economics as treated in *Capital*), mathematics, soviet structure, and geography.

A three-year study program was initiated in late 1922 to offer additional work in mathematics, biology, chemistry, and physics plus new courses on the history of the East, the national and colonial questions, history of the women's movement, and English language training. The university also set up new study groups in Leninism and Party structure, "economic sciences," natural sciences, Eastern studies and colonial politics, history, philology, and education.[18]

For the Chinese students, P'eng Shu-chih taught a course in 1923 on the History of the Development of Society and lectured on Marxist philosophy. Ch'ü Ch'iu-pai, who was a Chinese interpreter for the university, gave a course on Historical Materialism. On occasion Josef Stalin and international Communist leaders addressed university students. CPSU members on the regular instructional staff often punctuated their lectures with the Central Committee's views on current Party affairs.[19]

Group study was promoted at the university and at higher Soviet Party schools to raise the level of student interest and involvement. In conjunction with lectures, groups of twenty-five to thirty students met periodically under the guidance of discussion leaders to comment on materials[20] that were read independently. The group discussion leaders fielded questions from students and helped clarify the main points of the material under scrutiny.

In line with promoting independent study and research, the university for a time offered a program that concentrated study areas around a central theme such as "the processes of production." Separate "study rooms" were designated for the social sciences, history of technique, natural sciences, and languages and there was a psychometric study room for use in evaluating university teaching methods and curriculum. Students were also taken on excursions where they could select and analyze materials for research.

The "excursion method" of instruction, reinforced by the Marxist concern with "theory" and "practice," encouraged outside "practical work." University students participated in Party work in Moscow factories and tried to relate their classroom studies to actual conditions among the working masses. Whether the

Chinese students were actively involved in this aspect of the training program is unclear. The Asians did participate in military training, which helped bridge the gap between the requirements of an established socialist state and those of active revolutionaries. Military training during summer vacations was initiated during the early twenties and had become a regular part of the curriculum for foreign students by 1926.[21]

One should bear in mind that the study programs of Soviet Party schools changed periodically in response to developments within the CPSU.[22] During the early twenties, Party-political education aimed at producing reliable leaders for the new Soviet state. It tried to inculcate elementary Communist principles and challenged beliefs inherited from the old order, but it allowed some degree of debate and criticism. After the death of Lenin, however, the Party schools became Stalinist tools to train obedient apparatchiks.

From the mid-twenties onward the curricula of the Soviet Party schools, including the Communist universities, stressed as core courses the study of "Leninism," Party history, and Party organization. Research into Lenin's writings and descriptions of the triumph of the Bolshevik Party and the CPSU over deviationist groups were employed to demonstrate Stalin's legitimacy as the true heir of Lenin and his Party. Courses in Party organization emphasized problems of Party unity, discipline, intraparty democracy, and administrative questions such as "regulating the growth of Party membership" and "Party work in the villages." Classroom study was supplemented by "practical work" in Party organizations outside the school to test students' political reliability. With Stalin's rise to power in the CPSU, Party-political education became preoccupied with preventing deviation from ideological orthodoxy.

Because of the concentration of intellectuals concerned with Marxist doctrine on the staffs of Soviet Party schools, these institutions became major battlegrounds for factional struggle in the CPSU. Many schools were bastions for the opposition activities of those supporting Trotsky or Bukharin. Even after Communist intellectuals were replaced by Party-machine men in the early thirties, Party schools remained potential trouble spots for the Stalinists. During the Great Purge the entire system of Party schools was dismantled in favor of individual study. The Communist University of the Toilers of the East was closed in 1936.

Most of the Chinese Communists who studied at the Communist University of the Toilers of the East completed their training before 1925. Towards the mid-twenties they would have been exposed to the upsurge in training in Leninism, Party history, and Party work. However, they escaped the extreme emphasis on Party loyalty and ideological orthodoxy that characterized the training of the next generation of Chinese Communist leaders in Moscow.

Much of the knowledge that the Chinese Communists at the university acquired about Party life was imparted by Communist Party branches at the school. Representatives of the CPSU were assigned to groups of students to ferret out those with anti-Communist tendencies. Chinese students fell under the jurisdiction of a special Moscow branch of the Chinese Communist Party.23

Members of this Moscow branch were either Chinese Communist Party or Socialist Youth League members. P'eng Shu-chih remained secretary of the branch from August 1921 until the summer of 1924. He was succeeded by Lo I-nung, who in turn was replaced by Wang Jo-fei when Lo left for China in the spring of 1925. Wang returned to China that autumn.

A "Committee of Five" active Communists—P'eng Shu-chih, Lo I-nung, Yü Hsiu-sung, Ch'en Wei-jen, and Pu Shih-ch'i—stood watch over the Chinese students' ideological development. "Passive" Communists, such as Jen Pi-shih, objected occasionally to the committee's activities, and Chiang Kuang-tz'u, Ch'in Ti-ch'ing, Ts'ao Ching-hua, Wei Wu-yüan, and P'eng Lieh-wu claimed they were persecuted by its members.

University students also attended special "study-criticism" sessions led by members of the CPSU. Each student had to find a point on which to criticize another and had to answer similar charges against himself. In this manner one was supposed to learn how to conduct "emotionless struggle"24 against harmful habits and incorrect thoughts. The study-criticism sessions prefigured what later became one of the principal Chinese Communist techniques for maintaining group cohesion.

Study-criticism sessions were jolting experiences for the Chinese, challenging their deeply-ingrained sense of "face" and group harmony. To survive these sessions Chinese students had to break sharply with traditional patterns of behavior. Study-criticism encouraged militant attitudes for revolutionary conflict and individual subordination to the will of the group.

The "Concrete Guide to the Work of Training" issued in the mid-twenties by the Moscow branch of the Chinese Communist Party reveals the extent to which concern for group discipline pervaded Party life among Chinese Communists in the Soviet Union. Among its key articles are:

4. We should destroy family, local and national concepts—the proletariat has no family, no local or national limitations.
5. Destroy unity based on sentiment—sentimental unity is petty bourgeois unity—we build our unity on Party interests.
17. We must at all times and everywhere mutually correct each other's errors of thought and action.
18. When we have opinions, we must express them—if we hide our opinions and do not express them, we would be standing outside the organization and encouraging counterrevolutionary [tendencies].
22. Every comrade must develop close relations with at least two other comrades (exclusive of comrades belonging to the same small unit) in order to achieve solidarity among our comrades.
23. The organization's interest is the individual's interest. We must not obstruct the organization's advance because of individual interest. . . .
24. . . . We must have the psychology of thoroughly trusting the organization—it is counterrevolutionary conduct not to trust the organization.
25. Our lives and our will must not be based on individual beliefs or the individual will. . . . There is absolutely no such thing as individual life or individual free will.
26. We must strictly criticize our comrades' errors and humbly accept our comrades' criticism. . . . Wherever he may be, every Communist must at all times criticize and supervise his comrades in accordance with the relations of mutual supervision.[25]

The spirit of the "Concrete Guide" appears to have affected other aspects of student life at the Communist University of the Toilers of the East. Students maintained a rigorous schedule of classes and extracurricular activities during the week. On Saturdays they participated in obligatory "labor service." Digging ditches or repairing school grounds offset the costs of tuition and furnished another sample of proletarian life. School authorities hoped the tempo of student life would nurture students' fortitude and discipline for future revolutionary work.[26]

Some of the features of study life at the university, such as group study, the excursion method, labor service, and military drill, were incorporated into leadership training programs in China. This did not mean, however, that Chinese Communist Party life and training programs mirrored those of the Soviet Union. "Struggle and criticism" sessions did not become standard features of Chinese Communist Party-political education until the early thirties and played a different organizational role.

The first wave of Chinese Communists to return from study in the Soviet Union infused the Party with additional theoretical expertise and a firmer grasp of the membership and operational requirements of a revolutionary party. They were more adept at internal Party affairs than outside mobilization work. Most Chinese graduates of the Communist University of the Toilers of the East later occupied predominantly administrative positions in the Chinese Communist Party hierarchy.[27]

The Communist University of the Toilers of the East also furnished the leading Chinese Communist figures in Party-political education during the mid-twenties. These people directed propaganda work and leadership training programs in China, helping to transmit Soviet educational models to the Chinese Communist Party. They were vehicles for Soviet influence upon the upcoming generation of Chinese Communists who were trained under their guidance. Among them were Li Fu-ch'un, who returned from six months in Moscow in 1924 to teach in the Political Department of the Whampoa Military Academy and to head a Kuomintang political training class. In 1926 Li directed the Political Department of T'an Yen-k'ai's Second Army. Li Ch'iu-shih, who trained at the Communist University of the Toilers of the East between 1923 and 1925, became district secretary of the Communist Youth League in Honan in 1925. The following year, while propaganda chief of the Youth League Kwangtung Committee, he organized lectures for a cadre training class. Fellow Youth League activist Lo I-nung, who matriculated in Moscow between 1921 and 1925, returned to China as a delegate of the Krestintern. He headed a short intensive cadre training program in Peking at one of the Party schools authorized at the enlarged Chinese Communist Party Plenum of October 1925.

SHANGHAI UNIVERSITY

A group of Chinese Communist Party members associated with the Communist University of the Toilers of the East—Ch'ü Ch'iu-pai, Chang T'ai-lei, Chiang Kuang-tz'u, and P'eng Shu-chih—helped in 1923 to launch Shanghai University, the major training center for Chinese labor movement cadres before 1925. The Chinese Communists operated this school jointly with the Kuomintang prior to setting up their own training institutions.

By the mid-twenties Chinese Communist leadership policy attempted to produce two types of Party members—those in the higher levels of the Party supervising internal organizational operations, and lower-level functionaries concerned with establishing ties to the mass movements. As the Party matured and expanded its mass base, it began developing training programs for mass movement cadres, but before 1926 the Communist University of the Toilers of the East was largely responsible for the formal training of Chinese Communist leaders in the first category. By 1926 the Party had plans for a system of Party schools to prepare both higher- and lower-level leadership personnel.

Although Shanghai University was not a formal Chinese Communist Party school, it became a model for the Communists' Party school system. Most of the eminent Chinese Communists during the mid-twenties were Shanghai University instructors or students. Their activities at that institution have won praise in later Chinese Communist writings.

The university was founded under the sponsorship of the Kuomintang in 1923, a time of warm relations between the Kuomintang and the Chinese Communist Party. Its "united front" orientation enabled the Chinese Communists there to spread their influence in the Chinese labor movement and sheltered Party activities during the recovery from the setbacks of Wu P'ei-fu's "February Seventh Massacre." Eventually Shanghai University came under Chinese Communist domination and developed the reputation of a Communist training center.

When the university moved its quarters to Seymour Road in the International Settlement, it added the School for Common People and enlarged its middle school. Teng Chung-hsia became dean of studies and Ch'ü Ch'iu-pai headed the social science department. Yü Yu-jen remained the nominal president, but Ch'ü and Teng actually ran the school. In 1924 and 1925 prominent editor and Kuomintang radical Shao Li-tzu served as acting president. Some of the university funds were supplied by Kuomintang headquarters in Canton.[28]

Shanghai University consisted of four departments—social science, Russian language, Chinese language, and English language, all staffed by Kuomintang and Chinese Communist Party members.[29] Ts'ai Ho-sen, then editor of the Chinese Communist Party organ *Hsiang-tao chou-pao* (the *Guide Weekly*), lectured on the origins of private property and the family system. Chang T'ai-lei taught a political class in 1923 before departing for the Soviet Union. Ch'ü Ch'iu-pai, who had returned from the Soviet Union several months before, brought his experience at the Communist University of the Toilers of the East to courses on "Social Philosophy" and "Introduction to the Social Sciences."[30]

Despite the presence of Soviet-trained faculty members and a large contingent of Chinese Communists in the student body, Shanghai University did not replicate a formal Soviet-style Party school or train higher-level Chinese Communist directing personnel. It remained tied administratively to the Kuomintang and focused on the production of cadres for the mass movements. The Chinese Communist Party was able to profit from this situation by singling out promising young student activists for Party membership.31 Well-known Chinese Communist graduates of Shanghai University include Jao Shu-shih, Ch'en Shao-yü (Wang Ming), Ch'en Po-ta, Wang Chia-hsiang, Ting Ling, Li I-mang, Li Shih-hsun, Ch'in Pang-hsien (Po Ku), Chang Ch'in-ch'iu, Yang Shang-k'un, Yang Chih-hua, and K'ang Sheng. At Shanghai University the Chinese Communists learned techniques for educating "practical workers" in the labor movement which they applied to their own Party schools.

The study program at Shanghai University placed a great deal of emphasis on outside work. According to Yang Chih-hua, "progressive" students were permitted to work in the community outside the university. Many were active in the Shanghai labor movement. Yang was assigned to the women's department of the Kuomintang while Chang Ch'in-ch'iu worked at a part-time night school in an industrial district. Liu Hua, a printer attending the Shanghai University middle school, gained a reputation as "an expert at agitation." He became vice-president of the Shanghai General Labor Union and lost his life leading demonstrations for the May Thirtieth Movement. The call of outside work inspired Ch'in Pang-hsien to leave the university shortly after enrolling in the English department in the fall of 1924. Ch'in then worked full-time among the Shanghai proletariat.32

Through students' outside activities Shanghai University became the base for the Shanghai labor movement. Many of the night schools for workers that proliferated throughout Shanghai during the mid-twenties were staffed by Shanghai University students. University students were also instrumental in organizing the mass protests of the May Thirtieth Movement.

Contributions to proletarian unrest and the May Thirtieth Movement made Shanghai University a target of foreign reaction. Police from the International Settlement raided the university periodically throughout the winter and spring of 1924-25. American and British troops occupied the campus on June 4, 1925, forcing the university to move to other quarters. The school closed permanently after the Shanghai coup of April 12, 1927.[33] Many of its students lost their lives during the counter-revolution.

PARTY SCHOOLS AND EDUCATION AFTER THE MAY THIRTIETH MOVEMENT

To prepare large numbers of leaders with the organizational skills for a mass-based political movement, the Chinese Communists set up their own system of Party schools. At the higher levels the Party lacked competent directing personnel, and at lower levels there were no working-class leaders capable of understanding elementary Communist theory and organizational principles. Neither an isolated training program nor the skills developed through daily Party work could meet these needs.

By July 1926 the Chinese Communist Party had launched Party schools for both higher and lower-level leadership. Set up under local Party committees, general Party schools gave short courses, lasting two to four weeks, for the training of workers to agitate among the masses. Advanced Party schools, supervised by Party regional committees, trained experienced Communists as directing personnel; these courses lasted three months. The Central Committee cautioned both types of schools against separating classroom studies from outside work. Students were expected to work among the masses to acquire "true proletarian ideas."

The curricula for both types of Party schools differed mainly in degree of detail[34] and resembled that of Soviet Party schools in the early twenties. General and advanced schools used as texts Marx's *Wage-Labor and Capital, The Communist Manifesto,* Kautsky's *Economic Doctrines of Karl Marx* and *Class Struggle,* Bukharin's *Program of the Communists,* and Lenin's *Imperialism.*

Despite instructions that "training in the Party Schools" be "based on experience in the national revolutionary movement," the outline of lecture topics shows little attention to problems of Party organization, propaganda, and mass movement work. It is possible that the architects of the Party school system placed top priority on building students' commitment to Communism through theoretical training. They may also have felt that theoretical competence could solve most of the Party's movement-building problems or that organizational skills were best developed through "outside work." However, it may also be the case that Chinese Communist leaders were still confused about the appropriate forms of training for a critical period of Party expansion.

Type A Party schools for workers divided curricula into six lecture topics, each followed by a series of "problems" and suggestions for reference reading. The number of lectures for each topic and the distribution of teachers was fixed by local propaganda committees. In essence, instruction for low-level operatives consisted of a Marxist analysis of the dynamics of capitalism and imperialism and of the relationship of those systems to the Communists' political program. Teachers were encouraged to "pay special attention to facts which are easily observed and understood by local workers."

The main points of each lecture took the form of key questions. For example, the discussion on the nature of capitalism emphasized the progressive impoverishment of workers and peasants; the necessity of uniting to oppose capitalists; the inevitability of class struggle; the leading role of the proletariat in seizing political power; the eventual collapse of capitalism through contradictions; and the foundations for communism laid during the capitalist phase of history. Questions to develop these points proceeded as follows:

1. What is a commodity? What is commodity economy? What is hired labor?
2. How do capitalists exploit labor?
3. What is capital? What is surplus value?
4. Why is capitalist society divided into many classes? Explain the special characteristics of the following classes: (a) the bourgeoisie—big capitalists who own the instruments and capital of production (materials of production); (b) the petty bourgeoisie—the handicraftsmen and farmers who own the tools of production; (c) the proletariat (workers)—who are unable to own the materials of production but can only sell their labor.
5. What is the significance of class struggle?
6. What is industrial and commerical competition? Will small handicraft production or big production triumph in this competition? Why are the small farmer and small handicraftsman bankrupt? What is the meaning of concentration of capital?
7. Why do capitalists want to employ more female and child laborers? This is a capitalistic tactic of competition and exploitation of the working class.
8. What is the function of the state or government in the class struggle?
9. What is the phenomenon of anarchy of production in capitalist society?

10. What is economic crisis?
11. Why is it that as capitalism develops, economic crisis deepens and class conflict in society becomes more violent?
12. What is the result of concentration of capital? What is the meaning of corporations and trusts?
13. What are the merits of concentration of capital and mechanized production as compared with small handicraft and small business?
14. In what way does capitalist development prepare the social and economic foundations for communism?

Central ideas for the section on imperialism were the international character of the capitalist system that led to the struggle for colonies and the division of the world into advanced and oppressed nations. This framework was applied to conditions in China. Thus:

1. What is the organizational method of industrial production during the period of financial capitalism?
2. What is the function of banks during the period of financial capitalism?
3. What is the goal of capitalists when they unite in trusts and syndicates?
4. What is the tendency of concentration of capital during the period of financial capitalism? (must give illustrations)
5. What is imperialism?
6. Is it possible to avoid war between capitalist countries?
7. Why does the bourgeoisie of all countries fight for markets and colonies?
8. Give concrete examples of the partitioning of the world and seizure of colonies by the Powers during the second half of the nineteenth century (illustrated on simple maps of the world).
9. What is the condition of imperialist aggression in China? (Illustrate with unequal treaties, rights of customs administration, consular jurisdictional right to engage in railway, mining and industrial enterprises, foreign loans, securities, etc.)
10. What is the connection between militarists and imperialists?
11. What is the power of imperialists in Chinese industry?
12. Give concrete examples of direct exploitation and oppression of Chinese workers and the common people by the imperialists and foreign capitalists (including Christian mission schools).
13. Is China an independent nation or a semicolony?
14. During the imperialist period, why does conflict between the Powers and China and other oppressed peoples become daily more acute? (For material on the above questions use histories of Chinese foreign relations, current events, and articles on the movements of oppressed peoples in various magazines.)

There was also some attempt to introduce the vision of the classless society of the future and the intervening period of proletarian dictatorship:

1. Why does capitalist development inevitably lead to social revolution?
2. What is the system of proletarian dictatorship? What is a proletarian state?
3. Why is proletarian dictatorship transitional in nature? How will it be transformed from a proletarian state into a proletarian society?
4. Do classes still exist in a Communist society?
5. Does the system of private ownership of productive material still exist in a Communist society?

Two additional lecture topics and larger amounts of detail distinguished the curriculum of advanced Type B schools from that of Type A schools.   Such training could be used at the local level if local committees had suitable propaganda workers. However, the sophisticated terminology and developmental approach in the Type B curriculum appeared more suitable for intellectuals and Party members with some Marxist background. For example, the section on capitalism traced its historical evolution as well as contemporary characteristics:

A. The Development of Capitalism
   1. Period of natural economy
      a. Economy is the foundation of social development
      b. Primitive Communism
      c. Patriarchal society and slavery
      d. Feudalism
      e. The rise of private ownership and international trade during the period of natural economy
   2. Rise of capitalism and commerical capitalism
      a. Urban handicraft economy
      b. Commercial capitalism
   3. Basic contradictions between industrial capitalism and capitalist society
      a. Peculiar characteristics of capitalism
      b. Process of development of industrial capitalism
      c. Basic contradictions in the capitalist society
      d. Capitalist country
   4. Financial capitalism, imperialism and the World War
      a. Alliance of capitalists
      b. Bank capital
      c. The struggle of the Powers for markets and export—capital imperialism
      d. The World War
   5. Leninism

The section on imperialism and China was identical to that in the A schools, but could receive more detailed treatment. Like the section on capitalism, the section on communism viewed the socialist movement in historical perspective. The discussion of the history of early socialist movements, the three Internationals, and the Bolshevik Party furnished guidelines for the Chinese Communists' political strategy:

C. History of the Socialist Movement
   1. Evolution of socialism
      a. History is the history of class struggle
      b. Early communist theories—Christian communist movement
      c. "Heretical" communism
      d. The English and French bourgeois revolutions and the theory of communism (Babeuf)
      e. The Utopian socialists (Fourier, St. Simon, Owen)
      f. The revolutions of 1830 and 1840 and scientific socialism
   2. The three Internationals
      a. The First International
      b. The Paris Commune
      c. The Second International
      d. The Third International
   3. Communist society

D. History of the Russian social revolution (During lectures attention should be given to the history of the development of the Russian Bolsheviks and the internal conflict within the Russian Socialist Party.)
   1. History of the Russian revolutionary movement and the Bolsheviks
      a. The earliest revolutionary organization in Russia
      b. The rise of the Russian working class and its movement
      c. Before and after the 1905 Revolution
      d. From 1905 to 1914
      e. The European war and the Bolsheviks
   2. From the February 1917 Revolution to the October Revolution
   3. The October Revolution and the period of military communism
      a. Meaning of the October Revolution
      b. National construction by the working class
      c. The October Revolution and the Russian Communist Party (The Seventh, Eighth and Ninth Congresses of the Communist Party)

Outside Party schools many Party members received training during daily Party work. After July 1926 the propaganda department designed Party publications for instructing the rank and file. *Hsin ch'ing-nien* (*New Youth*), the organ of the Chinese Communist Party Central Committee, was to concentrate on theoretical articles, and *Hsiang-tao* (the *Guide*) would report on day-to-day developments in the labor and peasant movements.[35]

In routine Chinese Communist Party operations, education was structured through the Party cell. The Chinese Communist discussions of cells show considerable Soviet influence. As the "basic organ and organizational unit of the Party" that effected contact with the masses, the cell was the "center of life of the Party" and "the school of the Party for education and propaganda." Cell members were supposed to steel themselves with Bolshevik discipline. They were to submit to the authority of the Party hierarchy and learn to "collectivize life; oppose individualism; have absolute confidence in the Party; oppose all subjective points of view."[36]

As for all Communist parties, cell meetings had educational functions, and for the Chinese Communists these consisted of:

(a)   Political report
(b)   Discussion of concrete methods to realize the Party's policies
(c)   Discussion of means to develop the Party
(d)   Comment on the work of our comrades
(e)   Report and discussion of life within and outside the Party
(f)   Proposals

By listening to the political report and participating in discussions, Party members could deepen their understanding of Party policy and measure their activities relative to Party goals.

During this period special "educational propagandists" operated within Party cells to further "political education and ideological propaganda." They were responsible for helping "comrades in general to analyze current problems from the theoretical point of view." However, they were not supposed to "recite the propaganda outline word for word or pronounce stereotyped theories at cell meetings," but rather to facilitate Party members' comprehension of reports and Party Policies. The use of stimulating discussions and question-and-answer format was favored over "injection-type lectures." Special attention was given to cell members of proletarian background. It is likely that these guidelines for education in cell meetings were influenced by group study methods such as those at the Communist University of the Toilers of the East.

In addition to Party schools and daily Party activities, the Chinese Communist Party also organized special training classes. A directive of July 1926 ordered that training classes for low-level cadres in the labor movement be established in major urban centers. The Central Committee also instructed Party headquarters at all levels to set up classes to train women's movement cadres for agitation among female peasants and laborers.

Trained leadership at both lower and higher levels thus contributed to the Chinese Communist Party's rapid rise to political prominence in the 1920s. Yet the Party's early triumphs also contained the seeds of its downfall. The Chinese Communists had indeed created an impressive machine in the urban areas and had begun to penetrate the mass movements. However, they still could not control large populations to their satisfaction. New to the "game" of revolutionary politics, the Chinese Communist Party was unable to adequately prepare its membership—and its supporters—for the eruption of widespread class conflict. As an organization it could not keep pace with its phenomenal rise in membership and the growth of the mass movements. Success required sufficient numbers of competent directing personnel, strong local Party work, and effective propaganda activities among the masses—all conditions that the Chinese Communists failed to meet throughout the twenties.37

At this time the Chinese Communist Party was still unable to surpass the competition from other, more powerful political groups. The Kuomintang was also modelled along Leninist lines and had a monopoly on the armed forces. Both parties' constituencies and organizational boundaries were blurred by their mutual concern for anti-imperialist issues and the National Revolution. To overcome these obstacles Chinese Communism faced many more years of experimentation and struggle.

NOTES

[1] Figures on the growth of the CCP during the twenties can be found in Harrison, *March*, pp. 67-74, 84-86.

[2] Among the translations available in China in 1922 were Marx's "Critique of the Gotha Program" in *Chin-jih* [Today] monthly. Lenin's "Immediate tasks of the Soviet Government" appeared in the February 15 edition of *Ch'en-pao*. In 1924 portions of *State and Revolution*, under the Chinese titles "The Evolution of Communist Society" and "Marxian Politics," came out in translation. For additional details and a list of other translations between 1922-1927 see Chang Ching-lu, pp. 442-443, 452-454, 466-467.

[3] Even before the Comintern officially brought Chinese to the Soviet Union, a number of Chinese had been exposed to revolutionary influence as Soviet workers and residents. Forty to fifty thousand of some several hundred thousand Chinese workers in Russia were reported to have fought with the Red Armies during the civil war. In December 1918 a pro-Bolshevik Union of Chinese Workers was formed in Moscow. The Central Committee of the Russian Communist Party founded a Central Organization Bureau for Chinese Communists in Russia on July 1, 1920. Most of the Chinese in the Soviet Union during World War I returned to China between 1919 and 1920. See Chesneaux, pp. 207-210, and Harrison, *March*, p. 24.

[4] On Soviet activities in Asia see Harrison, *March*, pp. 24-27, and Xenia J. Eudin and Robert C. North, *Soviet Russia and the East* (Stanford, Calif.: Stanford University Press, 1957), p. 85.

[5]The closing session was in Petrograd on February 2. Among the Chinese was one Kuomintang representative. See Allen Whiting, *Soviet Policies in China, 1917-1924* (Stanford, Calif.: Stanford University Press, 1968), p. 78.

[6]See the biographies of all these figures in Klein and Clark, especially p. 141.

[7]Eudin and North, pp. 82-89. See also Kazama Jokichi, *Mosukō Kyōsan daigaku no omoide* [Recollections of the Communist University in Moscow] (Tokyo: Sangensha, 1949), p. 70.

[8]This discussion of the Foreign Language School is based on a transcript of an interview with P'eng Shu-chih by Robert A. Burton near Paris, August 11, 1966; "A Brief History of the Chinese Communist Party," in *Documents on Communism, Nationalism and Soviet Advisers in China 1918-1927*, ed. C. Martin Wilbur and Julie Lien-ying How (New York: Columbia University Press, 1956), p. 49; Harrison, *March*, pp. 31, 35; and Warren Kuo, *Analytical History of the Chinese Communist Party*, vol. 1 (Taipei: Institute of International Relations, 1966), p. 13.

[9]Among the Foreign Language School students to journey to the Soviet Union in early 1921 were P'eng Shu-chih, Liu Shao-ch'i, Lo Chüeh (Lo I-nung), P'u Shih-ch'i Yüan Ta-shih, Jen Pi-shih, Jen Tso-ming, Pao Pu (Ch'in Ti-ch'ing), Hsiao Ching-kuang, Ts'ao Ching-hua, Han Pei-hua, Chiang Kuang-chih, Ch'en Wei-jen P'eng Li-ho, Wang Jo-fei, Liang Pei-t'an, and Liao Hua-p'ing. Not everyone at the Foreign Language School travelled to the Soviet Union; according to P'eng Shu-chih, Wang Shao-hua, K'o Ch'en-shih, and Ho Chung-liang remained behind. The Shanghai Communist group planned to use some of the Foreign Language School students for work in China, especially organizing labor unions in Shanghai. See Burton interview with P'eng Shu-chih. See also "Brief History," Wilbur and How, p. 49, and Chang Kuo-t'ao, "Wo ti hui-i" [My Recollections] , *Ming-pao*, no. 30 (June, 1968), p. 91. Warren Kuo, *Analytical History*, vol. 1, p. 339, included among his list of Foreign Language School students Fu Ta-ching and Li Chi-han.

[10]There were also special Communist universities for specific fields, such as the Academy of Communist Education and the Leningrad Political Education Institute founded in 1919. See Zev Katz, "Party-Political Education in Soviet Russia" (Ph.D. dissertation, University of London, 1957), pp. 54, 340-341. The preceding discussion of Soviet party schools is based on Katz, pp. 54, 225-277, 306, 340-355, 376-378.

[11]Communist University of the National Minorities of the West trained "national minorities" of non-Russian nationality living in the European part of the Soviet Union or in Europe itself, such as Poles, Estonians, Latvians, Belorussians, Hungarians, Germans, Jews, French, etc. Regional Communist universities also spread throughout the USSR during the 1920s and by the early 1930s had been established in almost all important administrative and industrial centers. The most outstanding of those in the eastern areas were the Central Asian Communist University in Tashkent, founded in 1923, and the Tatar Communist University in Kazan, which opened in 1922. See Katz, pp. 379, 392, 394, 400.

[12]Sources vary on the opening date of the university. Wang Hung-hsün, one of the first Chinese at the school, said that the university was founded in the summer of 1921 and began classes in September. See Wang Hung-hsün, "Wei-ta shih-nien ti hsi-li," [Baptism of Ten Great Years] , in *Hung ch'i p'iao-p'iao* [Red Flag Flutters] , vol. 4, pp. 20-25, and the entry of July 31, 1921, in Chiang K'ang-hu's *Hsin O yu-chi* [Record of a journey to New Russia] (Shanghai: Shang wu ch'u-pan she, 1923), p. 35. See also Bernadette Yu-ning Li, "A Biography of Ch'ü Ch'iu-pai: From Youth to Party Leadership (1899-1928)" (Ph.D. dissertation, Columbia University, 1967), p. 66.

[13]That year CCP leaders Ch'en Tu-hsiu and P'eng Shu-chih, while attending the Fourth Comintern Congress in Moscow, decided to shift the locus of Chinese Communist activity abroad away from Western Europe. Ch'en began to encourage CCP and Socialist Youth Corps members to study at Communist University of the Toilers of the East. In addition to the Burton interview with P'eng Shu-chih, several other sources discuss Chinese enrollment at Communist University of the Toilers of the East. Ts'ao Ching-hua, "Tien ti i Ch'iu-pai" [A Bit of Recollection about Ch'iu-pai] , *Wen-i pao (Literature and Art)*, no. 11 (June 15, 1955), p. 47, lists 42 Chinese students in the first class. Katz, p. 383, points to

72 Chinese students out of a total of 713 in December 1921. Katz's figures show 900 students at the university in 1923 and 1,015 as of January 1924 (see pp. 363, 386). For another estimate see also Roger Swearingen and Paul Langer, *Red Flag in Japan* (Cambridge, Mass.: Harvard University Press, 1952), p. 24.

[14]On the language problem at Communist University of the Toilers of the East see Bernadette Yu-ning Li, "Ch'ü Ch'iu-pai," pp. 67-68; Ts'ao Ching-hua, p. 47; and Yang Tzu-lieh, "Mo-ssu-k'o tung-fang ta-hsüeh" [Eastern University in Moscow], *Chan-wang* [Outlook], no. 169 (February 16, 1969), p. 29. It took Japanese student Kazama Jokichi one year of Russian language study to read *Pravda* with the aid of a dictionary. Most students needed two to three years in the USSR before they felt comfortable with the Russian language.; see Kazama Jokichi, pp. 89, 99-100.

[15]Eudin and North, p. 86, and Swearingen and Langer, p. 24. See also S. Popov, "KUTV—kuznitsa Kadrov dlia sovetskogo vostoka," *Revolutsionni Vostok*, no. 2 (1935), pp. 189-190.

[16]Yang Tzu-lieh, "Mo-ssu-k'o tung-fang," p. 29, and Kazama Jokichi, p. 69.

[17]Kazama Jokichi, p. 89. According to Zev Katz, pp. 358 and 384, there was some consideration given to educational background as well as language in assignment of study groups. Separate seminar and instructors courses were in operation in 1921 with sixty-one and eighty-eight students, respectively. However, the materials on Asian revolutionaries at Communist University of the Toilers of the East do not mention these special programs and they may have only been available to Soviet nationals. The curriculum at Communist University of the Toilers of the East and other Communist universities was modelled after that of Sverdlov University, considered the most prestigious of such institutions. Katz also notes that the Agitprop (Agitation and Propaganda Department) of the Secretariat of the Central Committee of the CPSU established general curricula for all Soviet Party schools. However, not all of the Party schools were actually under Agitprop direction, especially in the twenties and thirties; see p. 546.

[18]Kazama Jokichi, p. 89; Yang Tzu-lieh, "Mo-ssu-k'o tung-fang," p. 29; Eudin and North, p. 86; and S. Popov, pp. 190-91. The Eastern studies course included topics on the economy, social structure, and revolutionary movements of the Soviet eastern republics and other Asian countries. Grigory M. Broido himself gave the general introduction to Eastern studies with Sultan-Zade lecturing on Persia and M. Pavlovich on Turkey. Discussions of world economic geography were entitled "European-American Imperialism and the Colonial World." See Katz, pp. 384-85.

[19]Only fifty percent of the instructors at the various Communist universities were Party members. Most of the non-Party instructors were specialists in technical subjects. The major theoretical courses were taught by Communists. Katz, p. 365.

[20]Books used by the Chinese students at Communist University of the Toilers of the East included Bukharin's *Historical Materialism*, Bukharin and Preobrazhensky's *ABC of Communism*. A.A. Bogdanov's *Short Course on Economics*, Mikhail N. Pokrovsky's *Concise Outline of the Russian History*, P.I. Stuchka's *Soviet Constitution*, and Nikolai N. Baturin's *Outline of the History of Social Democracy in Russia*. Bernadette Yu-ning Li, "Ch'ü Ch'iu-pai," p. 68.

[21]On the "excursion method" and military training see Kazama Jokichi, pp. 125-146; Katz, pp. 454-474; Wang Hung-hsün, p. 24; and S. Popov, pp. 194-195. Apparently the drive for military training grew out of the Comintern's concern over the possibility of another world war. However, military training did not dominate the educational experience at Communist University of the Toilers of the East as it did at the Whampoa Military Academy and the Peasant Movement Training Institute in China. While it may have instilled in students a sense of discipline and skills for armed class conflict, military training does not appear to have been used for character formation at Soviet Party schools at this time.

[22]On changes in the objectives and methods of Soviet Party schools during the twenties through the forties see Katz, pp. 63, 71-89, 91-96, 179, 211-224, 374, 408, 461-462, 486-489. A regular institutional system of Party education in the Soviet Union was revived around 1940-1941. By the end of World War II the Party school system again had become the principal method of Party-political education. However, even after a system of Party schools was reestablished, the use of

the press and private study, as emphasized during the late thirties, remained important features of political education. The most complete study of Soviet Party schools available in English is that of Katz. For another description of Soviet Party schools in the 1930s see Wolfgang Leonhard, *Child of the Revolution*, trans. C.M. Woodhouse (Chicago: Henry Regnery Company, 1958), pp. 163-98, 369-70. Gabriel Almond, on the basis of a survey of former Communist Party members of various nations, draws similar conclusions about changes in Communist Party-political educational trends. His respondents depicted training experiences of the 1920s as tolerant of lively doctrinal discussions and conflicting viewpoints. After Stalinization took root in the 1930s they found Party-political education more dogmatic, with considerable emphasis on rigid indoctrination. See Gabriel Almond, *The Appeals of Communism* (Princeton, N.J.: Princeton University Press, 1954), pp. 115-116. On Soviet philosophical debates and their effect on Soviet science and education (especially the controversy between the Deborinists and the Mechanists) see also David Joravsky, *Soviet Marxism and Natural Science, 1917-1932* (New York: Columbia University Press, 1961).

[23]Like the French and German branches of the CCP, the Moscow branch was established because of the language factor. Many Chinese Communists had language difficulties abroad and could not participate in the activities of the Communist Party in the countries in which they resided. Burton interview with P'eng Shu-chih.

[24]On "struggle and criticism" at the university see Yang Tzu-lieh, "Mo-ssu-k'o tung-fang," pp. 31-32, and the Burton interview with P'eng Shu-chih. Bernadette Yu-ning Li, "Ch'ü Ch'iu-pai," pp. 100-101, discusses the "Committee of Five."

[25]"The Concrete Guide to the Work of Training" is thought to have been drafted by the Moscow branch some time before February 1925. It is reproduced in Wilbur and How, pp. 135-137.

[26]Kazama Jokichi, p. 125, S. Popov, pp. 194-195; and Wang Hung-hsün, p. 24.

[27]In late 1924 Chao Shih-yen was appointed secretary of the CCP Peking Committee and chief of the propaganda department and secretary of the Labor Movement Committee of the CCP North China Regional Committee. Ch'en Yen-nien headed the CCP Kwangtung Regional Committee when he returned home in 1925. By mid-1925 Wang Jo-fei had become secretary of the CCP Honan-Shansi Regional Committee. Hsü Chih-chen headed the organization and later the propaganda department of the Hunan Party Committee in 1927. Proletarian Kuan Hsiang-ying became secretary of the Hunan provincial Party Committee in 1925. Ch'en Ch'iao-nien, the brother of Yen-nien, was reported working in the CCP North China Regional Committee in the mid-twenties and was a leading official in the Hupeh underground in late 1927. Yüan K'un, formerly secretary of the French CCP branch, first served on the CCP Shantung Provincial Committee when he returned to China in 1924. In early 1926 he took charge of propaganda for the Kiangsu-Chekiang-Anhwei Regional Committee. Ch'en Ch'ao-lin assisted P'eng Shu-chih in the CCP Central Committee's propaganda department before joining the Left Opposition in the summer of 1929.

Some graduates of Communist University of the Toilers of the East undertook somewhat different tasks in mobilization and military work. Ts'ai Ch'ang, Hsiang Ching-yü, Chang T'ai-lei, Liu Shao-ch'i, and Lo I-nung spent a portion of their time in "practical work" organizing laborers. Chu Te, Yeh T'ing, Nieh Jung-chen, and Hsiao Ching-kuang became commanders or commissars in the National Revolutionary Army and after 1927, the Chinese Communist Red Army. Their expertise was primarily military. Study at Communist University of the Toilers of the East helped to solidify their commitment to Communist beliefs and sensitized them to the rationale for political controls over the military. Biographies for all of these figures can be found in Klein and Clark. For the names of other figures who attended Communist University of the Toilers of the East see, in addition to Klein and Clark, the Burton interview with P'eng Shu-chih; Bernadette Yu-ning Li, "Ch'ü Ch'iu-pai," pp. 69, 98-99; Harrison, *March*, no. 32, p. 523; Yang Tzu-lieh, "Mo-ssu-k'o tung-fang," p. 28; and Yüeh Sheng, *Sun Yat-sen University in Moscow and the Chinese Revolution: A Personal Account* (Lawrence, Kansas: University of Kansas Center for East Asian Studies, 1971), pp. 25, 138, 171-172.

[28]On the organization of Shanghai University, see Hsiao Tu, "Yü Yu-jen yü Shang-hai ta-hsüeh," [Yü Yu-jen and Shanghai University], in *Hsien-tai shih-liao* [Materials on

Contemporary History], vol. 1 (Hai-t'ien ch'u-pan she, 1933), pp. 290-292. See also Bernadette Yu-ning Li, "Ch'ü Ch'iu-pai," p. 135, and the section on the May Thirtieth Movement of the manuscript by C. Martin Wilbur entitled tentatively "The National Revolution in China, 1922-1928," p. 28.

29During the 1923-1925 period the social science instructors included Ch'ü Ch'iu-pai, P'eng Shu-chih, Li Chi, Yü-han Tai-ying, Shih Ts'un-t'ung, Kao Yü-kan, Ts'ai Ho-sen. and Chiang Kuang-tz'u. Chiang Kuang-tz'u along with Ch'u Shih-ying was also listed as a Russian language instructor. The English department staff consisted of Ho Shih-chen, T'ien Han, Po Tung-hua, Hsieh Liu-i, Shao Li-tzu, Shen Yen-ping (Mao Tun), Yeh Ch'u-ts'ang, Hu P'o-an, Liu Ta-po, and Yü P'ing-po under the direction of Ch'en Wang-tao. The faculty roster also listed Chinese Communists Chang T'ai-lei, Jen Pi-shih, Hsiao Ch'u-nü, Li Ta, An T'i-ch'eng, Yun K'uan, Hsiao Ts'u-yu, and Shen Ting-i. In addition prominent Kuomintang and Chinese Communist figures visited the school as guest lecturers. Among them were Wang Ching-wei, Hu Han-min, Tai Chi-t'ao, Chang Chi, Sun K'o, Chang Hsü, Hsieh Chih, Shen Hsüan-lu, Kuo Mo-jo, Liu Ya-tzu, and Ch'en Tu-hsiu. See Hsiao Tu, pp. 290-291; Bernadette Yu-ning Li, "Ch'ü Ch'iu-pai," pp. 135-138; and Klein and Clark, p. 1,053. See also Yang Chih-hua, "I Ch'iu-pai" [Recalling Ch'iu-pai"], in *Hung-ch'i p'iao-p'iao [The Red Flag Flutters]*, vol. 8 (Peking: 1958), pp. 24-25.

30Counterbalancing politics and economics were literature offerings such as Shao Li-tzu's class on traditional Chinese literature, T'ien Han's discussion of the poems of Edgar Allan Poe, and Mao Tun's course on European and early Greek literature. See Helen Foster Snow, *Women in Modern China* (The Hague: Mouton and Co., 1967), p. 206. Ch'ü Ch'iu-pai's lecture notes for his Shanghai University courses were published in book form as the *Outline of the Social Sciences* [She-hui k'o-hsüeh kai-lun] and *Lectures on the Social Sciences* [She-hui k'o-hsüen chiang-i]. The *Outline of the Social Sciences* consisted of Ch'ü's notes for his lectures at Shanghai University in the summer of 1924 and was published by the Shanghai Bookstore attached to the university in October 1924. Ch'ü's *Lectures on the Social Sciences* were published in four installments between January and April 1924. Edited by Ch'ü himself, each volume contained six sections. The sections on "Contemporary Sociology" and "Outline of Social Philosophy" were written by Ch'ü himself, while the other four were written by instructors Shih Ts'un-t'ung (who had studied economics in Japan) and An T'i-ch'eng (who studied economics at Kyoto University). Ch'ü used as his main source for both works his text at Communist University of the Toilers of the East—Bukharin's *Historical Materialism*. However, Ch'ü's work was not a direct translation of Bukharin but a "severe condensation." Ch'ü was considered a leading Chinese Communist theoretician but lacked solid training in Marxist philosophy. Most of his works were translations and compilations of European Marxists. See Bernadette Yu-ning Li, "Ch'ü Ch'iu-pai," pp. 138-141, and Yang Chih-hua, pp. 24-25.

For analysis of Bukharin's *Historical Materialism*, which employed an equilibrium model to describe social change, see Cohen, pp. 109-120. Through the writing and teaching of Ch'ü Ch'iu-pai and others, the work of Bukharin appears to have been transmitted to the Chinese Communist movement. The *ABC of Communism* and other Bukharinist works continued to be utilized in Chinese Communist Party-political education even after Bukharin was discredited in the Soviet Union. Until the late twenties Bukharin's ideas were highly influential in the areas of Soviet political life to which many Chinese Communists were exposed—the Comintern and Soviet Party school system. For a time Bukharin's followers dominated the ideological organs and educational system of the CPSU, as well as the economic planning apparatus of the Soviet state. Bukharin himself served as general secretary of the Executive Committee of the Comintern between late 1926 and July 1929 and wrote on the question of the united front and revolution in China. His other writings on imperialism and economic development also touched areas critical to the Chinese revolution—imperialism and the role of the peasantry in industrialization. Bukharin was extremely sensitive to the plight of the peasantry under rapid modernization and warned of a "parasitic" effect of industrialization upon the countryside. In addition to focusing on rural economic problems, Bukharin championed the use of mass persuasion and education via voluntary organizations to forge links between the Party and the masses and to curb the coercive features of statization and Party dictatorship. One can also find affinities to later trends in Chinese Communism in Bukharin's discussion of economic development and social change in *Economics of the Transition Period*. Like Mao and the forces feeding Maoism in China, Bukharin emphasized "human" over objective material factors in modernization. His *Economics*

of the Transition Period has been described as "a theoretical justification of volunta-
rism and social leaps." Bukharin played a major role in adapting Marxist theory to
economically backward nations and as such represents one link between Soviet and
Chinese Communism. However, a precise assessment of Bukharin's impact on Chinese
Communism remains to be determined. It should also be pointed out that some
features of Bukharinism, such as his moderate, evolutionary approach to postrevolutionary economic policy and promotion of social harmony and class collaboration, ran
counter to other dominant trends in Bolshevik and Chinese Communist thinking. This
discussion of Bukharin's theoretical contributions is based on Cohen, especially pp. 25-
36, 87-109, 129-149, 170-227, and 253-261.

31There were KMT, CCP, and Socialist Youth League branches within the university,
but most students were either CCP or Youth League members; see Hsiao Tu, p. 290.
Prospective students were required to sit for an examination, but the main qualification
for admission appears to have been their potential as activists; see Yang Chih-hua,
pp. 24-31. Some female students, such as Ting Ling, entered Shanghai University
through a feeder institution called the Shanghai Masses Girls School. The Chinese
Communist Party opened this school in early 1922 to recruit poor (and hopefully,
working-class) women with middle-school training, who lacked funds for further
study, and uneducated older women. Chang T'ai-lei was in charge, assisted by
instructors Ch'en Wang-tao, Shen Yen-ping, Teng Chung-hsia, Chang Kuo-t'ao, Liu
Shao-ch'i, Ch'en Tu-hsiu, Shao Li-tzu, and Kao Yü-han. Shanghai University also
maintained its own middle school through which future Party leader K'ang Sheng
entered the university. See Snow, *Women*, p. 204, and Klein and Clark, pp. 50, 424,
and 843. Wang I-chih, p. 14, lists Li Ta as head of the Girls School. According to
Snow's biography of Ting Ling, the school suffered from shortages of funds and
instructional staff, forcing its closure after six months. Most of its sixty students
were from Kiangsu and had only a primary-school education.

32On Yang Chih-hua, Ch'in Pang-hsien, Jao Shu-shih, Yang Shang-k'un, K'ang Sheng,
Chang Ch'in-ch'iu, Ch'en Shao-yü, Ch'en Po-ta, Wang Chia-hsiang, and Li I-mang see
Klein and Clark entries. Other less renowned figures that attended the university
were Ts'ao Shu-ying, Wang Ch'iu-hsin, Li Ping-hsiang, and Liu I-ch'eng. Liu I-ch'eng
was involved in student activities during the May Thirtieth Movement. See Wilbur,
"May Thirtieth Movement," p. 61. On Wang and Ts'ao see Yueh Sheng, pp. 69 and
250. On Li Ping-hsiang see Yang Chih-hua. On Liu Hua, see William Ayers,
"Shanghai Labor and the May Thirtieth Movement," in *Papers on China*, vol. 5
(Cambridge, Mass.: Harvard University Committee on International and Regional
Studies, 1951), p. 14.

33On the closing of Shanghai University, see Hsiao Tu, pp. 292-295; Bernadette Yu-
ning Li, "Ch'ü Ch'iu-pai," p. 136.

34"An Outline of the Curriculum of the Chinese Communist Party's 'A' and 'B'
Party Schools," Wilbur and How, pp. 130-133. This discussion is based on the
"Outline" and Wilbur and How, pp. 90-98 and 128-133.

35"Resolution on the Work of the Propaganda Department," ibid., p. 127. *Hsin
ch'ing-nien* changed its format three times between 1915 and 1926. It was a CCP
organ between July 1922 and July 1926. See Lawrence Sullivan and Richard
H. Solomon, "Formation of Chinese Communist Ideology in the May Fourth Era: A
Content Analysis of *Hsin Ch'ing-nien*," in *Ideology and Politics in Contemporary
China*, ed. Chalmers Johnson (Seattle: University of Washington Press, 1973), p. 119.

36The "Plans for the Organization of Party Cells," issued by the organization department of the CCP Northern Regional Committee on December 10, 1925, has sections
that are almost exact replicas of documents drawn up in the Soviet Union. The
wording of "Standards for Internal Party Education and Propaganda" is nearly
identical to parts of the "Concrete Guide to the Work of Training" issued by the
Moscow branch of the CCP. See Wilbur and How, pp. 104-109. On the educational
value of Communist Party meetings, see Frank S. Meyer, *The Molding of Communists:
The Training of the Communist Cadre* (New York: Harcourt, Brace, and Co., 1961),
pp. 118-122.

37Wilbur and How, pp. 96-98, 111-112, 129, 289-302. See also C. Martin Wilbur,
"The Influence of the Past; How the Early Years Helped to Shape the Future of the
Chinese Communist Party," in *Party Leadership and Revolutionary Power in China*,
ed. John Wilson Lewis (London: Cambridge University Press, 1970), pp. 43-44, 51-61.

4   Politics and the Gun

One source of regret to the Chinese Communists in 1927 was the Party's failure to develop its own coercive apparatus. Most of the Chinese Communists' energy had gone into work with the masses, and the National Revolutionary Army remained the province of the Kuomintang. After near annihilation in 1927 the Communists began to build their own Red Army, which became one of their most important revolutionary instruments and took on substantial political responsibilities.

Much of the groundwork for the Chinese Communist Red Army was laid well before the army itself materialized. During the mid-twenties the Chinese Communists began acquiring the leadership skills for their own military arm. Through participation in the National Revolutionary Army and Soviet-sponsored training programs they developed the nucleus of their professional officer corps and procedures to put "politics in command" over the gun.

Within China, the most prominent training program that prepared military leaders for the Chinese Communist movement was the Whampoa Military Academy. This school, launched under Soviet guidance in the spring of 1924, contributed to the rise of both the Chinese Communist Party and the Kuomintang as major political forces in China. Whampoa educated many of the leading military figures in both camps. Its cadets helped lead the National Revolutionary Army to victory during the Northern Expedition.

Military schools in the Soviet Union also trained a number of Chinese Communist leaders from the mid-1920s through the early 1940s. Experiences at these schools and in the National Revolutionary Army gave Chinese Communists the technical expertise to run their own modern army. Equally significant, the Chinese Communists were introduced to the Soviet system of political education and Party controls that coordinated military activities with general political objectives.

THE WHAMPOA MILITARY ACADEMY

The Chinese Communist Party first became involved in military training through its policy of collaboration with the Kuomintang during the National Revolution. The Kuomintang, reorganized under Soviet guidance, set up the Whampoa Military Academy in May 1924 to prepare leadership for its own army. Through an intensive program of military training and political education, the school was to fashion a corps of politically reliable officers.[1] Because the new army was the Kuomintang's main instrument for the reunification of China, Soviet and Chinese Communists found the training of the officer corps a critical area for their influence.

Soviet advisers were largely responsible for the design of the Whampoa Military Academy and the supervision of its training program. A. I. Cherepanov, Vladimir Poliak, and Nikolai Tereshatov, members of the Soviet military mission to the Kuomintang, directed the instructional work at Whampoa. All were said to have graduated from the Red Army (Frunze) Military Academy in Moscow and had extensive combat experience.[2] Most of the initial contributions supporting the academy and a substantial portion of the school's military training equipment came from the Soviet Union.[3]

Leading Kuomintang members dominated the Whampoa staff, which was assembled during April and May of 1924. Sun Yat-sen, as premier of the Kuomintang, was titular head of the academy. He appointed Chiang Kai-shek commandant on May 3, 1924, and Liao Chung-k'ai was named Kuomintang Party representative on May 9. Both were on equal footing, in accord with the Soviet political commissar system which placed the military under Party control. Under Chiang and Liao there were six departments. Kuomintang Party theorist Tai Chi-t'ao headed the political department, which aided the Kuomintang Party representative in nurturing revolutionary spirit among the cadets. However, Tai, saddled with many other duties, left Canton within a month and his responsibilities at Whampoa later fell to Communist Chou En-lai.[4]

The instruction department, with a staff of fifteen, took charge of classroom functions. It was headed by Wang Po-ling, who had previously taught at the Yunnan Military Academy. Li Chi-shen was in charge of the training department, which dealt with cadets' technical military education. Ho Ying-ch'in served as chief instructor. The three lower departments consisted of administration, military supply, and medical work. Various lower-level officers, orderlies, and guards brought the total staff to about four hundred.5

Chinese Communist influence at Whampoa was heaviest in the political department, especially when the department was under the leadership of Chou En-lai. On the political department staff were Communists Ch'en I in 1926, Hsiao Ch'u-nü in 1924, and Li Fu-ch'un in 1925-1926. Nieh Jung-chen was political instructor for the fourth and fifth classes and department secretary-general. Yün Tai-ying was concurrently chief instructor of the department and lecturer for the sixth class of the Peasant Movement Training Institute in 1926.

Yeh Chien-ying, a member of the Whampoa teaching staff since 1924, commanded a Whampoa cadet training regiment in campaigns against Ch'en Chiung-ming. Other Chinese Communists who were Whampoa instructors included Chi Fang and Chou Pao-chung. Both Ch'ü Ch'iu-pai and Hsü Hsiang-ch'ien taught briefly at the Wuhan branch of Whampoa in early 1927.6 Chinese Communists in influential positions at the academy may have raised the respectability of Communism in the eyes of academy cadets, attracting prospective military leaders to the Party.

The Whampoa Military Academy was actually the school for what became the First Army Corps of the National Revolutionary Army. Commanders of other units continued to maintain their own schools. On January 12, 1926, the Military Council of the National Revolutionary Army ordered the formation of a Central Military and Political Academy incorporating all army corps schools. The core of this new school was the Whampoa Military Academy. The Central Military and Political Academy opened on March 8, 1926, and graduated a class of 2,500 in October. (This is considered the fourth Whampoa class.) A fifth class lasted from January to July 1927 and graduated 2,650 cadets, who were ordered to report to Nanking for duty. Altogether Whampoa and the Central Military and Political Academy graduated about 7,400 officers.7

Patriotic youth from primarily rural backgrounds flocked to Whampoa. They were selected through a competitive entrance examination that included questions on political background:

1. Why do you intend to enter the School?
2. Who are the chief enemies of China?
3. By what means can the Chinese people be helped?
4. What is the difference between imperialists and militarists?
5. What is the purpose of the National Revolutionary Army and how does it differ from the armies of the militarists?
6. Who are Chang Tso-lin and Wu P'ei-fu?
7. What is the basis of the doctrine of Dr. Sun Yat-sen?
8. What is the attitude of the Kuomintang Party towards the peasantry?
9. What are the "Three Principles" of Dr. Sun Yat-sen?
10. Who is Lenin?
11. Which branch of army service do you like most?
12. What are the problems with which officers and political workers of the National Revolutionary Army are confronted?
13. How does the policy of our Government differ from that of Chang Tso-lin?
14. For what purpose do Labor Unions exist?
15. Why was the strike declared? What are its purposes and aims?
16. What is Hong Kong? Who wields power there?
17. What are the fundamental theses of the Chinese Revolution?
18. Which country is the most hostile? Which country is the most friendly? (What is the chief occupation of the inhabitants of Kwangtung?)
19. Why does foreign capital strive to penetrate China?
20. Is there any difference between the doctrines of Confucius and Dr. Sun?
21. What is the purpose of political work in the Army?
22. What is the object of the Northern Expedition?
23. Can the National Revolutionary movement gain a victory without being supported by the world's revolution?
24. Who carries on the principal fight for the world's revolution?
25. What is the main force in the National Revolutionary movement?
26. What is the part of the peasantry in the National Revolutionary movement?
27. Can the National Revolutionary movement gain a victory without the participation of the peasantry and why?
28. To whom do the peasants pay taxes and in which way?[8]

Some of the students responsive to the anti-imperialist and "social revolution" issues explored in the entrance questionnaire may have been attracted to the Chinese Communist Party. More than eighty of the first class were either Chinese Communist Party or Socialist Youth League members. Few came from worker-peasant backgrounds. However, most Whampoa cadets did not become Chinese Communists. At most only several hundred Chinese Communist Party members were Whampoa students.[9]

The Chinese Communists who did emerge from Whampoa developed skills for future command positions in the Red Army. Military instruction consisted of class work and field training centered around a six-month course in infantry work. There were special classes for artillery (60 students in a nine- to twelve-month course); sappers (130 students, nine months); and supply (60 students, six months). A machine-gun class of 120 requiring twenty hours of training was selected from the infantry. Students could also pursue instruction in engineering service, military police work, Russian language, fencing, and gymnastics. During the fourth class the matriculation period was extended to one year.[10]

Although Whampoa training included some elements of traditional Chinese military practices, it was primarily modern and Soviet-inspired. Until Chiang's coup of March 20, 1926, the Soviet advisers supervised instruction at the school. Vladimir Poliak, working directly with Wang Po-ling, was the senior adviser in charge of the educational section. Nikolai Tereshatov and A.I. Cherepanov were in charge of combat, rifle, and tactical training. They worked primarily with Ho Ying-ch'in.

Modern Chinese military education faced two hurdles: one was the acquisition of a large array of modern military techniques in a short period of time; the other involved the transformation in thinking needed to apply these techniques. The modern-style military academies that had been set up in China during the late Ch'ing period had not solved these problems entirely. Many graduates who staff the "new-style" armies had absorbed modern military science through a superficial imitation of Western models.

To overcome reliance on form rather than substance, the Soviet advisers constantly stressed the application of students' classroom work to actual situations in the field. They used practical examples to explain essential concepts encouraged students to master practical skills, and tried to instill in students the meaning of combat training, constant combat readiness, and deprivation in the line of military duty.[11]

Above all, Whampoa considered political indoctrination to be its most important objective. The serious attention to political work at Whampoa was a feature of the Soviet military model and distinguished Whampoa from other modern-style military academies in China. On May 13, 1924, Sun Yat-sen appointed three distinguished Kuomintang leaders as academy political instructors. Hu Han-min was to lecture on the Three People's Principles;

Wang Ching-wei on Kuomintang history, and Shao Yüan-ch'ung on the politics and economics of Europe and America. Commandant Chiang and official political department head Tai Chi-t'ao also gave speeches to the cadets.[12] From time to time other Kuomintang luminaries gave special talks.

Chiang discussed patriotism, commitment to the National Revolution, group solidarity, reverence for the common people, and self-sacrifice. Representatives of the political department took up questions such as political economy, the theory of imperialism, Sun Yat-sen's Three People's Principles and political doctrines, the history of China, and the history of revolutionary movements in the West. The anti-imperialist and antimilitarist line was that of Kuomintang, but these themes could also be exploited by Chinese Communist Party members on the Whampoa staff.

As future officers of a Party army, all Whampoa cadets were required to engage in political study. In the Central Military and Political Academy those who were to become commanders spent two hours of the nine-hour school day in political training. A special political section of the academy prepared political officers to aid regular officers in political work among the troops. For these students the ratio of political to military education was reversed. They spent about six hours daily in political study.

Political work was divided into two parts: political study and general political work. Political study fell under the jurisdiction of the political department. It furnished cadets with a general theoretical background on the National Revolution. The topics selected for presentation and their analytical framework allowed for interpretations slanted toward—or highly sympathetic to—a Marxist-Leninist position. Topics included (1) Outlines of Political Economy and Political Science; (2) Imperialism in China; (3) Short History of Revolutionary Movements in Other Countries; (4) History of the Revolutionary Movement in China; (5) History of the Kuomintang and Its Future Prospects; (6) Kuomintang Political Platform; (7) The Land Question; and (8) The Labor Question.

For convenience the political subjects were divided into "ordinary political training" and "special political training." Reproduced here is an outline of the political curriculum for political instructors for the fourth and fifth Whampoa classes, after the school was renamed the Central Military and Political Academy. While the major objective was to inculcate loyalty to the Kuomintang, much of this curriculum could be invoked by Communist instructors to move students further toward the left.

Program of the Political Training
In the Central Military School of Whampoa

The subjects of the political training are as follows:

a. *Ordinary political training*
1, The history of the Chinese Kuomintang
2. The doctrines of Sun Yat-sen
3. The history of the imperalistic aggression in China
4. The Russian revolution
5. Imperialism
6. Outline of the political economy
7. Social problems
8. Political work in the army
9. Problems of party organization
10. Socialism
11. Special lectures

b. *Special political training*
[Items 1-3, 5, and 10-14 are the same as part a., items 1-3, 5, 7-11.]
4. The history of the world revolution
6. Outline of social sciences
7. Outline of politics
8. Outline of economics
9. History of social evolution

The political training is based on the following ten theses:

1. Students must be given to understand that the duty of the Kuomintang Army consists in elucidating the policy of Sun Yat-sen and the declaration of the Assembly of the National Representatives of China as well as the order of the Central Executive Committee to the effect that soldiers must obey the National Government and their commanders and sacrifice themselves for the sake of their party and their country.

2. Students must be taught the special spirit of the Kuomintang Army and to submit themselves to the political training and to accept political work of the party.

3. Students must know that the Chinese revolution is a part of the world's revolution, and the Chinese soldier is a part of the world army; that our life is closely connected with the life of the whole world.

4. Students must be taught that the object of the Chinese revolution from the inside point of view is to overthrow the militarists and from the outside point of view to overthrow the imperialists.

5. Students must be taught that the Chinese revolution is an *international revolution*, and by no means a local political revolution.

6. Students must be taught that the duties of the revolutionary soldier from the point of view of the army organization are to sacrifice his freedom to the army, and from the point of view of the party to sacrifice his freedom to the party.

If one serves in the army of the party one must not insist on personal freedom. To insist on it is unworthy of the revolutionary soldier.

7. Students must be taught that rank in the army is a duty imposed on an officer and by no means does it isolate him from the soldiers (as it was during the feudal times).

8. Students must be made to understand that everybody's duty is to die for the benefit of the party and of the people without regret.

9. Students must be taught that in order to be able to solve social problems it is above all necessary to comprehend historical and political motives, social phenomena, and conditions as well as the relations between social and natural phenomena. To be able to decide all these questions a good knowledge of the revolutionary social sciences is necessary.

10. Students must be taught that the life of our party depends upon all its members who uphold the discipline and program of our party and the principles of Sun Yat-sen. A very important duty towards the party is therefore incumbent on every member of the party. [13]

The format for political study was divided into lectures and seminars of ten to fifteen cadets. Under the director of special instructors, the seminars discussed in detail the content of the lectures. According to Wang Po-ling, this "group conference technique" (*hsiao-tsu hui-i*) was "the soul of Whampoa's training and the life-blood of the Academy's success." It efficiently conveyed information to cadets and provided a showcase for leadership talent. The group discussion method was an important technique for Chinese Communist leadership education in subsequent years and probably was introduced to Whampoa by the Soviet advisers. [14]

A Kuomintang Party branch had been formed at Whampoa on July 3, 1924, and all officers and cadets were expected to join. [15] General political work was carried on by this branch and also fell under the direction of the Kuomintang Party representative at the academy and the head of the political department. Participation in the Kuomintang Party branch was designed to inculcate Kuomintang principles among commanders and other academy personnel. Kuomintang activities also drew cadets into active political work and enabled them to apply their theoretical knowledge. General political work consisted chiefly of lectures and discussions on current political topics, meetings, and the distribution of political literature.

POLITICAL WORK IN THE NATIONAL REVOLUTIONARY ARMY

Through participation in political work at Whampoa and in the National Revolutionary Army, Chinese Communists were able to observe a politicized military in operation. Political workers were assigned to indoctrinate the rank and file and to organize Party cells at the lower levels of the military. Special political workers (commissars) served as watchdogs over the commanders. This system of political control was adapted from the commissar system of the Soviet Red Army,[16] where politically reliable personnel supervised former White officers who commanded Red Army units during the civil war. Liao Chung-k'ai, first at Whampoa and later in the National Revolutionary Army, was responsible for setting the political commissar system in motion.

Party members who had been appointed liaison officers with the army were empowered to countersign and, if necessary, countermand the orders of the military commanders. A group of political commissars supervised political operations in the army through the system of Party cells. Each political commissar in an army corps had about one hundred political workers under him. Approximately one political worker was assigned to every hundred fighting men.

Political workers also helped to organize the civilian population, establishing contact with local residents and explaining the aims of the National Revolution and its benefits to the Chinese peasant. Through political work among the masses and the exemplary behavior of well-indoctrinated troops, the forces led by Whampoa graduates were said to have won over the population of Kwangtung. This popular support, cultivated through political work, was considered a decisive factor in the early victories of the National Revolutionary Army.[17]

Chinese Communists also had the opportunity to observe the exercise of political controls over the military in the operation of the Political Council and the Political Directorate of the National Government. The Political Council was the most powerful group in the National Government and drew members from the Kuomintang's civilian and military leadership. With an auxiliary group of Soviet advisers in attendance, it decided all major military and political policy issues. The Military Council, modelled after the Revolutionary Military Council of the Soviet Union, enforced the directives of the Political Council and took charge of the routine and technical aspects of military administration. Its members included Kuomintang leaders and commanders plus the Soviet advisers, all on equal footing.

The National Government created the Political Directorate, about the same time as it set up the Military Council, primarily to supervise political instruction within the National Revolutionary Army. The directorate, composed of departments for general affairs, agitation and propaganda, and Party affairs, issued a three-month program for the political education of soldiers.[18] The program required three to six hours of political work per week by the soldiers and included a list of questions on major political and economic issues for each political hour along with directions to the political workers conducting the sessions.

A pamphlet on "Political Lessons for Enlisted Personnel," issued in late 1925, illustrates the types of questions employed for troop indoctrination and the number of hours spent on the various items:

(1) Why have you become a soldier?

(2) Who are the landowners and why have they so much land?

(3) Why couldn't you find work in the city?

(4-7) Who is guilty for your misfortunes?

(8-15) What are the unequal treaties? What is extraterritoriality? What are the concessions? What is tariff autonomy?

(16-21) Why are the landowners acting in concert with the imperialists? Who are the compradores and why are they also acting in concert with the imperialists? Who are the *shen-shih* (gentry), *t'u-hao* (local bullies), and why are they acting in concert with the landowners and imperialists? Why are some merchants, students and capitalists acting in concert with the imperialists?

(22) What and who are the imperialists?

(23-4) Invite the soldiers' attention to some militarists; Yang Hsi-min, Liu Chen-huan, Wu P'ei-fu, Chang Tso-lin, Sun Ch'uan-fang.

(25-7) What is the National Revolutionary Army? How is the National Revolutionary Army organized? What aims does it set before itself?

(28) Who are the enemies of the National Revolutionary Army?

(29-32) Discussions of struggles of the oppressed peoples of the Far East, and of workingmen and peasants in England, Japan, and China itself.

Hours 33 through 36 were kept in reserve in case discussion of the questions had not been completed or for the reading of newspapers, exchange of opinions, or more detailed discussion of the Kuomintang Party program.

The questions were designed to explain in the most simple terms the nature of imperialism and militarism and their effect on the soldiers' own lives—landlessness, industrial unemployment, starvation, and forced conscription. Political workers were encouraged to employ examples from the soldiers' own lives, concrete figures, and statistics. Their instructions cautioned:

Least of all, recourse is to be made to theoretical reasonings and definitions while dwelling on these subjects. In connection with each of
these questions it would be quite possible to find appropriate instances which are known to the soldiers. One must train the soldiers
so as to make their minds work in the direction of conscious understanding of the life which surrounds them. It would be much better
if the soldiers succeeded in finding such examples by themselves. . . .
to give the soldiers "lectures" is the worst method of this work. . . .

You must be well acquainted with your soldiers. You must know
their names, ages, their native provinces and districts, their family
conditions, their professions before entering the military service,
whether they know how to read and write, etc. Only such detailed
knowledge of each soldier will give you in their eyes the great
authority, which is based, not on the rank you are holding, but on
their confidence in you and respect. Thereby, your task in connection
with their political education will be greatly facilitated.

Pay attention to the language you use when speaking to soldiers. . . .
keep in mind that different people use different languages. When
speaking to soldiers, use only one language and cite corresponding
instances; when speaking to officers or students, use another language
and cite other instances.[19]

Officers as well as rank and file were required to attend a political
instruction hour. In early 1926 the Political Directorate issued
instructions for the political education of officers. Regimental
commanders had to organize weekly political meetings for all
officers. The political commissar took charge of organizing each
lesson, which involved colloquia-type discussion of selected topics
similar to those for the rank and file.

The Political Directorate sponsored various agitation and propaganda activities. It surveyed all of the books, pamphlets, leaf-
lets, magazines, slogans, songs, wall newspapers, and placards
employed by National Revolutionary Army political departments.
The directorate encouraged the formation of clubs in army units
and sponsored the production of a reading primer for soldiers
in October 1925. It also attempted to install Kuomintang Party
nuclei in all army units.

The Political Directorate's Publishing Committee, consisting of
representatives of political departments within the National
Revolutionary Army, supervised the political departments'
publishing activities. One of the committee's major productions
was the newspaper *Political Work*, issued by the Publishing
Section of the Department of Agitation and Propaganda. *Political Work* supplemented the political instruction given to workers,
officers, and soldiers on the work of the National Revolutionary
Army.

The articles were written by the local committee of the Chinese Communist Party and the editor was also a Communist. The paper's circulation was 18,000, distributed among the political sections of the army. Its "letters to the editor" section was heralded for promoting "living contact between the editorial office and the reading masses."[20]

Involvement with political work at the Whampoa Military Academy and the National Revolutionary Army may have helped the Chinese Communist Party to recruit new members. Before the end of 1925, 250 political workers, including 100 Communists, had joined the National Revolutionary Army. By March 1926 the number of political workers had jumped to 876. Though the Political Directorate's records of political work in the National Revolutionary Army were imprecise, it was estimated that by March 1926 seventy-five percent of the political workers were Communists and left-wing Kuomintang members; twenty percent were officials seeking to advance their careers; and five percent were right-wing Kuomintang members.

The Chinese Communists headed the political departments of the First, Second, Third, Fourth, and Sixth Army Corps. Prior to the March 20 Incident they were most firmly ensconced in the First Army Corps, where Chou En-lai headed the political department and where Chinese Communists also occupied a large number of commissar positions and headed political work in four out of five divisions. Political work in the First Army Corps was said to have been the strongest in the entire National Revolutionary Army.[21]

The Chinese Communists remained influential in the training of officers for the National Revolutionary Army after Whampoa was redesignated the Central Military and Political Academy. The vice-chairman of the academy's political department was Chinese Communist Lu I, and Nieh Jung-chen was department secretary. The Chinese Communist Party cell at the academy was directly supervised by the Military Committee of the Chinese Communist Party Kwangtung Regional Committee, headed by Chou En-lai. Li Chih-lung, a Chinese Communist graduate of the first Whampoa class, headed the political department of the Navy Bureau and was concurrently the bureau's deputy chief.

The Military Committee of the Chinese Communist Party Kwangtung Regional Committee supervised the work of Chinese Communists in the National Revolutionary Army. It planned to organize workers' and peasants' armed detachments in operations against the morale of enemy troops. By March 1926 the Military Committee had set up Party schools at Swatow for the First Army Corps and at Canton for other army units. The committee sponsored a special political training class headed by Li Fu-ch'un to prepare political workers for the Northern Expedition. The Military Committee also supervised the formation of Chinese Communist Party nuclei within various army corps and issued directives for the penetration of Kuomintang organizations.[22]

Rising Communist influence in the National Revolutionary Army and Central Military and Political Academy sparked fierce clashes with the Kuomintang, and the Kuomintang suppressed Chinese Communist activities in the academy and the army after the Chung-shan Gunboat Incident of March 20, 1926. Chiang Kai-shek tried to retain Soviet assistance for his Northern Expedition, but he reduced the influence of Soviet advisers in the Military Council, the Central Military and Political Academy, and all divisions of the National Revolutionary Army.[23]

Even before the break with the Communists, political work within the National Revolutionary Army had had very uneven results; it was least effective in former regional military units absorbed by the Kuomintang during the Northern Expedition. Political indoctrination failed to transform warlords into servants of the nation-state. The National Government did not acquire jurisdiction over much of China, and national unification existed only on paper.[24]

Political work in the National Revolutionary Army deteriorated further after 1927. Left-wing Kuomintang and Chinese Communist political workers were purged, severely depleting the army's political work force. After 1928 the National Government switched from a Soviet to a German military model. Political work came to play a negligible role in the preparation of officers and the indoctrination of the rank and file. Kuomintang Party branches within the military became increasingly formalistic devices for supervision and control.[25] The Chinese Communists' experience with political work within the National Revolutionary Army occurred earlier, when the work had been most effective. The Communists drew heavily on the Kuomintang's pre-1927 military-political model when they fashioned their own Red armies.

SOVIET MILITARY SCHOOLS AND MODELS

The Chinese Communists' exposure to the Soviet military model and training methods did not end with their expulsion from the National Revolutionary Army. From the mid-twenties to the early forties, the Chinese Communist leaders attended military schools in the Soviet Union. The most prominent of these schools were the Red Army (Frunze) Academy in Moscow and the Leningrad Military-Political Academy.[26]

Both the Soviet military schools and the Whampoa Military Academy generated a significant portion of the top command structure of the Chinese Communist Red Army. They provided the technical expertise that enabled the Chinese Communists to develop their own army within the space of a few years. In accord with the Soviet model, trainees at these schools specialized in either military or political skills. The Chinese Communist officer corps evolved into two basic leadership types with either commander or commissar functions.[27]

While the Soviet military model paid serious attention to political indoctrination, its approach to political questions and political controls shifted markedly after the mid-twenties. Chinese Communists educated by Soviet advisers at the Whampoa Military Academy or Soviet military schools between 1924 and 1926 were likely to have come in contact with M.V. Frunze's doctrine of "unified strategy," which then prevailed in Soviet military circles. Unified strategy emphasized military involvement with civilian activities and Party controls over the military in the form of political commissars within the military chain of command.

Chinese Communist leaders who trained in Soviet military schools from the late twenties onward were more likely to have come under the sway of "integral strategy." Promoted by the theories of Boris Shaposhnikov and Mikhail Tukhachevsky, integral strategy became popular among Soviet military thinkers after Frunze's death in 1925. In contrast to unified strategy, integral strategy subordinated military linkages with civilian activities and political controls in the military to professional specialization and purely military strategic and tactical imperatives.[28]

It is difficult to measure the effects of integral strategy or unified strategy among different Chinese Communist military generations. There appears to have been a tendency among the Chinese Communists exposed to formal military training to align with those favoring a professionalized military in the Chinese Communist movement. But the Chinese Communists' military did not become highly professionalized until after 1949. Until 1948 it had almost no experience with artillery and fought most battles as either guerrilla or semiconventional formations with light arms.[29] Nevertheless formal military education at Whampoa, Soviet military schools, and subsequent Chinese Communist training programs imparted technical skills associated with conventional military operations and respect for professional military expertise.

Concepts of military style and ethic later became a major source of cleavage in the Chinese Communist leadership. The founding of the Red Army triggered numerous policy debates on guerrilla versus conventional operations, military independence from political controls, and the compatibility of military professionalism with mass mobilization and base-building. Military perspectives—and personal ties—developed at the Whampoa Military Academy also produced factional alignments among Chinese Communist leaders in the early thirties. Members of a "Red Whampoa Faction," who were former students of Chou En-lai or members of the Union of Military Youth, were prominent soviet leaders, political commissars, and commanders of various Red Army units.[30] As professionally trained officers, this group objected to Mao Tse-tung's promotion of guerrilla warfare in Party policy-making. Chou En-lai was the leader of the faction and maintained his ranking positions in the Communist hierarchy with the help of this military backing.

Whampoa and the Soviet military schools attended by Chinese Communists were the early models for Red Army programs to train military-political leadership. A great deal of the content and learning practices of Chinese Communist Red Army training institutions was based on Whampoa and Soviet military school procedures, and graduates of Whampoa and Soviet military schools were active in the design and preparation of Red Army military-political leadership training programs. Among the Whampoa graduates, Lin Piao became president and political commissar of the Red Army Academy in Shensi and official head of the Anti-Japanese Military and Political University (K'ang-ta). Lo Jui-ch'ing, Chang Chi-ch'un, Hsü Kuang-ta, and Hsü Hsiang-ch'ien were also prominent members of K'ang-ta's administrative or instructional staff. Tso Ch'üan, Chou Shih-ti, and Hsü Meng-ch'iu were associated with the Red Army Academy in Juichin, and Ch'en Keng and Ch'en Ch'i-han were with the Red Army School. Among the graduates of Soviet military schools, Liu Po-ch'eng and Yeh Chien-ying headed the Red Army School in 1931 and 1932-1933, respectively. Wu Hsiu-ch'üan taught at the Red Army Academy and T'eng Tai-yüan headed one of the K'ang-ta branches in south Shansi.

There would be some differences between the Chinese Communists' practices and the model of the Party-army they encountered during the twenties. The Chinese Communist system of political work in the Red Army and later in the People's Liberation Army became much more elaborate than those of the National Revolutionary Army and Soviet Red Army forces. Chinese Communist political work has continued to use the commissar system to keep its military under Party control, but it has also placed more emphasis on political education among both officers and rank and file than did either the Soviet model or the National Revolutionary Army. And to a greater degree than that achieved by the National Revolutionary Army, the Chinese Communists have developed the nation-building role of the military.[32] They have taken up where the National Revolutionary Army left off in 1927 and have made the military a major instrument for transforming Chinese institutions and society. In this capacity the Red Army became the backbone of the Chinese Communist movement and the organizational model for other aspects of Communist political and social life. Nevertheless, despite these differences, the essential features of the Chinese Communists' system to harness military force to larger political ends—political commissars, political departments, political education of officers and soldiers, and military participation in mass mobilization—have their roots in the Chinese Communists' experiences during the twenties.

NOTES

[1] Roderick L. MacFarquhar, "The Whampoa Military Academy," in *Papers on China*, vol. 9 (Cambridge, Mass.: Harvard University East Asia Program of the Committee on Regional Studies, 1955), pp. 149-152. Plans for the Whampoa Military Academy materialized after Sun Yat-sen and Liao Chung-k'ai's conversations with Comintern representatives in 1923. Arrangements for Soviet aid to the Kuomintang included a mission of military advisers to Canton, the first five of whom reached Peking in June 1923. Chiang Kai-shek spent the autumn of that year in Moscow studying the Soviet military system, and he headed an eight-man committee to plan for the military academy. The Whampoa Military Academy was located on Ch'ang-chow Island, fourteen miles south of Canton, and occupied the former site of the Kwangtung Provincial Military Academy and Naval Academy. Preparations for Whampoa are discussed in C. Martin Wilbur, "Forging the Weapons" (unpublished paper, presented at Columbia University Seminar on Modern East Asia: China, February 19, 1966), pp. 71-72.

[2] Alexander Ivanovich Cherepanov, *Notes of a Military Adviser in China*, trans. Alexandra O. Smith (Taipei: Office of Military History, 1970), p. 118.

[3] Much of the financial support for Whampoa came from Soviet sources. The Russians also supplied the school with military equipment. The first Soviet shipment of eight thousand rifles reached Canton on October 7, 1924. Later the Soviets supplied an additional ten thousand rifles plus machine guns and artillery pieces. F.F. Liu, *A Military History of Modern China, 1924-1949* (Princeton: Princeton University Press, 1956), pp. 14-15.

[4] The exact date of Chou En-lai's appointment to head the Whampoa political department is unclear. Chou appears to have taken charge of the department some time in the spring of 1925. See Hsu Kai-yu, *Chou En-lai: China's Gray Eminence* (Garden City, New York: Doubleday Anchor Books, 1968), pp. 41-43 and n. 12, pp. 215-216.

[5] Most of the Chinese faculty at Whampoa had studied at the Shikan Gakko in Japan or the Japanese-influenced Paoting and Yunnan military academies in China; see F.F. Liu, p. 14, and Cherepanov, p. 119. Other military instructors at Whampoa included Hu Shu-sen, Ch'en Chi-ch'eng, Ku Chu-t'ung, Ch'ien Ta-chün, Wen Su-sung, Shen Ying-shih, Lu Fu-t'ing, Yen Chung, Wang Chun, and Liu Chih. Among the non-Communist political instructors were Hu Han-min, Shao Yüan-ch'ung, and Wang Ching-wei. See Ch'ien Ta-chün, "Huang-p'u chun-hsiao k'ai-chuang shih-ch'i chih tsu-chih" [The Organization of the Whampoa Military Academy at the Time of its Founding], in *Ko-ming wen hsien* [Documents on the Revolution], vol. 10 (Taipei: 1955), pp. 1465-1467. On the Whampoa staff, see also Wilbur, "Forging," p. 73 and MacFarquhar, pp. 154-157.

[6] See the individual biographies of the Chinese Communist leaders in Klein and Clark.

[7]The first Whampoa class consisted of 470 students who entered the school in May 1924 and an additional group of 143 students from Hunan and Kwangtung who joined the class in September of that year. Richard B. Landis in "The Origins of Whampoa Graduates Who Served in the Northern Expedition," *Studies on Asia* (University of Washington Far Eastern and Russian Institute Modern Chinese History Project Reprint Series, no. 9, 1964), p. 150 gives this breakdown of the first four Whampoa classes: the first class (May-December 1924), 613; the second class (October 1924-summer 1925), 449; the third class (summer 1925-winter 1925), 1,225;and the fourth class (spring 1926-October 1926), 2,650. The composition of the Whampoa student body is discussed in Richard B. Landis, "Institutional Trends at the Whampoa Military School, 1924-1926" (University of Washington, 1969), pp. 10-11, 27-37; Chang Ch'i-yün, *Tang-shih kai-yao* [Outline of Party History], vol. 1 (Taipei: Chung-yang kai-tsao wei-yüan-hui wen-wu kung-ying she, 1951), pp. 349-350; and Cherepanov, p. 120. Most of the students in the first three classes came from Hunan and Kwangtung. Most also appear to have had at least a middle-school background.

[8]The questionnaire and details on the reorganization of Whampoa can be found in "The Central Military Political School of the National Revolutionary Army, 1926-1927," in *The Whampoa Military School: A Report Compiled from Soviet Documents* (A-44), File 2657-I-281/120, Modern Military Records Division, U.S. National Archives, pp. 12-16.

[9]On Chinese Communist enrollment at Whampoa see Cherepanov, p. 120; Chang Kuo-t'ao, *Rise*, p. 451; and Harrison, *March*, p. 56.

[10]Cherepanov, pp. 116, 118, and MacFarquhar, p. 158. According to F.F. Liu, pp. 14-15, many of the texts used at Whampoa were Japanese and had been obtained through the Japanese assistant military attache in Canton.

[11]Cherepanov, pp. 115-124, and F.F. Liu, p. 11. Ralph L. Powell, *The Rise of Chinese Military Power, 1895-1912* (Princeton: Princeton University Press, 1955), pp. 236-237; 268, 290-295, discusses late Ch'ing military academies and military education.

[12]Chang Ch'i-yün, vol. 1, pp. 357-362; MacFarquhar, pp. 159-160; and F.F. Liu, p. 10. Chiang's speeches at Whampoa can be found abbreviated in Mao Ssu-ch'eng, ed., *Min-kuo shih-wu nien i-ch'ien ti Chiang Chieh-shih hsien-sheng* [Chiang Kai-shek before 1926] (Hong Kong: Lung-men shu-tien, 1936), pp. 278 ff.

[13]This outline and discussion of political courses at Whampoa is from "The Central Military Political School," pp. 19-22. The outline can also be found in the J.C. Huston Collection at the East Asia Collection of the Hoover Institution on War, Revolution and Peace at Stanford University.

[14]F.F. Liu, p. 12. Landis, "Institutional Trends," p. 174, states that the small groups (*hsiao-tsu*) numbered seven to eight men. Chapter 2 discusses group study methods at leadership training institutions in the Soviet Union.

[15]"The Central Military Political School," p. 22; Wilbur, "Forging," p. 74; Chang Ch'i-yün, vol. 1, pp. 362-364; F.F. Liu, pp. 16-19; and MacFarquhar, p. 162, discuss political work at Whampoa.

[16]On the political commissar system and political training in the Soviet Red Army see D. Fedotoff White, *The Growth of the Red Army* (Princeton: Princeton University Press, 1944), pp. 42-97, 233-234.

[17]Harold Isaacs, *The Tragedy of the Chinese Revolution* (New York: Atheneum. 1966), p. 111. One observer witnessed Whampoa cadets practicing mass organizing while still at the academy. They linked meetings and demonstrations with local public organizations and "faithfully took part in every mass undertaking." During maneuvers and field studies Whampoa cadets were seen fraternizing with peasants, issuing revolutionary handbills and proclamations and supporting struggles against landlords. See Vera Vladimirovna Vishnyakova-Akimova, *Two Years in Revolutionary China, 1925-1927*, trans. Steven I. Lévine (Cambridge, Mass.: Harvard University East Asian Research Center, 1971), p. 163.

[18]"Political Work in the National Revolutionary Army" (probable date: March 15, 1926), British Foreign Office Public Records Office Document Z 50 FO F8322/3241/

10, pp. 1-2. See also F.F. Liu, pp. 16-17, on the Political Council and Political Directorate.

19"Political Lessons for Enlisted Personnel" (late 1925), British Foreign Office Public Records Office Document Z 50, FO F8322/3241/10, Annex 2.

20Other publications of the Political Directorate included a Series for Political Workers with a *Monthly Magazine* on "What and How to Teach Soldiers," "How to Organize the Work in a Club," "The Methods of Political Work," "The Party and the Army," and "The *Vade-Mecum* of the Political Worker" (programs, regulations, and instructions). A General Political Series was to involve "The History of the Kuomintang," "The History of the Revolutionary Movement in China," "Unequal Treaties," and "Who are the Imperialists?" The publishing committee also planned a Soldiers' Series and The Officers' Library. By March 1926 it had in press *The Textbook for Reading and Writing*, "What and How to Teach Soldiers," "The History of the Kuomintang," "What Are the Unequal Treaties?", and "Regulations for Political Commissars." See "Political Work in the National Revolutionary Army," pp. 2-8.

21For figures on Chinese Communists in the National Revolutionary Army, see ibid., pp. 8-12; Alexander Ivanovich Cherepanov, *The Northern Expedition of the National Revolutionary Army of China (Notes of a Military Adviser 1926-1927)*, trans. Caroline Rogers and Lydia Holubnychy and ed. Lydia Holubnychy (unpublished manuscript, East Asian Institute, Columbia University, 1970), p. 4; Harrison, *March*, p. 56; and Wilbur and How, p. 218. None of these sources indicates what portion of the seventy-five percent of the political workers identified as either CCP or left-wing Kuomintang members were actually Communists.

22Wilbur and How, pp. 217-218; Li Jui, p. 249; and "Political Work in the National Revolutionary Army," pp. 10-11. "Political Work in the National Revolutionary Army," p. 15 describes a special political class at the Central Military and Political Academy with 430 students to be trained as political workers for the National Revolutionary Army (NRA). This is probably the same class as that run by Li Fu-ch'un. The Kuomintang also operated a special institute for propaganda workers called the Chinese Kuomintang Institute. It opened officially on June 29, 1924, and was under the jurisdiction of the KMT propaganda department. The institute training program ran for four weeks, offering forty-eight hours of classroom instruction to selected members of KMT party branches and their executive committees. At the Chinese Kuomintang Institute Hu Han-min lectured on "The Three People's Principles;" Liao Chung-k'ai on "The Five-Power Constitution," "Dealing with the Present Situation," and "Forward Strategy;" Lan Hsing-shih on an "Outline of Politics;" Chou Hai-pin and Wang Ching-wei on "History of the Chinese KMT;" Lin Yun-kai on "Principles of Economics;" Shao Yüan-ch'ung on "Methods and Strategy of Contemporary Revolution;" T'an P'ing-shan on "Explanation of the Constitution" and "Explanation of Various Diagrams and Charts;" Sun K'o on "Essential Points of the Rules of Business Organizations and Meetings of Associations;" and Liu Lu-yin on "Explanation of the KMT Political Program." A course on the "Condition of Political Parties in Germany, France, the U.S., England and Russia" was taught by Liu Lu-yin, Chang Shen-fu, Franke, Voitinsky, and Borodin. See *Chung-kuo Kuo-min-tang chou-k'an* [Chinese KMT weekly], no. 28 (10th session of CEC June 29, 1924); and Chung-kuo Kuo-min-tang chung-yang chih-hsing wei-yüan-hui hsuan-ch'uan pu, "Chung-kuo Kuo-min-tang chiang-hsi-so t'ung-kao" [Announcement of the Chinese KMT Institute], July 2, 1924, and "Chung-kuo Kuo-min-tang chiang-hsi-so yen- chiang shih-chien piao" [Chart of the Lecture Schedule of the Chinese KMT Institute], both at the Yokota Collection, Tokyo.

23Mounting tensions were visible even before the Chung-shan Gunboat Incident. To neutralize leftist strength, some KMT Central Executive Committee members sponsored the formation of a Society for the Study of Sun Yat-senism. Branches appeared at the Central Military and Political Academy and within the NRA to propagate the teachings of Sun and the KMT political platform. Chinese Communists countered with their own organization, the Union of Military Youth. See "Political Work in the National Revolutionary Army," pp. 11-12; F.F. Liu, p. 22; Hsu Kai-yu, pp. 48-50; Cherepanov, *Northern Expedition*, pp. 84-88; and Li Yün-han, p. 475.

24These points are developed in Diana Lary's study of *Region and Nation: The Kwangsi Clique in Chinese Politics, 1925-1937* (London: Cambridge University Press, 1974), especially pp. 53-114.

25After the anti-Communist purges of 1927, Chinese Communist influence vanished entirely from the NRA. In January 1928 the Central Military and Political Academy moved officially to Nanking and was known from then until 1937 as the Central Military Officers Academy. On the removal of Communists from the academy and NRA, see Landis, "Origins," n. 2, p. 162, and Chang Ch'i-yün, vol. 2, p. 502. John Gittings, "The Chinese Army," in *Modern China's Search for a Political Form*. ed. Jack Gray (London: Oxford University Press, 1969), p. 196, discusses changes in military-political education in the Kuomintang after 1927.

26On the complex of Soviet military academies in the mid-twenties see John Erickson, *The Soviet High Command: A Military-Political History 1918-1941* (London: Macmillan and Co. Ltd., 1962), pp. 194-195. Chinese Communists who studied at the Red Army (Frunze) Military Academy included Nieh Jung-chen (1924-25); Yeh T'ing (1925); Li Ta (late twenties); Yeh Chien-ying (1928-30); Whampoa alumni Hsiao Ching-kuang (1927-31), Tso Ch'üan (1928-1930), Wang Chen (1928-29), and Hsü Kuang-ta (1935-38); Liu Po-ch'eng (1928-30), T'eng Tai-yüan (1935-38); Chang Chen (1935-38); Fang Ch'iang (late thirties); and Liu Ya-lou (1938-42). Fu Chung, Li T'e, Liu Po-chien, and Hsiao Ching-kuang trained at the Leningrad Military-Political Academy around 1928-1930. Chou Pao-chung, a Whampoa instructor, trained at the Red Army Staff College between 1928 and 1931. Others reported to have studied at Soviet military schools include Liu Chen, Ch'ang Ch'ien-k'un, Wang Shang-jung, Hsieh Fang, Chung Ch'ih-p'ing, Li T'ai, Chu Jui, Wen Nien-sheng, and Wu Hsiu-ch'üan. See individual biographical listings in Klein and Clark; William W. Whitson, *The Chinese High Command: A History of Communist Military Politics, 1927-71* (New York: Praeger Publishers, 1973), pp. 36, 41, 54-55, 66, 105, 146, 159, 266, 472-473; and Huang Chen-hsia, *Chung-kung chün-jen chih* [Records of Chinese Communist Officers] (Hong Kong: Research Institute on Contemporary History, 1968), pp. 763-764.

27Those in the commander category would include Lin Piao, Hsü Kuang-ta, Hsiao Ching-kuang, Huang Kung-lüeh, Tso Ch'üan, Ch'en Keng, Sung Jen-ch'iung, Sung Shih-lun, Ch'en Ch'i-han, Chou Shih-ti, Hsü Hsiang-ch'ien, Liu Chih-tan, Chang Tsung-hsün, and Ch'eng Tzu-hua. Those in the commissar category include Lo Jui-ch'ing, Teng Fa, Huang K'o-ch'eng, Ouyang Ch'in, Chang Chi-ch'un and P'an Tzu-li. Chang Tsung-hsün and Ch'eng Tzu-hua graduated from the Wuhan branch of Whampoa. Both Lo Jui-ch'ing and Teng Fa subsequently went on to specialize in political security work. It is not always possible to establish a direct relationship between training at Whampoa or the Soviet military schools and later roles in the Chinese Communist military. For example, Chang Chi-ch'un specialized in infantry work at Whampoa before turning to political work in the Red Army after 1930. Ouyang Ch'in started out in the engineering section of the fourth Whampoa class. A number of those who became political commissars shifted after 1949 into civilian Party administration. See Whitson, pp. 56, 344-345, 437-443; biographies in Klein and Clark; and Huang Chen-hsia, pp. 763-764.

28This discussion is based primarily on Whitson, especially pp. 3-18, 54-67, 127-128, 146-147, 440-444, and 472-479.

29See Ellis Joffe's study of *Party and Army: Professionalism and Political Control in the Chinese Officer Corps, 1949-1964* (Cambridge, Mass.: Harvard University East Asian Research Center, 1965), especially pp. ix-xiii, and Joffe's review article on "China's Military Elites," *China Quarterly*, no. 62 (June 1975), pp. 315-316.

30Circa 1930 the members of the Red Whampoa faction included Ch'en I, Wang I-ch'ang, Yang Ch'i-kang, Li Chih-lung, Huang Chin-hui, Yang Po-hsien, Yü Ch'iu-tu, Lü Te-tso, Ma Chih, Lu I, Hsü Chi-shen, Wu Chung-hao, Liu Chiu-hsi, Chang Ho-k'un, Hu Kung-mien, and Chung Ch'ih-hsin.

Hsü Chi-shen was identified as commander of the Red First Corps; Wu Chung-hao, commander of the Red Third Army; Liu Chiu-hsi, commander of the Red Tenth Army; Chang Ho-k'un, commander of the Red Fourteenth Army; and Chung Ch'ih-hsin, commander of the Southeast Route Army in Kiangsi. Whitson, Chart C between pp. 124 and 125. See also Ozaki Hotsumi, "Shū On-rai no chii" [The Position of Chou En-lai], *Chūō kōron* [Central Opinion], 52, no. 12 (November 1937), p. 104; Hatano Kenichi, "Shū On-rai den" [Biography of Chou En-lai], *Kaizō* [Reconstruction], no. 7 (July 1937), pp. 89, 152; and Benjamin I. Schwartz, *Chinese Communism and the Rise of Mao* (New York: Harper Torchbooks, 1967), p. 181. Hatano and Ozaki both list Chiang Hsien-yün as a member of the Red Whampoa

Faction, but he died in action in 1927 in Honan. Chiang was a Hunanese whom Mao Tse-tung had assigned to work among laborers at Anyüan and later at Shui-k'ou-shan. He attended Whampoa and was a regimental commander in the Fourth Army during the Northern Expedition. See Hsu, p. 216, and the biographical files of Donald W. Klein at the East Asian Institute, Columbia University. Kai-yu Hsu, p. 217, also reported that Li Chih-lung, a native of Shantung and graduate of the first Whampoa class, was executed in Canton during the Northern Expedition.

Other Chinese Communists reported to have attended Whampoa included Kung Ho-ch'ung, Kung Ch'u, Wu Kuang-hao, Li Tzu-liang, Ts'ai Shen-hsi, Wu Ching-ming, Nieh Ho-t'ing, Ch'en Po-chien, Liang Kan-ch'ao, Li Wen-ling, Tuan Liang-pi, Li Po-fan, Li Hsiao, Liang Hsi-fu, Yang Chih-ch'eng, Ts'ao Yüan, P'eng Kan-chen, Chu Yün-ch'ing, Kuo Hao-jo, Ni Chih-liang, Tseng Chung-sheng, Chang Yün-i, Wang Chen, Wang Chün, and Wang I-fei. Wang Chün and Wang I-fei belonged to the Union of Military Youth and were responsible for issuing the union's publication, *Chung-kuo chün-jen* [Chinese Officers and Enlisted Men]. See Li Yün-han, pp. 475-476. Wu Kuang-hao was a graduate of the first Whampoa class and headed the Red Eleventh Corps between 1927 and 1929. Chu Yün-ch'ing and Kuo Hao-jo were on the staff of Chu Te in early 1931. Ni Chih-liang was chief-of-staff of the thirty-first division of the Red Eleventh Corps in 1929 and Tseng Chung-sheng was chairman of the Military Council of the Oyüwan Soviet in 1931. Chang Yün-i helped Teng Hsiao-p'ing build the Red Seventh Corps in Kwangsi in 1929 and led two divisions of the corps to Kiangsi in 1931-1932. For details on these figures see Whitson, pp. 55, 105, 124, 128, 133, 135, 214, and Chart C, between pp. 124 and 125. Li Wen-ling, Tuan Liang-pi, and Lin Po-fan had organized guerrilla bands in Kiangsi and joined with anti-Maoist forces when their troops were taken over by Huang Kung-lüeh in 1929. Li and Tuan were executed in 1931 by a Maoist faction as agents of the Anti-Bolshevik Corps. Li Hsiao and Liang Hsi-fu were among the dissidents executed by the CCP Chaochow Mei-hsien Special Committee. Ts'ai Shen-hsi commanded the Fifteenth Red Army in eastern Hupeh in 1930 and merged his units with the First Red Army in early 1931 to form the Fourth Red Army. Details on the above names can be found in Kuo, *Analytical History*, vol. 2, pp. 60, 65; Hsu, p. 217; Nym Wales, *Inside Red China* (New York: Doubleday, Doran and Co., 1939), p. 137; and Wales, *Dust*, pp. 153-55, 202.

[31]The biography of Ch'en Ch'i-han can be found in Union Research Institute, *Who's Who in Communist China* (Hong Kong, 1969-1970). On Hsü Meng-ch'iu, see Nym Wales, *Red Dust* (Stanford, Calif.: Stanford University Press, 1952), pp. 57-79. Details on the other figures are from Klein and Clark.

[32]See Ying-mao Kao, Paul M. Chancellor, Philip E. Ginsburg, and Pierre M. Perrole, *The Political Work System of the Chinese Communist Military: Analysis and Documents* (Providence, R.I.: Brown University East Asia Language and Area Center, 1971), pp. 9-46, and John Gittings, *The Role of the Chinese Army* (New York: Oxford University Press, 1967), pp. 100-105.

5 Communism and the Countryside

Revolution in the rural areas was not a serious prospect to the Chinese Communists until they were forced out of the cities in 1927. Before that time most Party leaders—with individual exceptions such as P'eng P'ai, Li Ta-chao, and Mao Tse-tung —were riveted to the proletariat. Though theoretically justified by the Comintern, agrarian problems[1] were considered a side-current to urban revolution. Nevertheless, a number of Chinese Communists did become actively involved in the Chinese peasant movement during the mid-twenties. Through participation in agrarian programs sponsored by the Kuomintang, the Chinese Communists developed their first organizational links to the countryside.

Most of the heads of the Kuomintang Peasant Bureau were sympathetic to the peasant movement and tolerant of the Chinese Communists' activities in the rural areas. Chinese Communists dominated the position of Peasant Bureau secretary—second in authority to the bureau chief—and thereby took charge of the detailed day-to-day operations of the bureau. Chinese Communist Party members also gained access to the peasant movement through provincial Kuomintang peasant bureaus and individual peasant associations.

As one of the "first steps" in the peasant movement, the Peasant Movement Training Institute was authorized at the thirty-ninth meeting of the Kuomintang Central Executive Committee on June 30, 1924. Most of its operating expenses were supplied by the Central Kuomintang Peasant Bureau.[2] A special Kuomintang Peasant Movement Committee took charge of the financing, housing, curriculum, and recruitment policies of the school.

The institute guided the Communists' early experiments with rural revolution and became the first formal school to train Chinese Communist Party members for work in the countryside. It left the Chinese Communist Party with a storehouse of information and techniques for peasant organizers that facilitated penetration of the countryside after 1927.

Seven training classes were held before the institute closed in May 1927, and approximately 1,700 peasant organizers were graduated (see Table 1).[3] The first six classes were conducted in Canton and the seventh in Wuhan. All of the institute principals, who taught as well as supervised the classes, and many instructors were leading Chinese Communists.

TABLE 1

Classes of the Peasant Movement Training Institute

Class	Date	No. Graduates	Principal
1	July 3-Aug. 3, 1924	33	P'eng P'ai
2	Aug. 21-Oct. 30, 1924	142	Lo Ch'i-yüan
3	Jan. 1-May 1, 1925	114	Juan Hsiao-hsien
4	April 1-Sept. 1, 1925	76	T'an Chih-t'ang
5	Sept. 14-Dec. 8, 1925	113	Lo Ch'i-yüan
6	May 3-Sept. 11, 1926	318 or 327	Mao Tse-tung
7	March 9-May 1927	500 or 950	Chou I-li (?)

Among the prominent Chinese Communists on the slate of instructors and guest lecturers were Chou En-lai, Wu Yü-chang, Ho Hsiang-ning, Ch'ü Ch'iu-pai, Teng Chung-hsia, Yün Tai-ying, Lin Tsu-han, Su Chao-cheng, Hsiao Ch'u-nü, Li Li-san, Chang T'ai-lei, Kao Yü-han, Ch'en Yen-nien, and Ch'en Ch'iao-nien. Ch'ü, Teng, Yün, Hsiao, and Chang had been instructors at Shanghai University and formed a tie between mass movement work in the city and in the countryside.. Chang T'ai-lei, Ch'en Yen-nien, and Ch'en Ch'iao-nien were graduates of the Communist University of the Toilers of the East. Along with Ch'ü Ch'iu-pai, who had acquired his theoretical expertise in Moscow, these "returned students" may have contributed to Soviet influence at the institute.

Ch'ü Ch'iu-pai lectured on the October Revolution and Socialist Construction; Hsiao Ch'u-nü spoke on Imperialism, History of the Chinese National Revolutionary Movement, Social Problems, and Socialism; and Yün Tai-ying gave an Outline of Chinese History. Chou En-lai discussed the Military Movement and the Peasant Movement and Li Li-san taught about the Chinese Labor Movement. Courses on the peasant movement generally fell to the institute principals, who were supposed to have demonstrated competence in rural work.4

Chinese Communists supervised the day-to-day operations of the Peasant Movement Training Institute, including administration of the admissions policy. Initially all candidates for the institute were required to have had at least a middle-school education, and they were evaluated through a written examination. Both Chinese Communist and Kuomintang accounts claim that nearly all the successful candidates were Chinese Communists. This most likely was the case for the first class of thirty-eight.5

However, shifts in recruitment patterns for subsequent classes probably precluded precise certification procedures. Class sizes increased sharply and the institute attempted to enlarge the proportion of students from worker-peasant backgrounds. Beginning with the second class, applicants were screened with a questionnaire to determine social background, political attitudes, and revolutionary experience. A series of questions probed:

1. Name of father and his address.
2. Father's occupation (for example, small farmer, rich peasant, petty merchant, compradore, official, miscellaneous, etc.).
3. Was your father a recognized man in the patriotic movement?
4. What are your feelings about your family?
5. Your present and former occupation and economic status..
6. From what school were you graduated? If you didn't graduate, can you read and write?
7. What are your political views?
8. Had you previously worked in the Chinese revolutionary movement?
9. Is there anyone who knew if you opposed the illegal movement before the Republic was founded?
10. Did you participate in the 1911 Revolution? Where? Can you prove it?
11. Did you participate in the revolutionary movement in the first year of the Republic? What kind of work?

12. State in detail your political activity within the Party (KMT), in the Constitution Protection Movement, or in the student, peasant or labor movement. Can you prove it by examples?
13. What year did you enter the KMT and to which local branch do you belong?
14. Did you go to prison for political reasons during the Manchu or Republican period?
15. Do you have relatives or close friends in the villages?
16. Were you born in the city or the country?
17. Are you familiar with peasant life?
18. When did you live in the countryside? What did you usually do and with what kind of people did you associate?
19. When you were in Kwangtung or another province from what *hsien* do people know you the longest?
20. In what area did you or your family have the most influence?
21. Have you ever done peasant movement work?
22. Which class in China do you feel should be the basis of the revolutionary movement?
23. Do you have dealings with gentry relatives. What kind of relatives?
24. Why do you want to enter the Institute?
25. Will your family oppose your political activities in the future? What will be your attitude toward this kind of feeling?
26. Have you decided what types of work you will do after graduation in the Peasant Associations—organizing, teaching, guiding?
27. Have you ever spoken before the masses?
28. Organizing, teaching, propaganda, industry, military—with which are you familiar or in which is your ability strongest?
29. Have you ever been a soldier? Where and with what military force?
30. Are you sound in body? How many *li* can you walk in one day? Can you ride horseback? Do you have physical defects or chronic illness?
31. What dialects do you know?
32. Who introduced you to enter this Training Institute? Where did you hear of the opening of this Institute?[6]

Admissions policy for the third through fifth classes focused on recruiting activists from among peasant associations and poor peasants. The middle-school education requirement was eliminated and the written admissions test replaced by an oral examination. To ensure dedication and loyalty the institute required all prospective students to bring written certification of their character from a Kuomintang or peasant association member.

Two factors precipitated this change in recruitment policy. The first class of 33 graduates measured pitifully against the 24 million inhabitants of the ninety-four *hsien* of Kwangtung province alone. Any serious effort to provide leadership for the peasant movement meant enlarging institute classes. Peasant movement strategists had also observed that fierce clashes between peasant and landlord often necessitated the use of arms. Production of able leaders for self-defense corps and peasant associations became a major concern of the peasant movement and the institute. Given the necessary changes in composition and size of the student body, the institute lacked the means to screen each student carefully and relied on the training program itself to weed out misfits.

As early as the second class the social background of institute students had changed to thirty percent peasants; ten percent "persons sent by peasant associations from various places;" thirty percent students; twenty-two percent workers: and eight percent women. Among the 128 original students in the third class (of whom 114 graduated), 92 were peasants and 72 were tenant farmers. The remainder consisted of 29 "rural students," 4 workers, 2 military men, and 1 petty merchant. Although there is no available information on the social background of the fourth and fifth classes, institute recruitment policy favored similar configurations.

However, the sixth class of the institute, headed by Mao Tse-tung, returned to the original admissions policy. The reintroduction of the middle-school education requirement suggests difficulty in rapidly training large numbers of uneducated peasants (or workers) for responsible leadership positions. It is also possible that the relaxed admission requirements produced many peasant trainees who proved unreliable after graduation. The reversal of admissions priorities presumably swelled the intellectual composition of the sixth class.

Expansion in institute class size was accompanied by gains in the number of geographical areas sending trainees. Most of the first class came from the immediate Canton region. The second class of 142 included representatives of twelve Kwangtung *hsien,* especially the *punti* areas of Hsiangshan, Shunte, and Kwangning. In the third session the 114 graduates listed thirty-three Kwangtung *hsien* as their home counties, with the majority born in the *punti* Pearl River *hsien* of Tungkwan, Hsiangshan, Hua, and Huoshan.

Non-Kwangtung students first appeared in the fourth class of 76 graduates, of whom 11 were from Hunan and 2 from Kwangsi. Beginning with the fifth class, which graduated 113, students from Hunan, Hupeh, Fukien, Kwangsi, and Shantung outnumbered the Kwangtung provincials. By the sixth class only 2 of the 327 students were from Kwangtung, with Kwangsi and Hunan, respectively, leading the nineteen provinces represented.[7]

Initially the training period of the institute was limited to one month. The first class lasted only from July 3 to about August 3, 1924. However, this short period of time proved insufficient for the task at hand. Subsequent classes averaged three to four months. Classroom work fell into four major divisions: the Party principles of the Kuomintang; basic knowledge of the National Revolution; theory and strategy of the peasant movement; and propaganda training. The longer training periods were accompanied by additional course offerings.[8]

In June 1924 the original plan for the institute had called for only subjects concerned with the peasant movement.[9] By the time the curriculum was published in 1925, the list of courses had grown to twenty-six. New areas of instruction elaborated on theoretical matters such as imperialism, political economy, and the history of world revolutionary movements. Other subjects, such as common legal knowledge, the history of Chinese secret societies, statistics, newspaper reading, article writing, public speaking, and singing, sought to prepare students for their future careers as organizers.[10] Given the political complexion of the institute staff and the focus on mass movement work, it is likely that these courses acquired a heavy Marxist orientation well before Mao Tse-tung's celebrated sixth class.[11]

PRACTICAL AND THEORETICAL TRAINING

Perhaps the most significant lessons occurred outside the classroom. Ten of the thirty days of training for the first class were devoted to military drill on the grounds of the Whampoa Military Academy. For the second class, a scheduled two weeks of drill turned into a baptism of fire. This group of Peasant Movement Training Institute students made up almost all of the "Peasant Corps Army" that Sun Yat-sen led to Shaokuan and against the Merchant Corps. The third and fourth institute classes explicitly emphasized skills for leaders of peasant self-defense corps. Military drill became a daily routine. During the fourth class, three hours every morning were devoted to military exercises. Mao's sixth class divided into two squads for a ten-week, 128-hour program of formal military training that lasted from May to July 1926. Presumably military education continued during the seventh class, held in Wuhan.

Even for those not marked for defense corps work, military training instilled an overall sense of discipline. The ability to withstand long hours on the drill field served as a test of stamina and dedication and clearly exposed misfits. As former institute student Wang Shou-tao observed,

We slept on double-decked wooden bunks, wore grey military uniforms and straw sandals. Grouped into twelve teams, we undertook strict military training and studied military subjects. This austere life formed a necessary preparation for us to become organizers and leaders of peasant revolutionary armies and to withstand trials and adverse circumstances.[12]

Military training became a standard feature of Chinese Communist leadership training programs from the mid-twenties on.

Another area of emphasis was "practical training" in actual peasant movement work. The trend started with the first class. Principal P'eng P'ai urged his students to spend as much time as possible in peasant movement work and he led expeditions every Sunday to villages on the outskirts of Canton. There trainees practiced marching, horseback riding, and organizing peasant associations. In fact, the first peasant associations in the Canton suburbs were founded by P'eng P'ai's students.

Even as the second class pressed on to Shaokuan, it divided into squads that canvassed neighboring villages for propaganda work behind enemy lines. Led by local students, the squads investigated conditions in each village and summoned inhabitants to form peasant associations and self-defense corps. Both the third and fourth classes practiced setting up various levels of peasant associations, giving special attention to linguistic and geographic differences. On Sundays they had outings to peasant villages or tried to cultivate group feeling through debating meetings, social gatherings, concerts, student clubs, and horticultural activities. The fourth class postponed its May 1 opening date to attend the first Kwangtung Peasant Congress. In twelve days of meetings, peasant movement leaders discussed their own experiences and various problems of the peasant movement.

Preparation for self-government received special attention during the fifth class. Students organized a "society for self-government" that took charge of all student affairs. The fifth class also attended founding meetings for a district-level peasant association outside Canton and for the Ch'u-chiang *hsien* peasant association. Mao Tse-tung led his entire sixth class on a two-week expedition to inspect peasant organizations in Hai-feng. Students in the fifth class had made a similar week-long trip to Shao-chou.[13]

With each class the orientation towards practical peasant movement work grew stronger. It was up to the institute to arm each student with the appropriate knowledge and skills to work in his or her native area. Yet from the students' enormously diverse geographic, economic, and linguistic backgrounds the institute also had to extract a method of analysis applicable to all peasant problems.

As principal of the sixth class Mao Tse-tung constantly underlined the significance of regional and local differences in revolutionary work.[14] He outlined the criteria for determining the revolutionary potential of a given area:

> land condition, style of living, social background, how Chang San became rich and Li Szu poor, how much public land that village maintains, who manages it, an index of who rents and rents out, number of households.[15]

On the basis of class background students learned to predict an individual's attitude toward revolution—whether he would be the friend or foe of class struggle—and the changes he would undergo during the revolutionary process.

To anticipate problems in future areas of peasant movement work activity, students formed research societies to study peasant problems for the provinces of Anhwei, Hunan, Kiangsi, Hupei, Szechuan, Yunnan-Kweichou, Kwangtung-Kwangsi, Fukien, Chekiang, Shantung, Hopei-Shansi, South Manchuria-Chihli, and three special areas. Each research society consisted of students from the one region being studied.

Meeting once or twice each week, the research societies investigated such factors as (1) rate of rent; (2) landlord-tenant relationships; (3) movement (uprisings) to reduce or withhold rent payments and rice price control; (4) interest rates; (5) nature of bills from unpaid debts in arrears; (6) land tax; (7) situation of peasants withholding grain; (8) miscellaneous taxes, *likin*, and temporary taxes; (9) comparison of number of self-cultivators, semi-self-cultivators, hired peasants, and poor peasants; (10) origins of landlords; (11) comparison of the value of agricultural products with the value of goods; (12) value of labor; (13) unemployment situation; (14) organization of temples and nature of clan rule; (15) organization of local public associations and property conditions; (16) local political organizations; (17) local political conditions; (18) factions and bandits; (19) militia defense conditions; (20) educational situation; (21) effect of boycott on Western goods; (22) military misfortunes and their effect; (23) natural calamities and their effect; (24) opium, gambling, brigands, and pilfering; (25) avaricious officials and their influence; (26) goods produced and points of blockade; (27) position of women; (28) peasants' conceptions, feelings, opinions; (29) comparison of past and present land value; (30) comparison of past and present value of agricultural products; (31) nature of peasant village organization; (32) quality and fertility of land; (33) degree of belief in religion; (34) weights and measures; (35) folk songs; and (36) proverbs.16

These forays into "practical" research were accompanied by individual "theoretical research" projects. The institute appointed special instructors (including Mao and Hsiao Ch'u-nü) to direct student investigations of theoretical issues apart from classroom work. The term "theoretical" applied not only to aspects of Marxism-Leninism but to the principles of the Kuomintang, issues in the contemporary peasant movement, and even "infantry drilling rules."

A distinct study technique was utilized for students' investigation of these problems.17 Before making assignments the special instructor examined prescribed books and outlined their essential sections and important questions. Students read these books with such questions in mind and wrote out answers to return to the instructor by a set deadline. The instructor selected the best set of answers and posted them on the wall as "model answers," returning the remainder to the students. The latter then traced their errors and corrected their papers to conform to the model essays. This pedagogical technique may have been inspired by the group study procedures used at Soviet schools such as the Communist University of the Toilers of the East, or may have been initiated by Mao Tse-tung himself. Mao may also have been responsible for the thrust toward independent research projects, since individual study had been encouraged at the Changsha Self-Education College.

THE INSTITUTE AND THE PEASANT MOVEMENT

From the findings of students' practical and theoretical research projects, translations of Krestintern literature, and various Kuomintang documents on agrarian questions, the Peasant Movement Training Institute compiled a set of reference material for rural operatives on all aspects of the peasant movement throughout China. Edited to delete references to the Chinese Communist Party, the documents served as discussion material for study meetings and were published in a volume called *Nung-min wen-t'i ts'ung-k'an* (*Collection on the Peasant Problem*).

This collection of information on fifty-two topics18 was prefaced by Mao Tse-tung's summary of his conclusions on the peasant movement. Through the reading of students' reports and the experience of directing the sixth class of the Peasant Movement Training Institute, Mao's appreciation of the revolutionary potential of the Chinese peasantry was increased.   In "The National Revolution and the Peasant Movement," his preface to *Nung-min wen-t'i ts'ung-k'an*, he wrote:

> [this book] enables us to understand the nature of the Chinese peasant movement and realize that the Chinese peasant movement is a movement of class struggle in which political and economic struggles are combined. What the contents reveal as most significant are the political struggles, and these are considerably different from the nature of the urban workers' movement. What the urban working class is struggling for politically at this time is only the freedom of assembly and association. It still has not demanded at this time to destroy the political position of the capitalist class. The peasants in the countryside, on the other hand, on rising up have clashed with the political power that the *t'u-hao lieh-shen* and great landlords have held for thousands of years to oppress the peasants. This landlord power is the real basis of warlord government.[19]

Three-fourths of the thirty-three graduates of the first institute class were immediately assigned as special deputies of the Central Peasant Bureau. One graduate died and one of the two female graduates went to work in the General Affairs section of the Central Peasant Bureau. The 142 members of the second class were dispatched on October 30, 1924, to organize their home villages around Canton.

The fifteen most outstanding pupils in military training in the third class were chosen to continue their military education. Most of them eventually joined peasant self-defense corps and four or five were assigned to help teach the next institute class. Twenty other graduates remained with the Central Peasant Bureau for further "practical training"—propaganda work in various villages around Canton. This group was to serve as "on the spot study personnel" for future institute classes. The remaining graduates of the third class returned to their native villages to assist peasant associations.

Soon after the fourth institute class had begun, its ninety-eight students were ordered to return immediately to their native areas as temporary leaders of rural work. By June 4, 1925, all of the trainees had begun to depart when the Yunnan Army suddenly attacked and occupied the school. It was not recovered until June 24 and classes did not resume until July 1. By that time many students had reached destinations that were too far away to permit return. To the shrunken class the institute added twenty-five auditors. The session lasted two months, graduating fifty-one regular students and the twenty-five auditors on September 1, 1925. Sixteen auditors stayed on for the next institute class.

The fifth class divided into two sections, each receiving different work assignments. After the graduation ceremonies of December 8, 1925, one section dispatched its sixty-four members to work in Honan, Hunan, Anhwei, Shantung, Kwangsi, and Fukien provinces. Those in the second section were sent to the East River area and along the Southern Route. Most of the Hunanese students worked as special deputies along the railroad to Changsha. The graduates of the sixth class all returned to work in their nineteen native areas.

The Peasant Movement Training Institute alone could not develop sufficient leadership for the Chinese Communists to harness the social forces in the countryside. Although the turnout of graduates continued to increase, it was always outpaced by the peasant movement. In working with the Chinese peasantry the Party found that it did not take many to arouse the masses.   However, to provoke an uprising and to sustain a revolutionary movement were two different matters. Building permanent mass organizations in the rural areas demanded a large corps of trained and dedicated leaders in numbers far beyond the supply of institute graduates. The Chinese Communists' failure to control the mass movements in the countryside in 1927 would teach this lesson at a cost of many lives.

The number of graduates of the institute barely sufficed to replenish the school's staff and that of the Kuomintang Peasant Bureau. It was calculated that one-third of all institute graduates remained with the Kuomintang central and regional apparatus. Even in Kwangtung, where the peasant movement had advanced farthest, in 1926 there was only one trained peasant movement leader for every thousand peasants already enrolled in peasant associations.[21] A resolution prepared for a meeting of Special Deputies of the Kuomintang Peasant Bureau on August 15, 1926, listed only 600 Communist Party members working among the 800,000 Kwangtung peasants enrolled in over 10,000 village associations. The thirty-five higher-level comrades in the six Kwangtung regional offices were constantly swamped with emergencies. During the first stage of the Northern Expedition the ratio of leaders to led diminished further.[22]

It has been estimated that less than 1,000 of the total 1,700 graduates of the Peasant Movement Training Institute actually operated on the village level. One-third of 454 graduates of the first five classes were reported to have been named special deputies of the Central Peasant Bureau in Kwangtung.[23] A large portion of the students, such as half the trainees from Hupeh, eventually dropped from sight. The problem of loyalty to the Chinese Communist Party thus arose. Neither careful screening nor rigorous training procedures could guarantee a turnout of one hundred percent revolutionaries. Even before the Wuhan class graduated, the Kiangsi peasant movement had turned anti-Communist, triggering a purge of institute students from that province.

In 1927 the counterrevolutionary activities accompanying the first stage of the Northern Expedition also took their toll. Violence in the rural areas served as a "screening process" for both the "faint-hearted" and for the talented leaders who lost their lives.[24] Unfortunately, there is little available information on the careers of most Peasant Movement Training Institute graduates. Since few distinguished themselves later in the Chinese Communist movement, one can surmise that most met one of three ends: death, defection, or obscurity.[25]

One has the impression that the institute functioned similarly to Shanghai University in the recruitment and preparation of Chinese Communist Party leaders. Both institutions operated under Kuomintang sponsorship and attracted young activists anxious to work in the mass movements. Through contacts with ranking Chinese Communist figures at both schools, promising leadership talent was recruited into the Chinese Communist Party.

In evaluating the impact of the Peasant Movement Training Institute on the evolution of the Chinese Communist movement, one must look beyond its production of Party members to its effect on Party rural strategy and leadership policy. Through Chinese Communist involvement in the institute and the Kuomintang Peasant Bureau, the Party began to acquire its first knowledge of rural areas and techniques for peasant mobilization. The institute itself, although not a formal Chinese Communist Party school, became a model for future Party leadership training programs for rural mass movement organizers. Its graduates were the prototype of the peasant movement cadre who played a critical role in Chinese Communist movement-building after 1927.

Despite some Soviet influence in training procedures and some linkages with the urban mass movements, the Peasant Movement Training Institute had a very strong native orientation. It encouraged students to turn inward to the countryside and pressed for knowledge of the specific dynamics of agrarian revolution in

China. In the institute training experience are perceptions of the need for a distinct work style for rural revolution. The approaches to agrarian work at the institute were experimental, but they helped to guide activities that turned defeat in 1927 into victory in 1949.

NOTES

[1]On the factors behind the Chinese Communist Party's decision to organize the Chinese peasants, see Carol Corder Andrews, "The Relationship between the Chinese Communist Party and the Peasant Movement, 1921-1927" (Masters essay, Columbia University, 1964), pp. 22-36.

[2]The relationship between the CCP and the Kuomintang Peasant Bureau is discussed in Roy Mark Hofheinz, "The Peasant Movement and Rural Revolution: Chinese Communists in the Countryside (1923-1927)" (Ph.D. dissertation, Harvard University, 1966), pp. 7-28.

[3]The chief source for the first five classes of the Peasant Movement Training Institute is Lo Ch'i-yüan, "Pen-pu i-nien lai kung-tso pao-kao kai-yao" [Outline of a Report on the Work of Our Bureau during the Past Year], *Chung-kuo nung-min* [Chinese Peasant], , no. 2 (February 1, 1926), pp. 168ff. On the sixth class see "Ti-liu chieh nung-min yün-tung chiang-hsi-so pan-li ching-kuo" [Experience of Managing the Sixth Class of the Peasant Movement Training Institute], in *Ti-i-tz'u kuo-nei chan-cheng shih-ch'i ti nung-min yün-tung* [The Peasant Movement during the First Revolutionary Civil War] (Peking: Jen-min ch'u-pan she, 1953), p. 20. Two other sources list a total of 327 students in the sixth class. They are Mao Tse-tung, "A General Explanation of the Chart for the Sum Total of Income and Expenditure of the Peasant Movement Training Institute of the Kuomintang," *Chinese Studies in History*, no. 3 (Spring 1973), pp. 28-29, and T.C. Chang, *The Farmers' Movement in Kwangtung*, trans. Committee on Christianizing Economic Relations (Shanghai: National Christian Council of China, 1928), p. 14. Figures for the Wuhan class are from *Ti-i tz'u*, p. 395. Roy Hofheinz's study of "The Peasant Movement and Rural Revolution" lists 950 students in the Wuhan class and March 7, 1927, for the beginning of classes.

[4]Tu Sung-shou, "Chi-nien Mao chu-hsi tsai Kuang-chou nung-min yün-tung chiang-hsi-so ti liang-san shih" [Remembering Several Things about Chairman Mao at the Canton Peasant Movement Training Institute], in *Hua-nan ko-ming shih-chi* [Records of the Revolution in South China], ed. Liao Yüan (Canton: Hua-nan jen-min ch'u-pan she, 1951), p. 17. T.C. Chang, pp. 7 and 14, lists as lecturers for the second institute class Liao Chung-k'ai, Kan Nai-kuang, Ch'en Kung-po, T'an P'ing-shan, and Michael Borodin. For the sixth class he lists Ch'en Kung-po, Kan Nai-kuang, Mao Tse-tung, Hsiao Ch'u-nü, Chen Chih-hsin, Yün Tai-ying, Chang Chin-jen, P'eng Shu-chih, and Chou En-lai. In the sixth class Mao taught courses on Chinese Peasant Problems, Village Education, and Geography. See "Ti-liu," p. 23.

[5]The Chinese Communists and student admissions policy is discussed in Tsou Lu, *Chung-kuo Kuo-min-tang shih-kao* [Draft History of the Kuomintang], vol. 1 (Shanghai: Shang-wu yin-shu kuan, 1945), p. 378; Eto Shinkichi, "Hai-lu-feng: The First Chinese Soviet Government," part 1, *China Quarterly*, no. 8 (October-December 1961), p. 182; and Lo Ch'i-yüan, "Pen-pu," pp. 168-187.

[6]See the chart between pp. 176 and 177 of Lo Ch'i-yüan, "Pen-pu."

[7]Hofheinz, pp. 36-37, points out that the recruitment pattern of the Peasant Movement Training Institute coincided with those areas the revolutionary movement had reached or hoped to reach.

[8]Lo Ch'i-yüan, "Pen-pu," p. 159. See also "Nung-min yün-tung ti-i pu shih-shih fang-an" [Plan for the First Step in the Peasant Movement], *Chung-kuo Kuo-min-tang chou-k'an* [Chinese KMT Weekly], no. 29 (39th Session of CEC, June 30, 1924).

[9]These courses were listed as (1) Theory of the Peasant Movement; (2) Program of the Chinese Kuomintang Concerning the Peasant Movement; (3) Agricultural Conditions in Kwangtung and Means of Improvement; (4) Condition of the Peasantry in Kwangtung; (5) Methods of Organizing Peasant Associations; (6) History of the Kwangtung Peasant Movement; (7) Relation of the Cooperative Movement to the Peasantry; (8) Condition of the Peasant Movement in Various Nations; (9) Relationship of Peasants and Workers to the Kuomintang; and (10) Peasant Self-Defense Corps. See "Nung-min yün-tung chiang-hsi-so tsu-chih chien-chang" [Simple Regulations for the Organization of the Peasant Movement Training Institute], *Chung-kuo Kuo-min-tang chou-k'an*, no. 29 (39th session of CEC, June 30, 1924).

[10]Lo Ch'i-yüan, "Pen-pu," pp. 168-171.

[11]Subjects for the sixth class consisted of (1) The Three People's Principles; (2) History of the Chinese Kuomintang; (3) Chinese Peasant Problems; (4) Village Education; (5) Imperialism; (6) History of the Chinese National Revolutionary Movement; (7) Social Problems and Socialism; (8) Chinese Political Situation; (9) Chinese Economic and Financial Conditions; (10) Elementary Economic Knowledge; (11) Situation in Soviet Russia; (12) Outline of Chinese History; (13) Geography; (14) Chinese Labor Movement; (15) Resolutions of the Second Kwangtung Peasant Congress; (16) High Demands and Wrongs in Kwang-ning and Kiangsi Peasant Movement Conditions; (17) Hai-feng and Tung-chiang Peasant Movement Conditions; (18) Military Movement and Peasant Movement; (19) Basic Legal Knowledge; (20) Statistics; (21) Basic Agricultural Knowledge; (22) Outline of Village Cooperatives (23) History of Revolutions in Various Nations; (24) Revolutionary Books; and (25) Revolutionary Songs. See "Ti-liu," p. 23

[12]Wang Shou-tao, "The Peasant's Role in China's Revolution: A Memoir of the National Institute of the Peasant Movement," *China Reconstructs*, vol. 12, no. 10 (October 1963), p. 26. The discussion of military drill is also based on Lo Ch'i-yüan, "Pen-pu," pp. 174-194, and "Ti-liu," p. 23. As principal of the second institute class, Lo Ch'i-yüan had suggested military training to determine which students could withstand hardship and group discipline.

[13]On "practical work" at the institute, see Lo Ch'i-yüan, "Pen-pu," pp. 174-200, T.C. Chang, p. 14; and "Ti-liu," p. 23.

[14]Two hundred eighteen of the 327 students enrolled in the sixth institute class graduated. Most came from the following provinces: Kwangsi, 40; Hunan, 36; Honan, 29; Hupei, 27; Szechuan, 25; Shantung, 23; Chihli, 22; and Kiangsi, 22. "Ti-liu," p. 20-21.

[15]Li Jui, p. 250. On Mao at the institute see also Tu Sung-shou, p. 16; Wang Shou-tao, p. 26; and Kaoputsebo, "I nung-min yün-tung chiang-hsi-so ti hsüeh-hsi sheng-huo" [Recalling Study Life at the Peasant Movement Training Institute], *Min-tsu t'uan-chieh* [People's Unity], no. 7 (July 1962), p. 9.

[16]"Ti-liu," pp. 26-28, and Wang Shou-tao, p. 25.

[17]The following bibliography of guided readings for the study of "theoretical" topics was related to peasant movement work, with titles such as (1) The Three People's Principles; (2) Results of Imperialist Policy; (3) Introduction to Imperialism; (4) Introduction to the Capitalist System; (5) Brief History of the Evolution of Society; (6) Proclamation and Resolutions of the Second Kuomintang Congress; (7) *Chinese Peasant Monthly* (periodical); (8) *Peasant Movement Weekly* (periodical); (9) *Dark Heads Weekly* (periodical); (10) Chinese National Movement and Policy; (11) Collection of Discussions on Sun Yat-senism; (12) Sun Yat-sen's Teachings Concerning the Peasants; (13) Chinese Kuomintang Peasant Policy; (14) Proclamation of the Revolutionary Government Concerning the Peasants; (15) Rules of the Kwangtung Peasant Association and Laws of Organization of Peasant Self-Defense Corps; (16) Important Resolutions of the First Kwangtung Peasant Congress; (17) Important Resolutions of the Second Kwangtung Peasant Congress; (18) Present Policy of the Hunan Peasant Movement; (19) General Discussion of Peasant Cooperatives; (20) Lenin and the Peasants; (21) Peasant International; (22) Russian Peasants and Revolution; (23) Research on Chinese Peasant Problems; (24) Land and Peasants; (25) Soviet Russian Agricultural Policy; (26) Socialist Revolution and the Peasant Movement; (27) Infantry Drilling Rules; and (28) The Peasant Movement in Japan, Germany and Italy. See "Ti-liu," pp. 24-26.

18 Seventeen of the topics in *Nung-min wen-t'i ts'ung-k'an* had been published by November 1926. They included (1) Sun Yat-sen's Teachings Concerning the Peasants; (2) Chinese Kuomintang Peasant Policy; (3) Proclamation of the Revolutionary Government Concerning the Peasants; (4) Rules of the Kwangtung Peasant Association and Laws of Organization of the Peasant Self-Defense Corps; (5) Important Resolutions of the first Kwangtung Peasant Congress; (6) Important Resolutions of the Second Kwangtung Peasant Congress; (7) Resolutions of the First Kwangtung Provincial Party Congress Concerning the Peasant Movement; (8) Present Policy of the Hunan Peasant Movement; (9) General Discussion of Peasant Cooperatives; (10) Lenin and the Peasant; (11) Peasant International; (12) Russian Peasants and Revolution; (13) Research on Chinese Peasant Problems; (14) Land and Peasants; (15) Soviet Russian Agricultural Policy; (16) Socialist Revolution and the Peasant Movement; and (17) The Peasant Movement in Japan, Germany, and Italy. At the printers or in the process of compilation were such topics as (18) General Explanation of the Kwangtung Peasant Movement; (19) Report on the Hai-feng Peasant Movement; (20) Record from Beginning to End of Kwang-ning Peasants' Opposition to Landlord; (21) Record from Beginning to End of P'u-ning Peasants' Resistance to Landlords; (22) Important Chinese Agricultural Products; (23) General Situation of Important Chinese Agricultural Products vis-a-vis Foreign Trade; (24) National Agricultural Administrative, Experimental, and Educational Organizations; (25) Agricultural Progress in Various Nations and Its Causes; (26) Problems of Chinese Agricultural Production; (27) General Situation of National Peasant Movement; (28) Problems of Chinese Land Rentals; (29) Landlord-Tenant Relations in Various Places; (30) Problems of Chinese Usury Exploitation; (31) Chinese Problems; (32) Movement to Withhold Grain in Various Provinces; (33) Problem of Cruel Taxation; (34) Analysis of Peasants in Various Provinces; (35) Origin of Landlords; (36) Temples; (37) Local Public Associations; (38) Local Political Organizations in Various Provinces; (39) Problem of Armed Chinese Landlord Class; (40) Problem of Natural Calamities; (41) Problem of Military Calamity; (42) Problem of Avaricious Officials; (43) Problem of Villainous and Despotic Large Landholders; (44) Value of Labor in Various Areas; (45) Weights and Measures in Various Areas; (46) Problem of Village Education; (47) Problem of Village Religion; (48) Position of Women in Chinese Villages; (49) Chinese Peasants' Conceptions and Feelings; (50) Village Literature; (51) Village Proverbs; and (52) General Discussion of the Chinese Peasant Problem. See "Ti-liu," pp. 28-32.

19 My translation of a portion of Mao's "Kuo-min ko-ming yü nung-min yün-tung," dated September 1, 1926. Mao's preface to *Nung-min wen-t'i ts'ung-k'an* was also printed in the publication of the KMT Central Executive Committee (CEC) Peasant Bureau, *Nung-min yün-tung* [The Peasant Movement], no. 8 (September 21, 1926), and is reproduced in *Mao Tse-tung chi* [The Works of Mao Tse-tung]. ed. Minoru Takenchi, vol. 1 (Tokyo, 1970), pp. 175-170.

20 On the disposition of the first five institute classes see Lo Ch'i-yüan, "Pen-pu," pp. 175-200. On the sixth class, see "Ti-liu," p. 20. Chang Kuo-t'ao, *Rise*, p. 630, mentions four hundred graduates of the Wuhan Institute class involved in preparations against the Hsia Tou-yin Mutiny. Most of the institute classes required a written and occasionally an oral exam for graduation. Special deputies spent most of their time in the countryside investigating rural conditions and supervising the organization of peasant associations. They were primarily graduates of the institute or experienced peasant organizers. In early 1926 fourteen members of the second institute class, fifteen of the third class, and ten of the first class were still listed among the sixty-five special deputies in service. See C. Martin Wilbur, "Socio-economic Conditions in Rural Kwangtung" (partial manuscript for a study entitled *The National Revolution in China: 1922-1928*), p. 2.

21 Hofheinz, pp. 51-52.

22 C. Martin Wilbur, "The Influence of the Past," pp. 44-45.

23 The other two-thirds returned home for local peasant movement work. See "Ti-liu," p. 7, and Lo Ch'i-yüan, "Pen-pu," p. 168. On student attrition see also Hofheinz, pp. 52-53.

24 Wilbur, "The Influence of the Past," p. 61.

25 The names of the students in the first five classes are included in Lo Ch'i-yüan, "Pen-pu,"

pp. 175-176, 182-186, 190-193, 197-199, and 203-207, but Lo's report offers no additional biographical information. Among the few Peasant Movement Training Institute graduates who rose to prominence in the CCP are Li Ching-ch'üan, Wang Shou-tao, Mao Tse-min (Mao Tse-tung's younger brother), Chang Ting-ch'eng, Feng Wen-pin, Fang Fang, and P'eng Kuei. Li Ch'ing-ch'üan also graduated from the first K'ang-ta class and Chang Ting-ch'eng underwent additional political education at the Central Party School in Yenan in 1942. Chang Ting-ch'eng and Fang Fang did spend most of the thirties and forties in the rural areas of Fukien as guerrilla leaders. They and other alumni may have immersed themselves in rural mobilization work after leaving the institute. However, the career patterns of most of these distinguished alumni were not limited to those of peasant movement "specialists." Biographies on all of these figures except P'eng Kuei can be found in Klein and Clark. **Kaoputsebo**, a Mongolian, was an institute student as was Tu Sung-shou. The former had trained at Whampoa before transferring to the institute in 1926. See **Kaoputsepo**, p. 7. See also Tu Sung-shou, p. 17, and Liu Chih-yüan, "Hai-lu-feng kung-nung cheng-fu ch'eng-li ch'ien hou shih-ch'i ti P'eng Kuei t'ung-chih" ["Comrade P'eng Kuei before and after the Hai-lu-feng Worker-Peasant Government"] , *Hua-nan*, p. 30.

6 Sun Yat-sen University in Moscow

The Chinese Communist Party dismantled its school system when it was forced underground in 1927. Until the early thirties formal training of most Chinese Communist leaders took place in the Soviet Union. This was not a period of great political gains for the Chinese Communists, and the preparation of leaders abroad had mixed effects.

Sun Yat-sen University of the Toilers of China supplanted the Communist University of the Toilers of the East as the principal Soviet institution developing Chinese Communist leadership. Sun Yat-sen University graduates returned home with theoretical and organizational expertise. However, their skills and outlook were not identical to those of the first generation of "Russian-returned" Chinese Communists and reflected shifts in Soviet leadership doctrine.

Stalinization in the Communist Party of the Soviet Union redefined the ideal Communist as the obedient servant of the Party line. By 1930 Soviet leadership education focused on promoting ideological conformity and ferreting out deviationist views. These concerns were not absent from training practices at the Communist University of the Toilers of the East, but they were emphasized beyond all other matters at Sun Yat-sen University.

Under this influence the second generation of "Russian-returned" Chinese Communists introduced a new set of organizational techniques to discipline intra-Party life. They developed the Chinese Communist Party's purge machinery and injected "struggle and criticism" sessions into the molding of Party membership. The Party made use of these procedures to deal with counterrevolutionary pressures and intra-Party disputes during its most trying period of existence. Compared to the years before 1927, Chinese Communist leaders had a heightened awareness of ideological issues, policy lines, and their implications for the Party's political strategy. The cost, however, was initial destabilization and raging factionalism in the early thirties.

ORGANIZATION AND STUDY LIFE

Sun Yat-sen University of the Toilers of China had been founded by the Comintern in 1925 to develop leadership for the National Revolution in China. Prior to 1927 it trained both Kuomintang and Chinese Communist Party members and operated under the joint administration of the Central Committee of the CPSU and the Central Executive Committee of the Kuomintang.[1]

Most of its students were selected through a series of entrance examinations administered by a Kuomintang screening committee, and the most important qualification for admission was loyalty to the Kuomintang. Over eighty percent of the six hundred students in the first two Sun Yat-sen University classes were originally Kuomintang members. Before 1927 most Chinese Communist students were of lower calibre than those who had trained at the Communist University of the Toilers of the East. Comintern policy in China and the Chinese Communists' leadership requirements after 1925 account for the Communists' minority position. The Comintern had designed the school primarily to radicalize left-wing Kuomintang members. The Chinese Communist Party itself could not spare many of its leaders and few Communists could afford the expense of travel to Moscow.[2]

Sun Yat-sen University occupied a four-story structure in a complex of buildings at Sixteen Volhonka Street in Moscow. Before it closed in the autumn of 1930 it was headed by three different rectors. The first was the renowned international Communist leader and scholar Karl Radek.[3] Radek was replaced by Pavel Mif[4] in the summer of 1927. Following a bitter dispute over Party affairs at Sun Yat-sen University with Chinese Communist representatives to the Comintern, Mif asked to be relieved of his position. He was succeeded by Veger, a veteran Bolshevik who had specialized in cultural and educational work.

The prescribed course of study[5] at Sun Yat-sen University lasted two years and followed the lines of the curriculum of the Commu-

nist University of the Toilers of the East. Intensive study of the
Russian language accounted for four hours a day, six days a
week. There were also elective courses in a second language such
as English, French, or German. History courses emphasized the
study of revolutionary movements and included the History of
the Evolution of Society, History of the Chinese Revolutionary
Movement, History of the Russian Revolution, History of Eastern
Revolutionary Movements, and History of Western Revolutionary
Movements.

A course on Materialism tried to steep students in Marxist-Leninist
concepts and develop their ability to analyze problems in terms of
dialectical and historical materialism. In political economy, the
University offered a two-year course dealing with Marx's *Das Kapital*; because of the complexity of *Das Kapital*, students used as
texts Karl Kautsky's *The Economic Doctrine of Karl Marx* in the
first year and Lapidus and Ostrovityanov's *An Outline of Political
Economy* in the second year. The latter work attempted to apply
Marxian economic theory to the building of a socialist economy in
the Soviet Union. Sun Yat-sen University apparently gave high
priority to this course and staffed it with well-known "first-class"
economists from Germany and the Soviet Union.

A course on Leninism was based on Stalin's lectures on the doctrines of Lenin, which were delivered at Sverdlov University in
Moscow in early April 1924 and published in book form as *Foundations of Leninism*. This course ranked with that on political
economy in the eyes of the university administration, and leading
Communist theoreticians were among its instructors. The university also offered a course on Economic Geography, analyzing the
influence of geography on the rate of development of a society.
Many of the lectures were delivered in English.

Other courses at the university were concerned with the practical
problems of political work that students would face when they returned to China. In their second year at the university, students
attended classes on Party Construction, Soviet Reconstruction,
and the Workers' Movement. Although these courses were deemed
crucial, they suffered from poor instruction.

With China on the verge of "armed revolution," the university also
offered a course in military science. Students attended lectures in
classrooms and in a special military research room which exhibited various firearms and topographical sand models. They also
toured military academies near Moscow and practiced marksman-
ship in neighboring army garrisons. Beginning in 1928 all the male
students at Sun Yat-sen University spent their summers in field
training at an army garrison near Moscow.

The students were divided into study sections based on language ability, length of Party membership, and educational attainment. The first and second graduating classes included an English Class, a Russian Class, and a Semi-Russian Class, with most of the instruction in the appropriate foreign language. For Chinese students who had not mastered any foreign language, instruction proceeded through interpreters.

In the first graduating class a Theoretical Class was set up for veteran Chinese Communist Party members who had sought refuge in the Soviet Union after 1927. The distinguished Chinese Communists Chou T'ien-lu, Shen Tse-min, Teng Hsiao-p'ing, Hu Chung, Li Chun-tse, Yü Hsiu-sung, Ch'u Wu, Tso Ch'üan, and Wang Pien were among its members. During 1928 another Special Class was formed for noted Party leaders such as Lin Tsu-han, Hsü T'e-li, Yeh Chien-ying, Wu Yü-chang, Chiang Hao, Hsia Hsi, Ho Shu-heng, Mme. Chang Kuo-t'ao, Fang Wei-hsia, Tung Pi-wu, Li Kuo-hsüan, Ch'ien Yi-shih, Yang Chih-hua (Mme. Ch'ü Ch'iu-pai), and Chao Ju-chih. Since several of the special students were past the age of fifty, their study program took into account their extensive education and diminishing capacity for memorization. The special students were subjected to a minimum of foreign language study. Other classroom work, however, was more advanced and the Special Class resembled a graduate seminar.

On the opposite end of the educational spectrum, Sun Yat-sen University also operated a Preparatory Class for undereducated workers. The school had made special provisions for proletarian cadres in response to the Comintern's drive to enlarge the working-class composition of the Chinese Communist Party. A large number of workers had entered Sun Yat-sen University after the collapse of the labor movement in 1927. Most of the proletarian students at Sun Yat-sen University were illiterate and joined the Preparatory Class for remedial work in reading, writing, and general education. The main courses for this class consisted of Chinese, history, geography, arithmetic, Russian language, and "political common sense." In addition, students spent some time in Party and student organizations outside of class to absorb practical elements of leadership.[6]

For courses other than Russian, group study methods similar to those utilized at the Communist University of the Toilers of the East predominated. Instructors first lectured for several hours to outline the problem under study. Students were handed notes and study outlines listing assignments in various reference books. During the following class session, students had the opportunity to ask professors questions concerning their assignments and were in turn examined orally. A final conference under the direction of the professor then synthesized the material. There were usually no written examinations and students were evaluated on the basis of class participation.

One former student evaluated the pedagogical effectiveness of this procedure:

> One, it stimulated thinking rather than emphasizing rote memory. Two, the student had to be active rather than passive. He had to choose his own special topic and reference material from the outline; he also had to analyze and criticize the works he read and benefited from the mutual discussions. He began to see the old solutions in a new light.... Four, the stress upon daily work and oral testing in the class, with the accompanying elimination of formal examinations, gave a true measure of the student's worth. Five, learning was like a battle. When one put forth his arguments it was like charging forward on a battlefield. If the student was defeated, he still learned perseverance in the face of adversity. He also learned grace in accepting defeat and complying with the will of the majority.[7]

Such learning procedures thus developed valuable attitudes and behavioral traits for revolutionary work. This is one reason why group study and discussion methods were encouraged in the Chinese Communist leadership training programs.

Besides classroom study Sun Yat-sen University organized numerous student outings that were intended to show a successful socialist nation in operation. There were excursions to Lenin's tomb, model factories, schools, museums, and tours of Leningrad, the Crimean peninsula, and the Caucasus. University students were also invited to attend meetings of the Comintern and the CPSU.[8]

IDEOLOGICAL "STRUGGLES"

The experiences in and outside the classroom at Sun Yat-sen University were overshadowed by the fierce ideological "struggles" that raged through the school. The university's close links with the Comintern and the CPSU and the presence of both Kuomintang and Chinese Communist Party branches on campus turned student life into an ideological battleground. Encounter with intraparty struggle was perhaps the most important lesson for Sun Yat-sen University students; graduates returned to China with experience in the management of ideological debates and purge activities.

Before 1927 the Comintern permitted the Kuomintang to maintain a branch at Sun Yat-sen University. At first over half of the university's students belonged exclusively to the Kuomintang, but as the Chinese Communists absorbed left-leaning Kuomintang students into their ranks, the Communists soon outnumbered the Kuomintang students two to one. Both parties quarreled constantly over issues such as the role of the class struggle in the National Revolution and the meaning of Sun Yat-sen's Three People's Principles.[9] Their relations worsened with the turn of events in China. Kuomintang students began returning to China in the summer of 1926; the Moscow branch of the Kuomintang was dissolved in the summer of 1927, and the remaining Kuomintang students at Sun Yat-sen University hurried home.[10]

Besides clashes with Kuomintang students at the university, Chinese Communist students engaged in factional warfare among themselves. The Moscow branch of the Chinese Communist Party had been responsible for all ideological training of Chinese Communist students at both the Communist University of the Toilers of the East and Sun Yat-sen University. As many Chinese students transferred from the Communist University of the Toilers of the East to Sun Yat-sen University, the center of branch activities shifted to the latter institution. There the branch was known for its "authoritarian control" over all aspects of student life.[11]

Under a slogan of "having meetings is first, going to class is second; action is first, theory is second," the branch called relentlessly for meetings morning and night. It insisted that students subject themselves to self-criticism involving family, social background, past activities, and present aspirations. The Moscow branch also made every member keep a diary of daily activities open to Party inspection, and required participation in "action study"--tasks such as copying or translating books and lectures.

Weekly meetings of the various cells of the Moscow branch tried to reinforce ideological and behavioral conformity. Each cell, with twenty to twenty-five members, was led by a guide. At every meeting each member was required to say something about the topic under discussion. This procedure tried to spot deviant ideas while encouraging budding Chinese Communist leaders to develop extemporaneous speaking skills.

The repressive nature of the Moscow branch eventually worked against its objectives. Factional struggles erupted among branch members. Chou Tao-ming and Yü Hsiu-sung led a protest against the authoritarian leadership of branch secretary Jen Cho-hsüan (later known as Yeh Ch'ing) and his policy of subordinating Russian language study to training in revolutionary theory. A four-day series of meetings in the summer of 1926 culminated in the dissolution of the Chinese Communist Party branch. Branch members were then absorbed into a branch of the CPSU at the university.

As a result, Sun Yat-sen University became more closely linked to policy disputes among Soviet Communist Party leaders. Its association with the Chinese revolution made it an obvious forum for debates on Comintern strategy for Eastern revolutionary movements. University members became involved in the struggle between Stalin and Trotsky.

Even after the Trotskyite faction within the CPSU had been defeated, Trotskyite dissidents remained active at Sun Yat-sen University; in August 1928 they founded a secret Trotskyite organization.[12] University rector Karl Radek was dismissed from his post in the summer of 1927 because he supported the Trotskyite line. He was replaced initially by an acting rector, Agoor, the former dean of academic affairs. Agoor tried to consolidate his position as rector by cultivating the former opponents of the Moscow branch of the Chinese Communist Party—Chou Tao-ming, Yü Hsiu-sung, and Tung I-hsiang— and thus set off another wave of factional strife. Eventually the situation became so complicated that the Central Committee of the CPSU ordered vice-rector Pavel Mif to head the school.

Under the rectorship of Pavel Mif the hunt for Trotskyite dissidents continued at Sun Yat-sen University. The Trotskyites were joined by other university students, known as the "Second Line," who were alienated by the policies of Stalin, the Comintern, and the CPSU.[13] Rector Mif and the CPSU branch cultivated a group of students to counter the Trotskyite - "Second Line" coalition. Members of the group, the "Twenty-eight Bolsheviks," later dominated Chinese Communist Party affairs and were known for their facility in Russian and the Marxist classics.[14]

Periodic encounters between the Mif - "Twenty-eight Bolshevik" coalition and its opponents continued from the late summer of 1928 through the autumn of 1929. Then came the crackdown as purge commissars descended upon the campus. They suspended classes and divided the student body into small groups for interrogation. Each student gave his name, social background, age, native area, period of Party membership, and work experience. The CPSU branch at the University employed the "Twenty-eight Bolsheviks" and other loyal followers to hurl accusations against suspected Trotskyites and other anti-Party elements. One participant described the meetings as shattering experiences for the individuals being scrutinized, for the slightest possible blemish from the past was apt to be publicly questioned. Even one's family history going back to remote ancestors was thoroughly investigated. It was a cruel method of inquiry. In the heavy crossfire and charges, many of the weak people simply broke down. Even the most robust and strong-willed among us were bathed in their own sweat at these inquisitions.[15]

A chairman, secretary, translator, and assessor presided over these sessions. As each participant responded the chairman summarized his answer. The entire "purification" process lasted three months. It was supervised by a Party Purge Committee headed by General Pavel Ivanovich Berzin, chief of intelligence for the Red Army General Staff.

The purge activities crushed the Trotskyite organization at the university. The group's most prominent members were imprisoned by the Soviet State Political Administration (GPU). Dissidents from the "Second Line" coalition underwent various types of "labor reform." Some were exiled to Siberian labor camps; those not expelled from the Party spent three to six months working in local factories.[16]

THE LEGACY OF SUN YAT-SEN UNIVERSITY

In what manner was the Chinese Communist Party affected by members' experiences at Sun Yat-sen University?[17] First of all, another wave of Soviet leadership models and training techniques was infused into the Party in the late twenties and early thirties. However, in its extreme emphasis on ideological purity and rigid organizational discipline, it differed from the influences on the earlier generation of Chinese Communists who had studied in the Soviet Union.

Sun Yat-sen University alumni can be credited with introducing into the Chinese Communist Party a style of Party life and Party-political education preoccupied with combating deviationism. "Struggle and criticism" sessions and regimented Party meetings had not been absent from the training experience at the Communist University of the Toilers of the East. But they did not become the highlight of the study program for Chinese Communists in the Soviet Union until the CPSU underwent Stalinization. After Sun Yat-sen University graduates returned to China, "struggle and criticism" sessions became standard features of Chinese Communist Party political education and Party life.

One cannot equate the leadership practices transmitted to China by Sun Yat-sen University graduates with the Stalinist model in the Soviet Union. The Chinese Communist Party never became a carbon copy of the CPSU. Conditions native to China continued to affect Chinese Communist Party life. It should also be pointed out that Sun Yat-sen University alumni exhibited a wide range of political tastes and personality types. Even the "Twenty-eight Bolsheviks," considered the most Stalinist of all the "Russian-returned" students, did not operate as a monolith back in China.

As Sun Yat-sen University graduates assumed ranking leadership positions in the Chinese Communist Party,[18] they infused Soviet leadership and organizational practices of the late twenties into Chinese Party life. University alumni also became dominant figures in Chinese education and propaganda activities during the thirties and forties. Tung Pi-wu, Hsü Meng-ch'iu, Wu Hsiu-ch'üan, Teng Hsiao-p'ing, Wu Liang-p'ing, and Tso Ch'üan were on the staff of the Red Army Academy in Juichin. Yeh Chien-ying headed the Red Army School in Juichin in 1932-1933. Tung Pi-wu was also principal of the Academy of Marxian Communism founded in Juichin in 1933 and of the Central Party School in Wa-yao-pao and Pao-an in 1936. Ch'en Po-ta taught at the Central Party School in Yenan and worked on the staff of the Central Research Institute. Also in Yenan, Wu Yü-chang headed the Lu Hsün Arts Academy (1939-41) and Yenan University (1941-44) as well as North China University in 1948. Party elder Hsü T'e-li was president of the Lenin Normal School in Kiangsi and of the Natural Sciences Research Institute in Yenan and vice-president of the Soviet College in Kiangsi.

Among the "Twenty-eight Bolsheviks" Ch'en Shao-yü served as president of Women's University in Yenan (1939-1941), with his wife, Meng Ch'ing-shu and Chang Ch'in-ch'iu on the university teaching staff. Chang also taught at the North Shensi Public School in Yenan. Wang Chia-hsiang served as an administrator and conducted an officer training class at K'ang-ta in Yenan. Chang Wen-t'ien lectured at the Red Army Academy at Pao-an and by 1940 headed the Academy of Marxism-Leninism in Yenan.

A number of Sun Yat-sen University alumni became leading Chinese Communist ideologues. Ch'en Po-ta rose to prominence as a pro-Maoist spokesman during the late thirties. Chang Wen-t'ien directed the Chinese Communist Party propaganda department between 1933 and 1935 and edited the Kiangsi edition of *Tou-cheng (Struggle)*, the official Party journal prior to the Long March. While teaching in Yenan, Chang took charge of the reference room of *Chieh-fang jih-pao (Liberation Daily)*. In the early forties he headed the Academy of Marxism-Leninism, which trained party theorists. K'ai Feng was an important contributor to *Tou-cheng* and *Hung-ch'i chou-pao (Red Flag Weekly)* in the early thirties. He was named head of the Chinese Communist Party propaganda department in 1937. K'ai also wrote numerous articles for *Ch'ün-chung (The Masses)* and *Chieh-feng (Liberation)* during the late thirties and early forties and played a major role in the *cheng-feng* movement.[19]

Another legacy of Sun Yat-sen University was the mounting factionalism in Chinese Communist Party life, culminating in widespread purges of all types of oppositionists—Anti-Bolsheviks, Trotskyites, Social Democrats, Third Party members, and Liquidationists—during the early thirties. The primary source of bitter struggles within the Chinese Communist Party at this time was conditions within China itself, especially the "white terror" that followed Chinese Communist setbacks in the urban areas. Perhaps the daily threat of annihilation made a strong case for harsh and sometimes desperate measures to keep the Party united. Difficulties in creating a viable power base in both city and countryside multiplied policy differences among the Chinese Communist leaders. And Comintern interference also fed factional strife, as the Comintern tried to play off rival groups of Chinese Communists against each other.

To all of these sources of intra-Party cleavage must be added the influence of the polarization of the CPSU during the period many Chinese Communists trained at Sun Yat-sen University. Soviet influence was partially responsible for encouraging the growth of Trotskyism in the Chinese Communist movement. Trotskyism in China did not originate with its most famous exponent, Ch'en Tu-hsiu, but with a group of students from Sun Yat-sen University.[20]

Intense concern with factional activity and the use of purges to eradicate oppositionist[21] views were legitimized as features of Chinese Communist Party life after Sun Yat-sen University graduates returned to China. From the 1930s on one sees in Chinese Communist leadership training manuals and policy debates frequent discussions of correct and incorrect "lines" that were originally fostered in a Russian climate. After the influx of "Russian-returned" students in the late twenties, training procedures at Chinese Communist Party schools began to regularize techniques that employed intragroup conflict[22] to build Party unity. As in the Soviet Union, Party schools in China became centers for ideological "struggles" and purge activities. A series of "struggle" sessions in late 1933 was conducted by Chou En-lai at the Red Army Academy in Juichin against Kung Ch'u and K'ung Ho-ch'ung.[23] "Specialists" in Party "struggle" from Sun Yat-sen University, Chang Wen-t'ien and K'ai Feng directed the "struggle" against Chang Kuo-t'ao in the spring of 1937.[24] "Struggle" procedures were widely applied throughout the Chinese Communist Party during the Party's first major rectification movement in 1942-1944. They eventually became an integral part of Chinese Communist Party life at all levels.

NOTES

[1] The KMT did not fund Sun Yat-sen University; most of the university expenses were paid by the Profintern. Permanent KMT representative to the Comintern Shao Li-tzu took up residence in Moscow in the summer of 1926. He was supposed to watch over KMT interests at Sun Yat-sen University and joined the university Board of Trustees. He left Moscow after the anti-Communist coup in China in April 1927. On July 26, 1927, the KMT Central Executive Committee announced the end of all ties with Sun Yat-sen University. Kuomintang organizations ceased sending students to Moscow and most of the KMT students at Sun Yat-sen University returned home. Thereafter the University trained only Chinese Communists. In 1928 its name was changed to Communist University for the Toilers of China in Memory of Sun Yat-sen. Details on the founding and organization of Sun Yat-sen University can be found in Yüeh Sheng, pp. 1-22, 42-58; Eudin and North, pp. 86-87; and Wang Chüeh-yüan, *Liu-O hui-i lu [Memoirs of Study in Russia]* (Taipei: San-min shu-chü, 1969), pp. 3-38.

[2] Student recruitment and admissions are discussed in Yüeh Sheng, pp. 16-22, and Wang Chüeh-yüan, pp. 3-28.

[3] In February and March of 1927 Radek began criticizing Comintern policy in China. After the Shanghai coup in April he came out for the formation of soviets in China. Unlike Trotsky Radek did not press for a complete break between the Chinese Communists and the Kuomintang at first nor did he espouse Trotsky's theory of "permanent revolution" for China. In June 1927, however, he joined the Trotskyites in calling for the CCP to split from the KMT left. For his differences with Stalin on international revolution Radek was removed from the rectorship of Sun Yat-sen University in May 1927. He was arrested and tried in January 1937 and died after deportation in 1939. On Radek's career and views on China see Warren Lerner, *Karl Radek: The Last Internationalist* (Stanford, Calif.: Stanford University Press, 1970), pp. 136-147. Radek was initially succeeded by Agoor, the former dean of academic affairs at the university, who served as acting rector while Mif was in China. Yüeh Sheng, p. 205.

[4] Mif had joined the Chinese Section of the Far Eastern Secretariat of the Comintern in the early twenties. A supporter of Stalin, he was appointed vice-rector of Sun Yat-sen University when it opened. Just before Mif became university rector he was promoted to the directorship of the Chinese Section of the Comintern. In this capacity he made several trips to China and helped to organize the Sixth Congress of the CCP. Yüeh Sheng, pp. 37-41, and Hsi-men Chung-hua, "Chung-kuo liu-O hsüeh-sheng cheng-chih tou-cheng shih" [History of the Political Struggles of the Chinese Students in Russia], in *Chung-kuo yü Su-O* [China and Soviet Russia], 1933, p. 160.

[5] Radek taught the course on the History of the Chinese Revolutionary Movement. B. F. Shumiatsky, an expert on Oriental affairs who took over the Communist University of the Toilers of the East in 1927, taught the course on History of Eastern Revolutionary Movements. Yüeh Sheng, pp. 61-66; Eudin and North, p. 87; and Wang Chüeh-yüan, p. 35, all discuss the curriculum.

6Yüeh Sheng taught the "political common sense course" for the Preparatory Class using Bukharin and Preobrazhensky's *ABC of Communism*. Yüeh Sheng, pp. 74-75; on the Special Class see pp. 68-73, and Yang Tzu-lieh, "Mo-ssu-k'o Chung-shan ta-hsüeh tou-cheng ti shih-k'uang" [The Real Story of the Struggles at Sun Yat-sen University in Moscow], *Chan-wang*, no. 173 (April 16, 1969), p. 28.

7Yüeh Sheng, pp. 80-81, and Wang Chüeh-yüan, p. 35.

8Wang Chüeh-yüan, pp. 29, 35-36, 175, and Yüeh Sheng, pp. 82-84.

9Wang Chüeh-yüan, pp. 9-10, 73-74, and Yüeh Sheng, pp. 98-100.

10After the KMT in China initiated its "party purification" drive, the Far Eastern Bureau of the Comintern issued resolutions to dissolve the Moscow branch of the KMT and send the Chinese students home. While many KMT students were able to reach China, those who had not left Vladivostok by December 15, 1927, were detained indefinitely in the Soviet Union. Many were sentenced to prison, Siberian labor camps, or tours of duty with the Red Army. Several, such as Lin Hsieh and Kao Ju-ch'en, ended their lives there. Others were released when Sino-Soviet relations improved, and a number were detained permanently. The remaining KMT left-wing students at the university were eventually absorbed into the CCP. On the KMT-CCP split in Moscow see Wang Chüeh-yüan, pp. 74-77, 199-207; Yüeh Sheng, pp. 102-104; and Wang Chien-min, *Chung-kuo kung-ch'an-tang shih-kao* [Draft History of the Chinese Communist Party], Vol. 2 (Taipei: 1965), pp. 85-86.

11On factional struggles and the Moscow branch of the CCP see Wang Chüeh-yüan, pp. 80-82, 162-163; Wang Chien-min, Vol. 2, pp. 83-87; Hsi-men Chung-hua, p. 159; and Yüeh Sheng, pp. 81, 108-112.

12Warren Kuo, *Analytical History*, Vol. 2, pp. 75-76. See also Wang Chien-min, Vol. 2, p. 119, and Yueh Sheng, pp. 165-166

13The best account of the "struggles" at Sun Yat-sen University is in Yüeh Sheng, pp. 174-183, 205-226. For other descriptions see Hsi-men Chung-hua, pp. 159-168, and Chang Kuo-t'ao, "Wo ti hui-i", *Ming-pao*, no. 30 (June 1968), p. 92, and no. 31 (July 1968), p. 87.

14Accounts differ on the composition of this group. However, "Bolshevik" Yüeh Sheng lists as his twenty-seven comrades Chang Ch'in-ch'iu (Mme. Shen Tse-min), Chang Wen-t'ien (Lo Fu), Ch'en Ch'ang-hao, Ch'en Shao-yü (Wang Ming), Ch'en Yüan-tao, Ch'in Pang-hsien (Po Ku), Chu A-ken, Chu Tzu-shun, Ho K'e-ch'üan (K'ai Feng), Ho Tzu-shu, Hsia Hsi, Hsiao T'e-fu, Li Chou-sheng, Li Yüan-chieh, Meng Ch'ing-shu (Mme. Ch'en Shao-yü), Shen Tse-min, Sun Chi-min, Sung P'an-min, Tu Tso-hsiang (Mme. Ch'en Ch'ang-hao), Wang Chia-hsiang, Wang Pao-li, Wang Sheng-ti, Wang Sheng-yung, Wang Yün-ch'eng, Yang Shang-k'un, Yin Chien, and Yüan Chia-yung. In his view "the 28 Bolsheviks were united more by their ideological position than by any formal organization....Mif did not create the 28 Bolsheviks. But because of their outstanding performance in the struggle in Sun Yat-sen University, they came to Mif's attention as a disciplined force which could be useful to him." For other, sometimes conflicting, lists of the twenty-eight Bolsheviks see Warren Kuo, *Analytical History*, Vol. 2, p. 234; Wang Chien-min, Vol. 2, p. 100; and John E. Rue, *Mao Tse-tung in Opposition* (Stanford, Calif.: Stanford University Press, 1966), p. 7.

15Yüeh Sheng, pp. 174-175. Sheng's account of these events again appears the most complete. See also Chang Kuo-t'ao, "Wo ti hui-i", *Ming-pao*, no 30, pp. 93-94; Warren Kuo, *Analytical History*, Vol. 2, p. 221; and the synopsis of the "Resolution on the Question of the Action of the Delegation of the CCP Central Committee to the Communist International in 1929-1930," in Hsiao Tso-liang, *Power Relations within the Chinese Communist Movement, 1930-1934* (Seattle: University of Washington Press, 1961), p. 145.

16For example, Yang Tzu-lieh was sent to the Seventh Printing Works in Moscow with eight or nine other Chinese students. There they were supposed to learn a new vocation and rebuild loyalty to the Soviet Party line. One contingent of students expelled from the Party was sent back to China. See Yang Tzu-lieh, "Mo-ssu-k'o Chung-shan," pp. 32-33; Chang Kuo-t'ao, "Wo ti hui-i," *Ming-pao*, nos. 30 and 31, (June and July 1968), pp. 94 and 88, respectively. See also Yüeh Sheng, pp. 179-180, 223-234.

17Yang Tzu-lieh, "Mo-ssu-k'o Chung-shan," p. 31; Yüeh Sheng, pp. 224-226; and Rue, pp. 134-35. It should be pointed out that Sun Yat-sen University and Communist University of the Toilers of the East trained the majority of Chinese Communists in the USSR but some attended other Soviet leadership schools. Chapter 3 has discussed those who sought military education in the Soviet Union, and a number of ranking Chinese Communists also attended the Lenin School. Also known as the *Mezhdunarodnye Leninskie Kursy* (International Lecture courses on Leninism), this institution furnished advanced training to leading communists of various nations. It was founded in 1924 and headed by Madame Kirsanova. Under the direct control of the Comintern, the Lenin School featured a one-year curriculum of political economy, history of the CPSU, history of the labor movement, party construction, and Russian language instruction; several sources also mention that students received some military training. The Lenin School allowed students to read on their own according to study plans approved by their instructors to complete course requirements. The training experience was complemented by student field work, such as manual labor in factories for about eight hours per week or investigations of industrial relations and factory management. Lenin School students also journeyed to various regions in European Russia, Siberia, and Tashkent to observe firsthand the Soviet government in action. Chang Kuo-t'ao recalled that while he attended the Lenin School there were about ten Chinese among three hundred students from various nations. Besides Chang, Chou Ta-wen, Yü Hsiu-sung, Tung I-hsiang, and Juan Chung-chao studied at the school early in 1929; Tung Pi-wu, Chuang Tung-hsiao, and P'an Chia-ch'en between 1928 and 1931, and Ts'ai Shu-fan in 1929. Li Li-san and Chou En-lai were reported to have attended the Lenin School while staying in Moscow. Several Chinese Communists, such as Ch'in Pang-hsien, Chang Wen-t'ien, Ch'en Shao-yü, and Wang Chia-hsiang (all members of the "Twenty-eight Bolsheviks") were reported to have attended courses at the "Red Institute of Teachers"—probably the Institute of Red Professors in Moscow. There is little information on Chinese Communists' experiences at these schools and their impact on CCP affairs. On the Lenin School, see Chang Kuo-t'ao, "Wo ti hui-i," *Ming Pao*, no. 31, pp. 86-7; Yang Tzu-lieh, "Mo-ssu-k'o Chung-shan," p. 29; Eudin and North, p. 88; and Benjamin Gitlow, *The Whole of Their Lives* (New York: Charles Scribners' Sons, 1948), p. 242. See also the biographies of Tung Pi-wu, Ts'ai Shu-fan, and Li Li-san in Klein and Clark; and Klein and Clark, p. 195 on the "Red Institute of Teachers."

18Most of the graduates of Sun Yat-sen University were placed in ranking positions as directing personnel in the CCP hierarchy or as political officers in the Red Army. In terms of career patterns one would want to distinguish between the "elders," or established Party figures at the Special Class or Theoretcial Class at Sun Yat-sen University, and the younger generation of Chinese Communists whose distinction in the CCP followed their return from the Soviet Union. Russian training may have contributed to the career of Wang Ts'ung-wu in Party organizational and control work. The activities of Teng Hsiao-p'ing, Wu Hsiu-ch'üan, Hsü Yi-hsin, and Wang Chia-hsiang in liaison work with foreign Communist parties may have been a product of their knowledge of Russian and world Communist affairs acquired during matriculation at Sun Yat-sen University. Hsü Ping, a Sun Yat-sen University graduate, became a translator of major works of Marx, Engels, Lenin, and Stalin, including Stalin's *Problems of Leninism*, during the early Sino-Japanese War. The biographies of most of these figures can be found in Klein and Clark. On Hsü Yi-hsin, see Union Research Institute, *Who's Who*, p. 281.

[19]Ho Shu-heng was also involved in training personnel for Soviet area work in the early thirties. Other "returned students," besides those previously mentioned and the Trotskyites, included Wang Ho-shou, Ulanfu, Kan Szu-ch'i, Fu Po-chien, Huang Wen-chieh, Kuo Shao-t'ang, Li Ching-hsiu, Li Han-fu, Li Po-chao, Liu Ch'ün-hsien, Shen Chih-yüan (Kuan-lan), Shih Tung, T'ang Han-hu, T'ang I-chen, Hsü I-hsin, Ch'en Wei-ming, Chao Ju-chih, Ch'ien Yi-shih, Chu Jui, Ch'en Hui-ch'ing, Wang Hsiu, Li Chin-yung, Tu T'ing, Yün Yü-jung, Kuo Miao-ken, Liu Ch'i-feng, Hsieh Chien-ming, Sun Tsung-fan, Chu Tzu-shun, Hu chung, Li Chun-tse, Ch'u Wu, Wang Pien, Li Chien-ju, Yu Tu-san, Hsi-men Chung-hua, Chang Ch'ao, Li Hsieh-yüan, Hsin Ping-chou, Ch'ing Man- yün (Mme. Sheng Yüeh), K'ang Yün-shun, Li Kuo-hsüan, Chu Mao-tseng, Wang T'ung-yung, Jen Cho-hsüan (Yen Ch'ing), Yen Yu-chih, Chou Tao-ming, Li P'ei-tse, Hsü Hsi-k'uei, Ch'u Ching-pai, Chuang Tung-hsiao, Li Yüan-ch'u, Fang Wei-hsia, Shih Shih, Kao Ch'en-lieh, Lin Ch'i-t'o, Ku Ku-i, Li Pen-yi, Chang Kuo-shu, Wang Yu-chih, Hsiang Yu-mei, Ch'iu Tung-wan, Li Yao-k'uei, P'an Wen-yu, Wang Lan-yin, and possibly Lu Ting-i. Biographical information for most of these figures can be found in Klein and Clark; Yüeh Sheng; Nym Wales, *Red Dust*; Edgar Snow, *Random Notes on Red China* (Cambridge, Mass.: Harvard University Press, 1957), pp. 34, 313; and Harrison, *Peasant Rebellions*, pp. 23-24.

[20]A secret Trotskyite organization at Sun Yat-sen University was alleged to have received instructions from Soviet Trotskyites and translated their documents into Chinese. The group advanced the theory of "permanent revolution" and associated Stalin's "opportunism" with the CCP's censure of Ch'en Tu-hsiu. By August 1928 some of these Trotskyites were en route to China. The first general meeting of Chinese Trotskyites took place in Shanghai in January 1930. It elected a General Committee of Executives that was composed entirely of Sun Yat-sen University alumni such as Liang Kan-ch'ao, Shih Shou-yün, Ch'en I-mou, Li Mei-wu, Sung Feng-ch'un, Chang T'e, and Lu Yen, with alternate members Hsiao Pin-yang, Ou Fang, T'ang Yüeh-po, and Hsü Chen-an. Ch'en Tu-hsiu joined the Chinese Trotskyites after his formal expulsion from the CCP in November 1929. The Trotskyite coalition soon proved unstable and splintered into four major groups who were decimated by raids by KMT intelligence agents. Oppositionist activities in China ground to a halt after the arrest of Ch'en Tu-hsiu and P'eng Shu-chih in October 1932. Other Sun Yat-sen University graduates involved in Trotskyite opposition in China were An Fu, Wang Wen-kuang, Li P'ing, Ta Fu-lin, Fang Ching-piao, Lu Ch'ing, Ch'u Fang, Chang Fang, Fan Ken-piao, Li P'in, Fu Jen-lin, Liu Jen-ch'iung, Hsiao Pin-yang, and Chou T'ien-lu. Yüeh Sheng, pp. 3, 70, 164-173; Warren Kuo, *Analytical History*, Vol. 2, pp. 75-76; and Rue, pp. 146-159, 167. The most complete account of the Trotskyite movement in China is the dissertation by Richard Clark Kagan, "The Chinese Trotskyite Movement and Ch'en Tu-hsiu: Culture, Revolution and Polity" (Ph. D. dissertation, University of Pennsylvania, 1969).

[21]Individuals trained in the Soviet Union also appear to have been instrumental in the operation of the CCP's organs to combat counterrevolutionary and oppositionist activities. The head of the State Political Security Bureau of the Central Soviet Government was Soviet-trained Teng Fa; Teng also headed the Central Party School in Yenan. His biography can be found in Klein and Clark. On Soviet influence in the State Political Security Bureau, see Trygve Lötveit, *Chinese Communism 1931-1934: Experience in*

Civil Government (Lund, Sweden: Studentlitteratur, 1973), pp. 115-116; and Harrison, *March*, pp. 212-222.

[22]Within specific bounds intra-Party conflict was seen as productive to Party unity and is discussed again in Chapter 7 in relation to the *cheng-feng* movement. Current literature on conflict suggests that conflict within a group may help strengthen its cohesion. A group (such as a Communist party) that defines itself as in constant conflict with the existing social order tends to be small in size, select in membership, and aiming toward the total personality involvement of its members. Such a group may profit from maintaining a strict definition of "purity." Perceptions of "dangerous" tendencies within a group may increase members' awareness of issues at stake, intensify participation, and bring members closer to each other. That the use of "struggle" sessions and group criticism was originally foreign to the Chinese is suggested in David Nivison's essay on "Communist Ethics and Chinese Tradition." Nivison finds precedents for the Chinese Communists' concern with self-cultivation in Chinese philosophical trends inspired by the Ming thinker Wang Yang-ming. Wang's attempts to unify "knowledge" and "action" included rigorous self-scrutiny (similar to self-criticism) to determine if an individual's behavior was in accord with his morality. However, Nivison distinguishes between this form of "self-criticism" and the mutual criticism of group "struggle" meetings, pointing out that Wang Yang-ming advised against the criticism of others. See David Nivison, "Communist Ethics and Chinese Tradition," *Journal of Asian Studies*, Vol. 16, no. 1 (November 1956), pp. 58-59. On the functions of intragroup conflict see Lewis Coser, *The Functions of Social Conflict* (New York: The Free Press of Glencoe, 1956), pp. 38-118.

[23] Kung was chief-of-staff of the Red Army during the Fourth Encirclement Campaign and K'ung Ho-ch'ung was identified as commander of the Sixteenth Corps of the Red Third Army around 1930. See Whitson, p. 129 and chart G between pp. 288 and 289. Kung Ch'u describes the "struggle" against him in his memoir *Wo yü Hung-chün* [I and the Red Army] (Hong Kong: Nan-feng ch'u-pan she, 1955), pp. 101-102, 381-384. He was reinstated into the Party but defected in May of 1935.

[24]On the "struggle" against Chang Kuo-t'ao at K'ang-ta, see Warren Kuo, *Analytical History*, Vol. 3, pp. 237-245; Whitson, pp. 154-155; and Chang Kuo-t'ao, *The Rise of the Chinese Communist Party, 1928-1938* (Lawrence: The University of Kansas Press, 1972), pp. 504-517. From Yenan the "struggle" against the "erroneous right opportunist Chang Kuo-t'ao line" spread throughout the CCP and various military units.

7 New Methods of Leadership

The most painful and creative years for Chinese Communism were those between the evacuation of the cities and the Long March. They represented a period of bitter factional disputes, bloody purges, and erroneous "lines." But these years also brought a population of nine million in an area of several hundred thousand square miles under Communist rule.1

One of the Chinese Communists' major accomplishments was their organizational transformation enabling them to penetrate the Chinese countryside. The Party underwent structural reforms that enlarged the scope of its activities. More heavily than in the past, it relied on trained leadership to extend its communications system and organization into the rural areas. It developed a new model of leadership and leadership style—the "cadre" concept and "mass line"—to link its apparatus with local society and to win the support of the peasant population. These gains were the products of refinements in the Chinese Communists' leadership policy and system of leadership education.

Programs for leadership education also helped the Chinese Communist Party to curb the autonomy of its Red armies, which often overshadowed the Party in base-building and mobilization work. Through careful indoctrination and supervision of military leadership, the Chinese Communist Party began to place its military operations under centralized direction. Fears of "mountaintopism"—the creation of independent military "kingdoms"—persisted until the end of the Sino-Japanese War.2 However, the Chinese Communists were able to keep militarization in check and even creatively adapted their military model to general political work. Chinese Communist activities during the Kiangsi period were the groundwork for future success in Yenan.

LEADERSHIP POLICY AFTER THE FOURTH PLENUM

Leadership policy became a major issue in the Chinese Communist Party after the "Twenty-eight Bolsheviks" had captured the key leadership positions at the Fourth Plenum in Shanghai in January 1931.[3] Following the Plenum the Party center, which continued to operate in Shanghai until early 1933, instituted measures to assert control over Chinese Communist activities in the hinterland. In order to bring autonomous guerrilla groups and Red Army units under centralized control, the top Party leadership launched a massive program to restructure the Party apparatus for the countryside.

Later Chinese Communist accounts[4] have asserted that the "Twenty-eight Bolsheviks" tried to undermine the Maoists by reorganizing the Party at all levels to replace veteran cadres. While scanty documentation cannot separate naked power rivalries from necessary Party reforms, there were strong grounds for improving Party work. Up to early 1933 the Party as a distinct organization in the countryside was very weak.[5] Most of the Chinese Communist personnel were associated with the various Red armies or scattered guerilla groups. Most of the veteran rural cadres placed local concerns above loyalty to the central leadership and were hostile to Party discipline. The growing peasant composition of the Party also slowed down implementation of Party directives.

Recent interpretations have described the relationship between the "Twenty-eight Bolsheviks" and other Chinese Communist leaders as one of mutual accommodation rather than open antagonism. Policy differences were not coterminous with narrow factional lines, and different segments of the Party leadership could achieve consensus on some broad issues.[6] However, most of the Party reforms that followed the Fourth Plenum reflected mainly "Bolshevik" views.

These reforms tried to improve communication and coordination between various levels of the Party hierarchy. The "Resolution on the Question of Party Reconstruction," adopted at the First Party Congress of the Soviet Areas in November 1931, called for a strengthening of Party committees from provincial to branch levels under the principle of "collective leadership." It also advanced an inspection system through which higher-level cadres supervised

Party activities at the grass-roots level.[7] Party discipline was to be prompted through a system of regular oral or written reports and intra-Party self-criticism.[8] All of these measures were to extend the Communist organizational apparatus further into the country-side.

"MASS LINE" AND THE "CADRE" CONCEPT

Reforms to establish a firm Party structure down to the local level were responsible for the "new method of leadership," which put unprecedented emphasis on the role of the individual Party leader as the Chinese Communists' organizational link with local society. The "new method" was designed to maximize support for the Party and to develop effective policies for the rural areas.

The principal exponent of the "new method of leadership" was Chang Wen-t'ien. Chang emerged as a leading voice in Chinese Communist Party life in early 1933 when he became director of the Chinese Communist Party propaganda department and editor of *Tou-cheng (Struggle)*, the organ for Party affairs. He also worked with Mao Tse-tung in formulating the operational principles of soviet government[9] and shared some Maoist views on economic policy.

Chang elucidated "On the New Method of Leadership" in a four-part series of articles in *Tou-cheng* in 1933.[10] He listed as "the most important components of the new method of leadership.... the questions of whether or not the Party is actually performing the leadership function of leading the masses [and] whether or not the Party is able to meet quickly the aspirations of the masses and arouse the masses to respond to the call of the Party's policy line." If Party policies were to win popular support, Party leaders at the grass-roots level had to understand the interests and aspirations of the masses and the types of appeals to which they responded.

Chang detailed the prerequisites for this style of work. Every provincial Party committee was expected to closely watch every *hsien* committee; the *hsien* committee to watch every district committee; and the district committee to watch every Party branch. Chang instructed provincial committees to discuss the work of several core districts and branches to determine their degree of coordination. He encouraged improved communication between higher and lower levels of the Party to increase local leaders' input into policy decisions.

Reports on work in the soviets, political work in the Red Army, union work, and cultural and educational activities had been too superficial. Chang condemned reports from lower levels and work plans from higher levels that were full of hollow phrases. He instructed upper levels of the Party to dispatch inspection personnel or work teams to test policy against actual local conditions.

Chang also drew attention to propaganda work among the masses. He criticized previous propaganda work as being limited to issuing statements or posting slogans. He called for propaganda work that would arouse the masses to respond actively to Party policies, with language and objectives geared to the nature of the audience—its social composition, cultural level, and mode of speech. Propaganda teams were to avoid abstract issues, such as the "glory" of joining the Red Army, in favor of economic appeals such as the threat of Encirclement Campaigns to employment or landownership.

The kernel of Chang Wen-t'ien's description of the "new method of leadership" incorporates the essential features of the Chinese Communist leadership style heralded as the "mass line": (1) efforts by the Party leadership to maintain continuous contact with its base of support; (2) serious attention by the Party representative to the actual needs and concerns of the people; (3) Party policy formulated on the basis of these concerns; and (4) a Party organizational structure and communications system capable of testing and adjusting Party policies to elicit positive mass response.[11] Broad Party contact with the masses in mass organizations, mass movements, and propaganda with mass appeal are all part of the "mass line."[12] But the "mass line" designates a specific leadership style that develops policy through a process of sustained interaction between the Party leader and the elements of the population he wishes to cultivate. As early as the twenties there were glints of elements of the "mass line" in Chinese Communist statements on movement-building, statements which stressed the need for mass support, mass work, organizational ties with the masses, and effective propaganda.[13] But the documents on Party reform dated from about 1932 on were the first to bind up all of these activities into a systematic leadership style.[14]

Was the "mass line" or "new method of leadership" a Chinese creation, or was it imported from abroad? Certainly veteran rural leaders such as P'eng P'ai, Mao Tse-tung,[15] and Fang Chih-min contributed to its operational principles. However, the conceptual terms for the "new method of leadership" and the Party reforms to implement it show considerable Soviet influence. For theoretical justification of the "new method of leadership" Chang Wen-t'ien invoked both Lenin and Stalin. He sprinkled his essays "On the New Method of Leadership" with passages from Stalin's *Problems of Leninism* such as these:

> It means, firstly that the Party must closely heed the voice of the masses; that it must pay close attention to the revolutionary instinct of the masses; that it must study the practice of the struggle of the masses and on this basis test the correctness of its own policy; that, consequently, it must not only teach the masses, but also learn from them.

> It means, secondly, that the Party must day after day win the confidence of the proletarian masses; that it must by its policy and work secure the support of the masses; that it must not command but primarily convince the masses, help them to realize by their own experience the correctness of the policy of the Party; that, consequently, it must be the guide, the leader and the teacher of its class....

> It is quite opportune to call attention to these dangers precisely at the present moment, when the political activity of the masses is rising; when the readiness of the Party to heed the voice of the masses is of particular value; when regard for the interests of the masses is a fundamental precept of our Party; when it is incumbent upon the Party to display particular caution and particular flexibility in its policy; when the danger of becoming conceited is one of the most serious dangers confronting the Party in its task of correctly leading the masses.[16]

Chang also extracted from the *Problems of Leninism* Stalin's citation of Lenin's address at the Eleventh Party Congress of the Communist Party of the Soviet Union:

> Among the people we are after all but a drop in the ocean, and we can administer only when we properly express what the people are conscious of. Unless we do this the Communist Party will not lead the proletariat, the proletariat will not lead the masses, and the whole machine will collapse.[17]

It is difficult to determine if Chang Wen-t'ien was attempting to emulate Soviet theoretists in the hope of replicating the CPSU in China. Conditions in China were very different from those that inspired Lenin's and Stalin's statements in the Soviet Union in the 1920s. The two Communist leaders were calling for a strong presence in Soviet society of a Party that had already seized state power. The Chinese Communists in the 1930s, however, had yet to win the revolution and called upon Party-building to win broad mass support.

One can look at the effort to promote a "new method of leadership" from two perspectives. On the opportunistic side, it may have been employed to make the Party into a power base so that the "Twenty-eight Bolsheviks" could challenge veteran rural and military leaders. It is equally likely that the "new method of leadership" and Party reforms were conceived as legitimate solutions to the Chinese Communists' rural movement-building problems and contained input from experienced rural organizers. Given the Party's difficulties with peasant apathy, the "mass line" leadership style may have been recognized by most segments of the Party leadership as an appropriate work style for peasant mobilization.[18]

While the proponents of the "new method of leadership" looked to Lenin and Stalin for formal doctrinal backing, the "mass line" took on its own meaning in its Chinese context—a more serious concern with the Party's relationship to the masses, popular participation in the political process, and homage to the creativity of the masses in nation-building. The emphasis on the "mass line" in Chinese Communist writings on leadership reflects the nature of the Party's route to power through popular mobilization. It is also linked to the Party's continuing concern with maintaining a strong presence in local society.

Another influence on the "mass line" leadership style has been the traditional Chinese political heritage. During the Imperial era the personal leadership qualities of elites were recognized as the vital link between state and society. Administration was "by men, not by methods." Confucian-inspired standards exhorted officials to be close to the people and to take responsibility for their welfare. Ch'ing administrative writings frequently discussed the problem of maintaining a close relationship between leaders and led.[19]

Was the "mass line" or "new method of leadership" a hollow prescription on the pages of Party journals or an actual working leadership style during the Kiangsi period? Unfortunately, there are few reports on the activities of Party members during this phase of the Chinese Communist movement. The Chinese Communists did not succeed in establishing a strong Party organization in most of the soviet areas. In many cases Red Army units remained in charge of both military and administrative tasks. Most competent Party leaders were assigned to the Red Army, leaving the Party infrastructure severely understaffed at lower levels.[20] Some Red Army political workers may have used "mass line" methods for political work in the course of base-building. However the Communist infrastructure as a whole was very weak during the Kiangsi period. Under such circumstances, it is difficult to imagine a flourishing "mass line" in operation.

During the Yenan period, stable conditions allowed the Party to develop stronger local work. Mass organizations multiplied, providing another avenue of contact between Party representatives and the general population. All of these factors allowed the "mass line" to become a working leadership style in some Communist areas after the Long March.

Whether the "new method of leadership" became operational immediately or not, it did begin to transform the role of leadership in Chinese Communist organizational life. Its emphasis on the input of the individual leader in movement-building gave rise to more systematic policies to recruit and train leadership personnel. One indicator of this change was the redefinition of the term "cadre" (*kan-pu*). In the past the term was used to designate only ranking Party leaders, but following the Fourth Plenum a "cadre" came to mean one with the ability to lead and organize the masses. The association between the "cadre" and the "mass line" leadership style grew closer in the years thereafter.[21]

The enlarged role of leadership in revolutionary strategy was reflected in the expansion of Chinese Communist resources devoted to leadership education. Party resolutions on cadre recruitment and training together with large quantities of instructional materials for cadres produced in the soviet areas and Red Army units testify to the high priority placed on preparing leadership cadres during the Kiangsi period.

Following instructions in various Party reform documents issued after the Fourth Plenum, the Chinese Communist Party attempted to set up facilities to train cadres of all levels. The scope and objectives of cadre education were more ambitious than at any point earlier in Chinese Communist history. The Kiangsi cadre training system set the basic pattern for Chinese Communist leadership education during the Yenan period and thereafter.

A network of Party schools extended from central to district levels in the Central Soviet and outlying areas. The Central Bureau of Soviet Areas operated its own schools in Juichin to train elite cadres, while provincial and *hsien* Party committees operated their own Party schools for lower-level leaders. Training programs in the schools run by the provincial, *hsien*, and district committees were aimed at administrative cadres, with attention to specialization in secretarial, organizational, propaganda, agitation, and cultural activities.

The content of instructional material was similar for all Party schools, with some exposure at lower levels to practical work experience. But there was some variation in the quality of instruction among the various levels of Party schools. For example, central schools featured lectures by leaders such as Po Ku (Ch'in Pang-hsien), Lo Fu (Chang Wen-t'ien), Chu Te, Chou En-lai, and Mao Tse-tung. While graduates of the high-level Party schools often served as instructors for the training programs at provincial or *hsien* levels, the majority of the teaching staff for programs at the *hsien* level and below were graduates of provincial Party schools.

Besides regular Party schools, Party committees at various levels operated short-term training programs. A notable example was the Kiangsi Provincial Party Committee's short-term training program in Ning-tu *hsien* during July 1932. The education of leadership cadres also took place through the inspection system and in-service training programs. These programs supplemented local leaders' theoretical knowledge as applied to practical work and literacy skills. Because the Party suffered a perpetual cadre shortage, the in-service program became the most popular form of leadership education.

Training through the inspection system was reserved for cadres who had graduated from formal instructional programs but lacked practical work experience. After graduation these "intellectual cadres" were assigned to provincial, *hsien*, or district inspection committees to observe local Party branches and mass organizations. In investigating and evaluating local operations, they were expected to develop valuable insights into local problems and share with local cadres their "theoretical" expertise.[22]

Party publications furnished teaching materials for various instructional programs and also served as training instruments for cadres unable to undertake formal study. The most widely used in Party education was *Tang ti chien-she [Reconstruction of the Party]*, issued by the organization department of the Central Bureau of Soviet Areas. Its contents included Soviet and Chinese theoretical pieces and reports by cadres active in local work and Party-building. Resolutions of the Chinese Communist Party Central Committee and the Central Bureau of Soviet Areas were also popular educational devices. Given the limited resources and publishing equipment of the soviet areas, the volume of material issued by the Chinese Communist Party for propaganda and Party-political education is quite impressive.[23] It is another indicator of the Party's commitment to leadership education during the Kiangsi period. However, Party-building and leadership training programs failed to take root on the local level in many areas.[24] The scope of Chinese Communist leadership education before the Long March remained quite limited.

HIGH-LEVEL SCHOOLS

The most effective instructional programs were those at the highest level, generally located in Juichin. These schools were organized along specialist lines to develop the skills required for maintaining sizable territorial areas. The trend toward specialization would become stronger as the Chinese Communist movement grew in size and complexity. Curricula during the Kiangsi period began to cater to various types of leadership models, reflecting more division of labor among Chinese Communist leaders than in the past. There were training programs for Party administrators, "white area" operatives, military commanders, political commissars, and personnel with technical skills. Most of the leadership training for peasant mobilization work took place in lower-level programs; however, even the production of specialists in high-level schools was closely linked to the Chinese Communists' new conception of leadership and strategy for peasant revolution.

The Academy of Marxian Communism specialized in training staff for the Party organizational hierarchy, thus feeding the developing Communist infrastructure needed to penetrate the soviet areas. The academy was founded in March 1933 to commemorate the fiftieth anniversary of Marx's death. Classes began on March 15. Originally called the School of Marxian Communism, the academy was first situated in Chi-an in Kiangsi but later moved to Sha-chou-pa. Tung Pi-wu, who had attended Sun Yat-sen University and the Lenin School in Moscow between 1928 and 1931, was superintendent. He was assisted by Lo Ming, the acting secretary of the Fukien Party Committee until his removal from office in February 1933. From his lectures at the academy, Lo compiled a famous textbook, *Tang ti chien-she (Reconstruction of the Party).*25

Three types of classes operated within the academy: (1) a training class for new soviet area work personnel, consisting of eighty students (after two months of study graduates of this type of class were assigned to work in soviet or "white" areas); (2) a four-month training class, divided into four sections for Party, Communist Youth Corps, soviet, and labor union work, with fifty students per section; (3) a high-level training class lasting six months consisting of forty students sent from provincial committees, provincial soviet governments, and provincial labor unions. Although the curriculum for each type of class varied, all students received instruction in basic principles of Marxism-Leninism, Party construction, history of the labor movement, geography, principles of soviet organization, labor and peasant union organization, mass organization, and basic knowledge of the natural sciences. Lecture courses centered on Problems of Agrarian and Industrial Economy (peasant and worker problems), Cultural Work (propaganda), and Partisan Organization and Training.[26]

According to Lo Fu, the Academy of Marxian Communism offered the first "full course" in Marxism in the history of the Chinese Communist Party.[27] A test on *Basic Problems of the Chinese Revolution* analyzed Chinese history from the Marxist standpoint. It covered topics such as the feudal nature of traditional Chinese society; disruption of the Chinese economy under imperialism; rising tides of revolutionary change in the May Fourth Movement, labor movement, and May Thirtieth Movement; and the rise and fall of the Wuhan government and the Canton commune. In depicting these events the text introduced an economic interpretation of history and the concepts of imperialism, class struggle, and the revolutionary party.[28]

Po Ku (Ch'in Pang-hsien), who had acquired some theoretical training in Moscow, lectured at the academy in early 1933 on the history of the Communist Party of the Soviet Union. This course examined the features of a "model" Bolshevik Party that had risen from a small group to lead an "antilandlord, anticapitalist"civil war and the first successful socialist revolution. Po praised the CPSU for adapting to changing conditions, especially in its "struggle against opportunism." He encouraged the Chinese Communist Party to emulate the CPSU in practicing internal struggle. He also emphasized that Bolshevik strategy was appropriate to its time and place and could not be applied mechanically to China.[29]

An institution called the Soviet College, founded in August 1933 at the forty-eighth session of the Council of the People's Commissars, trained working cadres for the soviet areas. Its president was Mao Tse-tung and its vice president was either a figure identified as "Shakov" or Hsü T'e-li. The college's fifteen hundred students were divided into a "general" class and a "special work" class. The "special work" class had eight sections devoted to land, national economy, finance, worker-peasant inspection, education, labor, law, and domestic government affairs.[30]

Special propagandists, who used dramatic arts in their political work, were trained at the Gorky School of Dramatics outside the western gate of Juichin. Headed by Li Po-chao, a graduate of Sun Yat-sen University, the staff included Wei Kung-chih, Chang Ai-p'ing, Ts'ai Ch'ien, Hua Ch'ing, Ts'ao Hsin, and Ts'ao Ping-san. The Gorky School was reported to have graduated over one thousand students and trained sixty theatrical troupes for propaganda work in villages and army units.[31]

Most of the high-level specialized training institutions prepared personnel for military work. This is not surprising in view of the Chinese Communists' dependence on the military for defense and base-building throughout the Kiangsi period. These schools upgraded Chinese Communist leaders' military skills and their political awareness. They were part of a coordinated effort to place Red Army operations under centralized control.

Red Army units changed constantly in number and designation throughout the Kiangsi period. Between 1928 and 1931 there were about ten army corps operating in widely scattered areas; Party reforms after the Fourth Plenum introduced measures to coordinate military activities from the Party center. In 1931 the Party established a Central Soviet Government Revolutionary Military Council (headed by Chu Te), a political commissar system (headed by Mao, followed by Chou En-lai in mid-1932), and a General Political Department (headed by Mao, followed by Wang Chia-hsiang). The Military Affairs Committee of the Central Committee, headed by Chou En-lai for most of the time before 1935, had ultimate authority over the military at all levels.

These measures set representatives of the Party to watch over Red Army commanders. They stepped up political education for both officers and rank and file. They promoted a "scientific" division of labor between commanders and commissars, limiting the former's authority to purely military matters. This system of political controls was a modification of the system of political work used in the National Revolutionary Army. Since the early thirties it has undergone few changes. It established the basic system of political work in the military that still operates in the People's Liberation Army today.

Various training schools for Red Army leaders were set up near the Party center in Juichin. These schools tried to raise the quality of command personnel and to regularize army tactical doctrine, equipment, and organization according to professional military standards. Most of the training programs were not very sophisticated, and technical training was limited by shortages of equipment and ammunition. Although they made some contribution to Red Army leaders' professional skills, their major function appears to have been political.[32] A large portion of their curricula consisted of ideological education that would increase the commanders' loyalty to the Party and their sensitivity to political controls.[33] Many training programs had special sections for political commissars and political workers that focused mainly on building political skills. By bringing commanders and commissars from scattered base areas together in one central location, leadership training programs for commanders and commissars also promoted centralization.

The Worker-Peasant Red Army Kung Lüeh Infantry School, established around 1930 near Hutu, trained company and platoon leaders. Originally called the Red Army Second Infantry School, its name was changed to commemorate Huang Kung-lüeh, a former commander of the Red Third Army who was killed in the Third Encirclement Campaign. The school graduated between eight and nine hundred students in a four-month training course. It was headed by Liu Yen, a native of Lung Yen in Fukien who had joined the Red Army in 1929 and become chief-of-staff of the Red Twelfth Army in 1931.

The Worker-Peasant Red Army Special Arms School was located in Wu Yang Yüan in Juichin. Its commandant was Hu Kuo-chieh, a native of Szechuan. The Special Arms School featured courses for artillery corps and engineer corps, a light and heavy machine gun class, and an antiaircraft class. About four to five hundred students were reported to have graduated. Also in the Juichin vicinity, the School for Guerrilla Cadres offered a three-month course in guerrilla warfare. Over three hundred students were selected from among cadres in various guerrilla and Red Guard units. The school opened around 1930 and was headed by Liu Hai-yün, a former head of the tenth division of the Red Fourth Army.

The Worker-Peasant Red Army P'eng and Yang Infantry School was set up in 1930 at the ninth fortress in Juichin. Originally called the Red Army First Infantry School, it changed titles to honor martyred Communist leaders P'eng P'ai and Yang Yin. Its commandant was Ch'en Keng, who had been a division commander in the Oyüwan soviet area. The school trained company and platoon leaders in a four-month course and graduated one thousand students. In the autumn of 1931 the P'eng and Yang Infantry School combined with the camp training class of the Red First and Third Army Groups and was renamed the Worker-Peasant Red Army School (*Kung-nung hung-chün hsueh-hsiao*). The Red Army School trained lower-level Red Army cadres and graduated four classes. On November 7, 1933, the school was again reorganized and renamed the Worker-Peasant Red Army Academy (*Kung-nung hung-chün ta-hsüeh*), and shortly thereafter was renamed the Worker-Peasant Red Army Hassis Academy, in honor of M. Hassis, a Soviet vice-consul in Canton who had been killed during the Canton uprising. The commandant of the academy was Chou K'un, formerly a high-level military official in the fifty-second and fifty-ninth divisions of the National Army.[34]

Among these institutions the most significant developments in leadership training took place at the Red Army School and the Red Army Academy. The curriculum and organization of the two schools were based on the model set by the Whampoa Military Academy. All students studied both military and political subjects, with the balance between subjects determined by specialization in either purely military or military-political work. Both schools apparently placed a high premium on professional military standards and were run by a number of Red Army commanders influenced by training in Soviet military institutions in the late twenties. Despite strong military emphasis, however, both schools devoted considerable attention to political education and the production of political commissars. Red Army political work remained an important element in base-building as well as troop indoctrination and the training methods at these Red Army schools took into account popular mobilization and "mass-line" operations. Because so much of the political life of the soviet areas continued within the framework of the Red Army during the Kiangsi period, Red Army schools were pioneers in political education. Their innovations in political work were later applied to the preparation of nonmilitary cadres.

THE RED ARMY SCHOOL

The Red Army School was headed by Liu Po-ch'eng in 1931-1932 and Yeh Chien-ying in 1932-1933. Ch'en Keng, who directed the Worker-Peasant Red Army P'eng and Yang Infantry School, was also said to have been president of the Red Army School in 1933. Altogether the school graduated about two thousand students in four classes, the last on February 16, 1933. The students were drawn primarily from the lower-level Red Army leadership. They were divided into two infantry groups, one special task group, one women's group, and a children's group.[35]

The Red Army School began to train high- and middle-level cadres in September 1932 and organized a "training battalion." The battalion consisted of 120 students above the regimental level and presented a three-month course. Later the school set up a "political battalion" to prepare middle- and high-level political cadres for the Red Army. Most of its students were company and regimental political commissars, heads of political departments at various levels of the Red Army, middle-level Party cadres, and local Party secretaries. The 360 political-battalion students were divided into three companies which were to train for three months, but acute cadre shortages forced battalion members to cut short their studies by one month.

Only thirty percent of the course work in the political battalion was devoted to military subjects. The most essential courses dealt with political work among the masses and with prisoners of war. The principal means of developing disciplined behavior was through group criticism.

Teaching methods at the school tried to elicit maximum participation from each student. Influenced by Soviet methodology, the Red Army School staff avoided "dry" classroom teaching and employed group discussions that featured question and answer sessions. Students were issued research materials and divided into discussion groups. Each group appointed a leader to draw conclusions from the results of the group's research. This study method helped to dissolve boundaries between student and teacher while maintaining a high level of student interest.

Party meetings at the school operated along similar lines. In the high-level "training battalion" there was a Party branch supervised by the Communist Party Committee of the Red Army School. The branch was divided into nine cells in which instructors and students mixed together. Branch meetings took place once a month and included political reports on topics such as the international and domestic situation, Party policies, and the tasks of the Red Army. At cell meetings, which were held weekly, members discussed documents issued by higher levels of the Party. Much of the cell meeting time was devoted to discussion and criticism of members' activities and life histories.[36]

Course outlines from the Red Army School depict the main themes of political education as self-discipline, activism, leadership, and concern for the welfare of the Red Army rank and file and the masses. Most of the political leadership prepared at this school was assigned to Party work and mobilization activities within the Red Army. Some of the leadership qualities to be developed in the political curriculum involved aspects of the "mass line" work style. For example, one "Lecture on Political Work" for the political battalion discussed these topics:

> 1. The Mission and Function of Political Instructors:[37] political education among the troops; inculcation of activism and military spirit; the work of the Lenin Room; direction of mass organizations; dealing with immoral acts and breaches of discipline; liaison with local Party leaders; propaganda work under fire.
>
> 2. How to Be an Instructor: requirements of experience in "outside mass work" as well as political education; ability

to be "close to the masses" and to understand the needs and feelings of the rank and file; serving as an example of a heroic fighter to others.

3. Leadership in Time of War: insuring that both troops and the Party representatives understand the functions of a mission and that each individual is prepared to fulfill his assigned role.

4. Relationship between Political Instructor and Company Commander: assisting the commander in elevating and consolidating troops' fighting power; maintaining discipline.

5. Functions of the Political Commissar: to lead Party work and political education within the Red Army; to enforce Party supervision over all military and political activities; to curb anti-Party tendencies within the ranks through "education and struggle."

6. The Political Department: its function and relationship to the political commissar and the masses.

7. Relationship between Political Organs in the Red Army and Local Party Branches.[38]

Following each topic were a series of questions on the key points and a list of reference materials.

Another series of "Political Questions and Answers" dealt with the fundamentals of Communism and the Chinese Communist Party. In very simple language the text posed questions such as:

1. What is Communism? What are classes and how do they arise? (To show the evolution of the system of private property.)
2. How do revolutions occur? What is their aim? What is a socialist society?
3. What is the Communist Party? (To distinguish between a Communist Party with its vanguard functions and other political parties and the present program of the CCP.)
4. What are the differences between the Chinese Communist Party and the Kuomintang? (To contrast the class nature and political positions of both parties and furnish a critique of the Three People's Principles.)[39]

The school's political department also issued the periodical *Hung-hsiao tou-cheng (Struggle in the Red School)* for political education Although the frequency and publication dates of this periodical are unknown, one available issue, dated July 8, 1933, furnishes some indication of its contents. Several articles concerned military affairs, such as the formation of military research groups and the use of hand grenades. Others dealt with "revolutionary competition" work; incorrect tendencies from changes in work patterns; self-criticism; and a July 6 meeting of activists and youth workers.40

Exchanges between members of the Red Army School were also furthered through the "wall newspaper," another indoctrination technique borrowed from the Soviet Red Army. Wall newspapers supplemented the activities of political discussion groups. The wall newspaper was published each week by a committee selected from the student body. In the paper students reported their opinions of the instructional program, interpretations of Communist theory, suggestions for future activities, and the results of their studies. Some wall newspapers featured "red" and "black" columns that praised or criticized army personnel. These columns served as guidelines for desired behavior and indicated the criteria for promotion. The Chinese Communist Red Army considered wall newspapers very effective for making the teachings of the Party meaningful to the ordinary soldier.41

"Saturdays" were modelled after "labor activity" in the Soviet Union and drew students and teachers into outside mass work. Every Saturday afternoon, Party, government, and army leaders spent two hours in manual labor. Students in the Red Army School political battalion divided into forty small groups and moved into nearby villages. Without compensation they assisted the inhabitants in such chores as cutting grass and firewood and harvesting grain. The students used these occasions to investigate local conditions and conduct propaganda work.42

Another feature of the Red Army School was its "revolutionary competition" movement. Students contended in groups for first place in academic achievement, discipline, wall newspaper activities, shooting, and hygiene. This form of competition bolstered both individual achievement and group spirit, promoting Chinese Communist ideological and organizational objectives. The exact date on which the Chinese Communists initiated revolutionary competition campaigns is unknown, but they were widely used in political education during the Kiangsi period.43

THE RED ARMY ACADEMY

Unfortunately, there is almost no information on the careers of graduates of the Red Army School or the institution's impact on the Chinese Communist leadership structure. The Red Army Academy was more prominent in producing high-level military leadership and refinements in leadership training methods. One factor behind the reorganization of the Red Army School into a higher-level training institution was its difficulty in eradicating "low" political and cultural standards among Red Army leaders of worker and peasant origins. The reorganized Red Army Academy hoped to circumvent this problem by limiting the student body to command personnel above the regimental level.[44]

Under the jurisdiction of the Chinese Communist Party Central Committee and the Revolutionary Military Council, the Red Army Academy opened officially on November 7, 1933. Its campus was nestled in a forest ten to fifteen miles from Juichin. Apparently the first class at the academy participated in the construction of the school, making use of the surrounding timbers.[45]

The academy consisted of four departments: a command class, an advanced command class, a senior political class, and a staff class.[46] The command class consisted of 480 Red Army youth and military cadres of the rank of company commander or above. There were only 12 students in the advanced command class, recruited from among high-level military and political officers.[47] Their studies consisted of research on military strategy and the problems of directing large troop units. The staff class trained Red Army middle-level cadres who had a relatively high "cultural" level. It totalled 45 students.

Closely tied to the student body, the staff of the academy was an amalgam of veteran Party leaders and recent converts from the Nationalist camp. Chou K'un, the academy director, was formerly a ranking officer in the fifty-second and fifty-ninth divisions of the National Army. After joining the Communists, he commanded the Red Fourth Army and later the Eighth Red Army. While repulsing the Fourth Encirclement Campaign he was seriously injured and became a student in the advanced command class of the Red Army School. After he was selected to head the academy he continued to participate in the advanced class. Another former Nationalist commander, Ch'en Shih-chi, and Li T'e (Otto Braun), the Comintern adviser to the Chinese Communist Party, were also instructors at the academy.

There were sixteen full-time members of the instructional staff.
Sporting a beard more than five inches long, Chou En-lai lectured
on combat techniques and quoted profusely from Soviet Red
Army manuals. His favorite subject was the political significance
of military action. Sun Yat-sen University graduate Teng Hsiao-
p'ing taught the "Construction of the Party," and Liu Po-ch'eng, a
graduate of the Frunze Military Academy, gave military reports.
Political work reports were delivered by Wang Chia-hsiang and
Mao Ch'ang. Li Pi-t'ing and Li Hsiang-wu, respective heads of the
organization department and the enemy work department of the
general political department of the Revolutionary Military Council, also served as instructors before their deaths.[48]

At the outset the Red Army Academy faced problems in student
quality and teaching materials comparable to those at the Red
Army School. Its student body numbered six to seven hundred
and was drawn from all military areas.[49] The teaching staff was
criticized for overly abstract lectures and its failure to organize debates in study groups. In the military area the staff was assailed
for ignoring the strong points of the Red Army in discussions of
new military techniques and for giving insufficient attention to the
Regulations for Warfare. These difficulties were exacerbated by
shortages of teaching materials and study aids.

At stake was a fundamental contradiction between "theory" and
"practice," heightened by wartime conditions. If the Red Army
Academy hoped to fashion seasoned commanders in six months, it
had to develop an effective instructional program on short notice.
Education in a crisis environment had to be ultimately "practical,"
pared of all but the essentials. It had to aim directly at the actual
conditions graduates would face on the battlefield.

Out of this state of emergency the Red Army Academy developed
a number of educational refinements that later became important
principles of leadership education. A report of the Revolutionary
Military Council encouraged the academy administration to solicit
students' opinions of their teachers. It instructed the teaching
staff to observe each others' classes. Each lesson plan was to undergo careful examination and revision. The format for courses
was rearranged so that students in the political class, for example,
discussed materials in the classroom only after reading them individually and analyzing them in study groups. For students in the
military classes, each course was broken down into sections. In
addition to periodic tests, instructors were to give surprise oral
quizzes to measure on-the-spot comprehension of material.[50]

The report of the Revolutionary Military Council also made recommendations for tailoring military training to the Red Army's

actual wartime needs. Students were to learn how to pinpoint the geographical features of each area of operation, to prepare for long distance marches, and to anticipate countermoves by the enemy. The report put strong emphasis on the principles of night combat and the study of past battle experiences. It was hoped such preparation would help graduates deal with rapidly changing conditions on the battlefield.[51]

Pedagogical practices favored independent and streamlined thinking, a type of "battlefield methodology." Each lesson topic was designed exactly for one class period (three hours). Topics could be subdivided if class time was insufficient. For example, a discussion on encounter in battle could be broken down into separate classes on (1) intelligence work and advance units and (2) selection of the method of attack. Students were encouraged to exhibit initiative in their design of battle plans.[52]

Careful planning in all aspects of the learning experience was supposed to teach students and staff how to distinguish between essential and nonessential points in each lesson. The academy favored the question and answer format for extracting the optimum learning value from each unit of class time. At all costs teachers were to avoid lecture classes and rote memorization. The thought process that emerged from this type of educational format was called *ch'i-fa*, "self-enlightenment."[53]

The Revolutionary Military Council condemned examinations at set times as too "bureaucratic." It recommended short surprise quizzes that would condition students to sudden decisions on the battlefield. It considered real military experience and political work the most valuable type of teaching material and encouraged academy students to exchange their own fighting experiences in and out of class. To test the quality of academy training against actual conditions at the front, the Council tried to obtain evaluations of the instructional program from graduates on active combat duty.[54]

Systematic efforts to link classroom "theory" with battlefield "practice," the use of streamlined lesson plans, and the *ch'i-fa* learning method helped to overcome some of the early difficulties of the Red Army Academy. Because these procedures helped to prepare students for emergency situations, they were considered valuable for producing desirable leadership qualities—a sense of clearcut organization, iron discipline, self-reliance, and group solidarity—in other types of Communist cadres. These learning practices could also justify—and find justification in—the Marxist concern with relating theory to practice. Thereafter the "battlefield methodology" became a standard form of preparation for political as well as military leadership.

Courses for the advanced command class consisted of military history, strategy, staff operations, study of arms, command of unified fighting with various types of forces, and building fortifications. A series of "Lectures on Strategy" published by the Red Army Academy training department included these topics: (1) purpose and means of warfare; (2) relationship between strategy and tactics; (3) essentials of troop strength; (4) essentials and mutual use of offense and defense; (5) "principles" (first to tenth); (6) strategic position and essential points of strategy; (7) significance of line of communications; (8) essential points of military action; (9) selection of line of action and objective of action; (10) attack and phases of action; (11) procedures for defensive warfare; (12) influence of supplies upon warfare; and (13) military encounters.[55]

Military subjects predominated in the command class but they were only a fraction of the curriculum of the political class. The political class emphasized mass mobilization techniques for rural base-building and procedures for political work within the military. All military instructors were required to participate in political classes and discussions along with the students.

Subjects in the political course were (1) Party construction; (2) history of the development of society; (3) political work in the Red Army; (4) regulations for infantry warfare; (5) basic tactics, with regulations for irregular skirmishing; and (6) basic military knowledge and training from squad to regimental level, including skills such as firing a gun, stabbing with a bayonet, and some civil engineering.[56]

An outline of lectures on political work for the high-level political class of the Red Army Academy dealt with the conduct of political work in the midst of ongoing warfare. A discussion of "Politics and the Military" explained in simple language the military basis for class rule and the need for military power to overthrow the landlords. The lectures made reference to a quotation attributed to Engels, stating that men were more important than military techniques, and contrasted the class basis and organization of the Red Army with that of the Nationalists. The outline gave considerable attention to political work in the Red Army and to the organization of various political organs. It underscored the importance of political work for maintaining Party leadership over the military, heightening troop morale, and mobilizing inhabitants of the surrounding areas to oppose the enemy. Like the "Lecture on

Political Work" at the Red Army School, these lectures detailed the relationship of commanders to political workers, the role of political workers in the Red Army, and political operations with enemy troops and local inhabitants. They spelled out procedures for propaganda work among the masses, initiating revolutionary committees and mass organizations, land reform work, and intelligence gathering. In addition, the lectures pointed out particular features of political work during offensive and defensive operations, retreats, and guerrilla activity.57

Another series of "Lectures on Political Work" at the Red Army Academy explored in even greater detail the functions of political leaders among the troops and the political commissars. For this type of political instruction, reference materials were mainly publications of the Red Army political department.58

Lectures on "Problems of the Chinese Revolution" tried to develop students' identification with the Chinese Communist Party and its general political goals. Questions for study focused on a Marxian analysis of the impact of imperialism on Chinese economic and political life. They also took up "problems of the nature of the motive force and leadership of the Chinese revolution." The questions took forms such as (1) "What stage is the Chinese revolution in? Where are the Trotskyites mistaken when they say that 'the Chinese revolution is at present a socialist revolution?' What conditions determine the nature of a revolution?" (2) "Why are only workers and peasants the motive forces of the Chinese revolution? Why can't peasants lead the revolution?" and (3) "Why are the proletariat and its Communist Party the leaders of the Chinese revolution?"

The section on the "present and future of the worker-peasant democratic dictatorship" dealt with the preconditions for socialism in China. It compared the "worker-peasant democratic dictatorship" with the "dictatorship of the proletariat" and asked "How can we prepare for the transition toward the dictatorship of the proletariat?" The selection of assigned readings bore the imprint of the "Twenty-eight Bolsheviks": Lo Fu's "Basic Problems of the Chinese Revolution," "The International Line," and "Two Strategies"; Stalin's *Problems of Leninism*; and an article by Po Ku from the eighth issue of *Tou-cheng*.59

As at the Red Army School, the Red Army Academy promoted a spartan atmosphere. Students were subject to frequent military inspections that were observed by ranking Party officials such as Mao Tse-tung, Chu Te, Chou En-lai, and Po Ku. The Revolutionary Military Council often sponsored "revolutionary competition" campaigns that developed students' grasp of military affairs and enthusiasm for collective life.60

Several former students recall physical labor as a vital part of the training experience at the academy. One remarked that the construction of the school buildings

> was the first lesson of the Red Army Academy....Through
> this labor to build the school students' mass viewpoint and
> labor viewpoint were strengthened, and it elevated and con-
> solidated thinking to "serve the people."61

Even after the school buildings were completed, physical labor remained part of the curriculum. Students maintained herds of cattle and pigs, tended a vegetable garden, and operated a mill. They also assisted local inhabitants with planting and harvesting and repairs during the New Year period. From such experiences students were supposed to realize that "labor became the most honorable thing and not to work became shameful."

Like the graduates of Whampoa, those who attended the Red Army Academy later became commanders or commissars.62 They and the graduates of other military-political training programs replenished the officer corps of the Red Army to counteract an annual casualty rate of fifty percent.63 Military leaders with formal training upgraded the quality and fighting capability of the Red Army at a time when the Chinese Communist movement relied most heavily on the power of the gun. Undoubtedly, political commissars and political workers who were developed in training programs elevated the Red Army's morale during the Long March.64 Red Army political workers also contributed to mobilization activities after the Chinese Communist Party reached Yenan.

One should not attribute the Chinese Communists' failure to hold their rural bases in the south entirely to erroneous policies. Most current interpretations of Kiangsi Communism agree that the major factor behind the loss of the soviets was the overwhelming military superiority of the National Government during the Fifth Encirclement Campaign.65 Severe material deprivation and constant military pressure throughout the Kiangsi period tinged Chinese Communist activities with a harsh and desperate quality. Many of those who served in the Party infrastructure at this time were illiterate peasants, which perhaps accounts for some faulty implementation of what may have been basically sound policies. All of these difficulties were further exacerbated by factional differences and the fragmentation of Chinese Communist leadership in scattered soviet areas. Nevertheless, further experience would show that many of the tentative and ad hoc approaches to rural revolution in the Kiangsi period proved major breakthroughs for Chinese Communism.

NOTES

[1] Conflicting estimates of the Chinese Communists' strength during the Kiangsi period range from two to thirty million inhabitants and sixty to three hundred *hsien* under Communist jurisdiction. See this discussion in Harrison, *March*, pp. 190, 199; and Ilpyong J. Kim, *The Politics of Chinese Communism: Kiangsi under the Soviets* (Berkeley and Los Angeles: University of California Press, 1973), p. 119.

[2] Whitson, pp. 442-443.

[3] On the results of the Fourth Plenum see Wang Chien-min, Vol. 2, p. 99; Rue, p. 245; Warren Kuo, *Analytical History*, Vol. 2, pp. 235-236; and Harrison, *March*, pp. 187, 222-223.

[4] Mao Tse-tung, "Resolution on Certain Questions in the History of Our Party," April 20, 1945, in *Selected Works*, Vol. 3 (Peking: Foreign Languages Press, 1965), pp. 187-194. One would also want to question views of the "Twenty-eight Bolsheviks" challenging their competence to deal with serious policy issues. Analysts such as John Rue, Warren Kuo, Li Ang, and Hsiao Tso-liang have upheld Mao's charge that "Bolsheviks" were totally devoid of work experience, "cloaking themselves in Marxist-Leninist theory" and the prestige of the Comintern as their only qualifications for Party leadership. While it is true that the majority were a youthful lot from intellectual backgrounds, with little contact with the countryside, they were not entirely ignorant of practical Party affairs. Ch'en Shao-yü, Ch'in Pang-hsien, Chang Ch'in-ch'iu, Wang Chia-hsiang, and Yang Shang-k'un had attended Shanghai University, where mass movement work outside the school was an essential ingredient in their training. The "Bolsheviks" had also worked underground in local Party organizations between their return from Moscow in the summer of 1930 and the Fourth Plenum in early 1931. At Sun Yat-sen University the group may have been preoccupied with "struggles," but it was exposed to some instruction in Party operations as well as theory.

[5] It is extremely difficult to develop a comprehensive picture of institutional development during the Kiangsi period. Each of the Communist rural bases had unique institutional patterns. Some soviet areas, such as the Central Soviet area, were better consolidated than others. Even within one base area Chinese Communist control could vary considerably from *hsien* to *hsien*. The network of soviets appears to have been better developed in many areas than the organization of the Party itself and frequently extended to the grass-roots level. In well-developed base areas, such as the Central Soviet area, the Party, soviet government, and Red Army maintained separate organizational hierarchies. However, virtually all of the base areas suffered from shortages of trained cadres and from loose coordination between local organizations and the Party center. See the discussions of soviet and Party development in Kim, *Politics*, pp. 40-53, 160-170, 178; and Lötveit, pp. 34-38, 58-59. The Red Army appears to have continued to have been active in mass work and drew off much of the best leadership talent from the Party and soviets. See Kim, *Politics*, p. 49; and Lotveit, pp. 25, 53.

[6]For example, Chang Wen-t'ien sided more closely with Mao Tse-tung than his fellow "Bolsheviks" on the issues of mobilization techniques for the land investigation movement and soviet construction. Discussions of the relationship between "Bolsheviks" and Maoists can be found in Kim, *Politics,* pp. 10-11, 87-88, 184-188; Lötveit, pp. 72-73; and William F. Dorrill, "Party Reform and Structural Change under the Returned Student Leadership" (unpublished paper presented at Connecticut Symposium on the Chinese Communist Movement, March 25-27, 1971), pp. 1-6.

[7]In the inspection system higher-level cadres were dispatched to lower levels of the Party. This enabled Party committees from provincial to district levels to check on local work and provided "intellectual" Party members with an opportunity for "practical work." Inspectors examined and assisted work at lower levels and transmitted policy directives downward. "Chung-yang kuan-yü kan-pu wen-t'i ti chüeh-i" [Central Committee Resolution on the Cadre Problem], August 27, 1931, *Hung-ch'i chou-pao [Red Flag Weekly],* no. 18 (October 13, 1931), reprinted in Hsiao Tso-liang, *Power Relations within the Chinese Communist Movement,* Vol. 2 (Seattle: University of Washington Press, 1961), pp. 381-382.

[8]On the report system see "Chiang-hsi sheng Su-wei-ai cheng-fu hsün kuan-yü shih-hsing pao-kao chih-tu" [Instructions from the Kiangsi Provincial Soviet Government on Implementing the Report System], April 13, 1933, in the Shih-sou Collection, reel 10. The Party reforms are also discussed at length in "Su-ch'ü tang ti-i-tz'u tai-piao ta-hui t'ung-kuo tang ti chien-she wen-t'i chüeh-i-an" [Resolution of the First Soviet Area Party Congress on the Question of the Reconstruction of the Party], Central Bureau of Soviet Areas, November 1931, in Hsiao, Vol. 2, pp. 397-404.

[9]Their writings on this subject were issued by the Council of People's Commissars in 1934. Chang Wen-t'ien and Mao Tse-tung, "Ch'ü hsiang Su-wei-ai tsen-yang kung-tso" [How to Work for a District and Township Soviet], Juichin, April 1934, Shih-sou Collection, reel 10.

[10]Lo Fu, "Kuan-yü hsin ti ling-tao fang-shih" [On the New Method of Leadership] serialized in *Tou-cheng,* see especially no. 2 (February 4, 1933), no. 5 (March 15, 1933), no. 20 (August 5, 1933), and no. 28 (September 30, 1933).

[11]The most extensive discussion of the "mass line" can be found in John Wilson Lewis, *Leadership in Communist China* (Ithaca, New York: Cornell University Press, 1963).

[12]In the current literature on Chinese Communism there are varying interpretations of the "mass line." Some studies see its origins in the Yenan period and rely on Mao Tse-tung's statement of "mass line" principles in "Some Questions Concerning Methods of Leadership" issued on June 1, 1943. Other proponents of Maoist authorship of the "mass line" base their arguments on definitions of the "mass line" as organizational and propaganda techniques that maximized popular support for the CCP. Studies in the former category include Mark Selden, *The Yenan Way in Revolutionary China* (Cambridge, Mass.: Harvard University Press, 1971), pp. 274-276. In the latter category would fall Chalmers Johnson, "Chinese Communist Leadership and Mass Response: The Yenan Period and the Socialist Education Campaign Period," in *China in Crisis,* vol. 1, book 1, ed. Ping-ti Ho and Tang Tsou (Chicago: Uni-

versity of Chicago Press, 1968), pp. 400-402; and Jerome Ch'en, "The Development and Logic of Mao Tse-tung's Thought, 1928-49," in *Ideology and Politics*, pp. 109-110.

[13]See, for example, CCP Central Committee "Resolutions on the Question of Propaganda," October 1925, in Wilbur and How, pp. 122-126, including the statement, "The most important principle of mass agitation is that it must be concretely based on facts immediately confronting the peasant and working masses" (p. 122). The CCP Central Committee "Resolution on the Peasant Movement" of July 1926 instructed that "Persons working in the peasant movement must first do as the peasants do in speech and action. Their living conditions and clothing must also be similar to those of the peasants. Only thus can they gain close contact with and disseminate propaganda among the peasants....It is necessary thoroughly, to understand the sufferings of the people in order to express the demands of the peasantry; to know the objective limits of action in order to lead the peasantry to struggle; and to utilize the tactics of united fronts in order to prevent the peasants from being isolated and defeated." The entire resolution can be found in Wilbur and How, pp. 296-302; this statement is from p. 301.

[14]In CCP documents on Party reform one begins to see statements on the "new method of leadership" appearing around mid-1932. It is interesting to compare the "Resolution on the Question of Party Reconstruction" adopted by the First Party Congress of the Central Soviet Area in November 1931 with the "Working Program for Party Development and Party Reform" issued by the CCP Central Bureau of the Soviet Areas on June 12, 1932. The November 1931 resolution discusses the question of winning the masses' confidence in terms of Party members' exemplary conduct. Its wording is similar to earlier CCP documents that describe mass work in terms of "agitation and propaganda." The "Working Program" of June 1932 shows more sensitivity to the dynamics of contact and interaction with the masses. It enjoins Party branches to improve and tighten relations with the masses and to understand adequately the real conditions in the masses' lives. Lower levels of the Party were to try to hear the masses' "real opinions" to determine appropriate policies for each concrete problem. See "Su-ch'ü tang," in Hsiao, vol. 2, p. 402; and "Fa-chan tang ho kai-tsao tang ti kung-tso ta-kang," June 12, 1932, in Hsiao, vol. 2, pp. 625-626.

[15]Mao Tse-tung has frequently been cited as the CCP's foremost authority on mass work. Although criticized by the Party Central in 1931-1932 for sacrificing mass work to coercive military methods, he devoted considerable attention to mass mobilization problems. He encouraged "investigation and research" and the immersion of leadership personnel into local society, both later components of "mass line" operations. His articles such as the "Letter to Yüan Kuo-p'ing" of March 6, 1932, and "Conclusions Reached by the Conference of Responsible Soviet Personnel of Eight Counties on or above the District Level on the Land Investigation Movement" of June 21, 1933, discuss mass work and mobilization techniques in the land investigation movement for building local political organs. Even if Mao did not invent the "mass line," he can be credited with sponsoring many of the techniques of "mass line" operations. See "Mao Tse-tung kei Yüan Kuo-p'ing ti hsin" and "Pa hsien ch'ü i-shang Su-wei-ai fu-tse jen-yüan ch'a-t'ien yün-tung so t'ung-kuo ti chüeh-lun," reproduced in *Mao Tse-tung chi*, vol. 3, pp. 95-97 and 251-270, respectively.

[16]Lo Fu, "Kuan-yü," *Tou-cheng*, no. 20 (August 5, 1933), pp. 10-12. One can find an English translation of these passages in J. Stalin, *Problems of Leninism* (Moscow: Foreign Languages Publishing House, 1953), pp. 174, 187.

[17]Lo Fu, "Kuan-yü," *Tou-cheng*, no. 20, p. 12. His citation of Lenin can be found in Stalin, *Problems*, p. 188.

18On the "mass line" as a leadership style for peasant mobilization, see James R. Town-send, *Political Participation in Communist China* (Berkeley and Los Angeles: University of California Press, 1969), p. 83. See also Alan Liu, *Communications and National Integration in China* (Berkeley and Los Angeles: University of California Press, 1971), pp. 9-10; 115-116, on the importance of oral face-to-face communication for effective Party relations with the peasantry.

19For example, Ch'eng Han-chang wrote that "Among the troubles of a district, there is nothing like above and below being divided and the sense of feeling of not getting across. ...I wish that all *chün-tzu* would be diligent at government and be close to the people in order to communicate feeling between above and below." Another authority on administration, Wang Hui-tsu, contended that "The official must also take account of feeling and circumstance. If your judgments are not in accord with popular feeling, they will stir up murmurings—And if you maintain your decisions afterwards, the employment of force will be comparatively difficult." See John R. Watt, *The District Magistrate in Late Imperial China* (New York: Columbia University Press, 1972), pp. 85-87, 227.

20See Davis Bernard Bobrow, "Military in the Chinese Communist Movement," part 2, "Political and Economic Uses of the Military" (Ph.D. dissertation, Massachusetts Institute of Technology, 1966), pp. 377-378.

21Kim, *Politics*, pp. 181-182, 191-192.

22This discussion of Kiangsi cadre education is based on ibid., pp. 192-198.

23Over seventy-seven publications are listed in the Shih-sou Collection alone. *Tou-cheng*, founded in February 1933, replaced *Tang ti chien-she* and *Shih-hua* [True Words] as the leading journal of Party affairs. It too was used for training purposes. For a list of other journals used in leadership training see Wu Tien-wei, "A Selected and Annotated Bibliography of the Ch'en Ch'eng Collection (unpublished manuscript), pp. 2-15.

24See "Fa-chan tang," in Hsiao, vol. 2, pp. 623-624; Chang Kuo-t'ao, *Rise, 1928-1938*, pp. 341-365; and the report by Tu Chen-nung, "Kan tung-pei Su-wei-ai ch'ü ti kung-tso pao-kao [Report on the Work of the Northeast Kiangsi Soviet Area], December 1932, reproduced in Hatano Kenichi, *Chūgoku kyōsantō shi [History of the Chinese Communist Party]*, vol. 3 (Tokyo: 1962). pp. 343, 375.

25Wang Chien-min, vol. 2, p. 415; Nym Wales, *Red Dust*, p. 43. See also Warren Kuo, *Analytical History*, vol. 2, p. 490, and vol. 3, p. 7.

26Wang Chien-min, vol. 2, p. 415.

27Edgar Snow, *Random Notes on Red China, 1936-45* (Cambridge, Mass.: Harvard University Press, 1957), p. 86.

28The text also contains some interesting discussions of strategic problems in the Chinese Communist movement. For example, the author distinguishes between revolution in a capitalist country and in a "semi-feudal, semi-colonial" country such as China. In the former the proletariat can triumph by taking over several key cities, whereas in the latter it can only take one region at a time where counterrevolutionary forces are weakest. Ibid., p. 138. This is similar to the description of Mao's views on revolutionary strategy described in Shanti Swarup, *A Study of the Chinese Communist Movement* (London: Oxford University Press, 1966).

29Po Ku, *Lien kung-tang shih yü Lieh-ning chu-i* [History of the Communist Party of the Soviet Union and Leninism] (Ma-k'o-ssu kung-ch'an chu-i hsüeh-hsiao chiao-yü ch'u, July 8, 1933), reprinted by Kung-nung hung-chün hsüeh-hsiao [Worker-Peasant Red Army School], August 15, 1933, Shih-sou Collection, reel 12, pp. 3-10. In addition to the history of the CPSU from the rise of the Russian Social Democratic Party to the New Economic Policy and anti-Trotskyite struggle, Po's course contained a section on Leninism. This part of the course dealt with the operations of the revolutionary party, definition of Leninism, proletarian revolution and dictatorship of the proletariat, transition from bourgeois-democratic to proletarian revolution, peasant and national minority problems, and Bolshevik organization, strategy, and tactics.

[30]Soviet College was located in Sha-chou-pa, near the headquarters of the Central Soviet Government in Juichin. See Wang Chien-min, vol. 2, p. 415; Wang Hsüeh-wen, "Chinese Communists' Yenan Spirit and Educational Tradition," *Issues and Studies,* 7, no. 5 (February, 1971), p. 59; and the biography of Hsü T'e-li in Klein and Clark.

[31]Wang Chien-min, vol. 2, p. 416. See also Edgar Snow, *Red Star over China* (New York: Grove Press, 1961), p. 114; Nym Wales, *Red Dust,* p. 183; and Klein and Clark, p. 987. Chang Ai-p'ing was denounced as a Trotskyite in August 1932. See Warren Kuo, *Analytical History,* vol. 2. pp. 475-478.

[32]This discussion of political work and political controls is based on Whitson, pp. 421-423, 441-443; Harrison, *March,* p. 202; Joffe, *Party and Army,* pp. 14-26; Kao et al., *Political Work,* pp. 10-17; and Gittings, *Role,* pp. 100-116. Before 1931, Party representation in the Red Army was first handled through the Front Committee. In 1928-1929 it took the form of the Party representative and Party committee system. The elaborate system of political commissars, political departments, and Party committees within the military went into operation in the early thirties.

[33]It should be noted that certain conditions that prevailed during the pre-1949 period helped to minimize the differences between the Chinese Communists' political and military activities. Commanders and commissars were usually ranking Party members. Political tasks were much more closely related while the Chinese Communists were struggling for survival. In some cases the commander and commissar of a given military unit were the same person. See Joffe, *Party and Army,* p. 68.

[34]These schools are discussed in Wang Chien-min, vol. 2, pp. 415-416; and Wang Hsüeh-wen, p. 59. Separate schools for military and political cadres in Chingkangshan, Tzu-p'ing, and Mao-p'ing were in operation as early as 1928. In the early thirties the Chinese Communists were known to have run a communications school headed by Liu Mou which graduated over one hundred students for radio communications work. Medical personnel were trained at a hygiene school headed by Ch'en I-hou.

[35]Accounts differ on the organization of the Red Army School. According to one, the school was run by a five-man committee consisting of Chu Te, commandant; Mao Tse-tung, political commissar; Ch'en Tung-jih, secretary; Ch'en Ch'i-han, education director; and Ping Cheng-ch'iu, Central Kiangsi Bureau representative. "Hung-chün hsüeh-hsiao chih tsu-chih" [The Organization of the Red Army School], in *Ch'ih-fei chi-mi wen-chien hui-pien [Collection of Secret Documents on the Red Bandits],* vol. 2 (June 30, 1931), Shih-sou Collection, reel 20. It also describes an eleven-member School Committee set up by the group in charge of the All-China Soviet Congress as the directing body for the school. Committee members included Ch'en Tung-jih, Ch'en Ch'i-han, Tseng Tu-fei, Chou Sung-shan, P'i Chi, Chia Ching-lien, Ho Ming, Lo Hsing-heng, Lai Ch'in, Shou P'u-piao, and Lan Chih-yung, with Ch'en Tung-jih, Ch'en Ch'i-han, Tseng Tu-fei, Chou Sung-shan, and Chia Ching-lien on the standing committee. Other sources with somewhat different descriptions of the organization of the school are Whitson, p. 147; Wang Chien-min, vol. 2, p. 415; Wang Hsüeh-wen, pp. 58-59; and Hsieh Chung-liang, "Tsai hung-hsiao tang kung-ping" [In the Engineering Corps at the Red School], in *Hsing-huo liao-yüan [A Single Spark Can Start a Prairie Fire],* vol. 2 (Peking: Jen-min wen-hsueh ch'u-pan she, 1961), p. 161.

36This discussion of study life is based on Kung Ch'u, pp. 339-343, 364. Kung was formerly chief-of-staff of the South Kiangsi Military District and chief-of-staff of the Red Army during the Fourth Encirclement Campaign.

37Political instructors were lower-level political officers in charge of indoctrination, cultural and recreational work, and mass campaigns. They were supposed to set an example for the rank and file and raise morale. Their functions were primarily educational and should be distinguished from those of the political commissars. The political commissar was the Party representative appointed to each military unit to supervise Party work and day-to-day operations, especially the activities of commanders. His functions were primarily control and supervision. The political department carried out the policy decisions of the commissar and Party committee in each unit and took responsibility for the education of the rank and file. Party committees within the military were not well developed before 1949 and their authority was exercised by the commissars. On the nomenclature and evolution of the political work system, see Gittings, *Role*, pp. 106-116, and Kao et al., pp. 7-50.

38Some of the texts for this course on political work were "Provisional Regulations for Political Work," "Regulations for the Work of the Political Commissar," "Regulations for the Work of the Political Instructor," "Outline of the Report on the Consolidation of the Political Commissar System," "Wartime Political Work," "The Political Department and Political Work," and "Lessons from the Civil War of the Soviet Union." Tsung cheng-chih pu (General Political Department), "Cheng-chih kung-tso chiang-i" [Lectures on Political Work], prepared for the political battalion of the Red Army School, pp. 1-31.

39Kung-nung hung-chün hsüeh-hsiao cheng-chih pu (Political Department of the Worker-Peasant Red Army School), "Cheng-chih wen-ta" [Political Questions and Answers], July 1933, Shi-sou Collection, reel 8.

40*Hung-hsiao tou-cheng [Struggle in the Red School]*, no. 5 (July 8, 1933), published by the Red Army School Political Department.

41Kung Ch'u, p. 341; Bobrow, p. 319. Wall newspapers and student meetings also encouraged students to exchange battlefield experiences. This later became a regular learning practice in Communist leadership training schools. On the use of "wall newspapers" in the Soviet Red Army, see D. Fedotoff-White, p. 337.

42Kung Ch'u, p. 344.

43Ibid., p. 345. For other discussions of "revolutionary competition" during the Kiangsi period, see Ch'en Shou-ch'ang, "Min, Yüeh Kan-tung ch'ün-chi ch'ung-feng chi chi szu-yüeh ching-sai kung-tso ti tsung-chieh yü chiao-hsün," *Tou-cheng*, no. 12 (May 20, 1933), pp. 1-4; Kim, *Politics*, pp. 38-39; and Mao Tse-tung, "Hsing-kuo Changkang hsiang ti Su-wei-ai kung-tso," *Tou-cheng*, no. 42 (January 12, 1934), Shih-sou Collection, reel 18.

44Hsü Meng-ch'iu, "I-yüeh lai ti hung-chün ta-hsüeh [The Past Month at the Red Army Academy], *Ko-ming yü chan-cheng [Revolution and War]*, no. 2 (April 1934), Shih-sou Collection, reel 16, p. 29. See also Bobrow, p. 253; and Kung Ch'u, p. 385.

45Kung Ch'u, p. 385; Wang Hsüeh-wen, p. 59; Liu Tao-sheng, "Sen-lin chung ti Hung-chün ta-hsüeh" [The Red Army Academy in the Forest] in *Hung-ch'i p'iao-p'iao*, vol. 3, p. 46.

46When the Red Army School was reorganized, high-level cadres from its training battalion were transferred to the Red Army Academy and divided into four intermediate battalions. On types of classes at the academy, see Kung Ch'u, p. 385; and Liu Tao-sheng, p. 46.

[47]Sources vary on the head of the advanced command class, naming either P'eng Hsüeh-feng or Ho Ti-chou, a former Nationalist engineering corps battalion head. See Liu Tao-sheng, p. 46; Kung Ch'u, pp 385-386; Wang Hsüeh-wen, p. 59; and Klein and Clark, p. 719.

[48]Other military instructors included Kuo Hua-yu, a respected author of numerous articles on strategy; Tso Ch'üan, a graduate of Whampoa, Sun Yat-sen University, and the Frunze Military Academy; Wu Hsiu-ch'üan, a graduate of Sun Yat-sen University and a Soviet Red Army artillery school, who was concurrently chief-of-staff of Red Army headquarters in Kiangsi; and Chou Shih-ti, another graduate of Whampoa. Tung Pi-wu, who headed the Academy of Marxian Communism, served as political director for the Red Army Academy, with Hsü Meng-ch'iu as his political commissar, between February and July 1934. Both Tung and Hsü had studied at Sun Yat-sen University in Moscow. Ho Ch'ang-kung, a member of the French branch of the CCP and former commandant of the Eighth Red Army, was associated with the academy. Between 1933 and 1934, Lo Kuei-po, a former Nationalist soldier turned deputy-commander for the Communists in Kiangsi, served as deputy-commandant. Wei Kung-chih, of the Gorky School, lent her talents to the role of cultural instructor at the Red Army Academy. See the biographies in Klein and Clark; Warren Kuo, *Analytical History*, vol. 2, p. 479; and "Hui-i Hung-ta," K'ang-ta yü Chün-ta," [Recalling the Red Army Academy, K'ang-ta and the Military Academy], *Kuang-ming jih-pao*, September 15, 1957, p. 3.

[49]Figures compiled during the first week of class show that over 92 percent of the student body were from the soviet districts and came from primarily poor peasant (46.4 percent) and "handicraft worker" (25 percent) origins. Over 72 percent were between the ages of twenty and thirty and 80 percent were Chinese Communist Party members. (Only 3.5 percent belonged to neither the Party nor the Youth Corps.) Over 46 percent spent three years or less in the Red Army, followed by 22.1 percent with two years or less, 17.1 percent with four years or less, 8 percent with five years or less, and 5 percent with six years or less. Hsü Meng-ch'iu, p. 30. See also Liu Tao-sheng, p. 46.

[50]See Hsü Meng-ch'iu, pp. 31-33, on the reforms at the Red Army Academy.

[51]Chung Wei-chien, "Tse-yang shih Hung-ta chiao-yü shi-chi hua" [How to Practicalize Education at the Red Army Academy], *Ko-ming yü chan-cheng*, no. 2 (April 1934), pp. 37-38, Shih-sou Collection, reel 8. This article is dated the last day of 1933.

[52]"Chung-yang ko-ming chün-shih wei-yüan-hui t'iao-ling chiao-ts'un pien-chi wei-yüan-hui kei yü Hung-chün ta-hsüeh-hsiao kuan-yü shih-hsing chan-shu ti fen-tsu shang-k'o ti chih-shih" [Instructions of the Editorial Committee for Prescribed Teaching Materials of the Revolutionary Military Council to the Red Army Academy-School concerning the Divided Group Class on the Implementation of Tactics] *Ko-ming yü chan-cheng*, no. 1, p. 12. Article dated October 31, 1933.

[53]Ibid., p. 13. See also "Tse-yang shih Hung-ta chiao-yü," p. 41. The term *ch'i-fa* also appears in "Fa-chan tang ho kai-tsao tang ti kung-tso ta-kang" to describe procedures for raising the level of a Party member's participation in Party life. Then the term appeared to denote the use of criticism and "struggle" to elevate members' activist spirit. Later the term was associated with a certain process of thinking. On the evolution of the meaning of *ch'i-fa*, see the section on K'ang-ta in Chapter 7.

[54]Hsü Meng-ch'iu, p. 34; Liu Tao-sheng, p. 48. One former student, perhaps reading a bit of the present into the past, claimed that battlefield experience was at the core of the study program. He recalled students pooling fighting experiences from various base areas to teach each other, with the lessons thus extracted systematized for further use. Some academy students were temporarily sent to the front lines to replace officer cas-

ualties and shared their experiences with fellow classmates when they returned to their studies. See "Hui-i Hung-ta," *Kuang-ming jih-pao*, September 15, 1957, p. 3.

[55] Kung Ch'u, p. 387; Kung-nung Hung-chün ta-hsüeh hsün-lien pu (WPRA Red Army Academy Training Department), "Chan-lüeh chiang-i" [Lectures on Strategy], January 16, 1934, Shih-sou Collection, reel 8.

[56] Liu Tao-sheng, p. 47.

[57] Hao-hsi-shih ta-hsüeh hsün-lien pu [Hassis Academy Training Department], "Hung-chün ta-hsüeh shang-chi cheng-chih k'o cheng-chih kung-tso chiang-shou ta kang" [Lecture Outline on Political Work for the High-level Political Class of the Red Army Academy], November 25, 1933, Shih-sou Collection, reel 8, pp. 1-9.

[58] Among them are "Political Work in the Red Army"; "Political Work in Wartime"; "Regulations for Infantry Work"; "Regulations for Open Field Maneuvers"; "The Political Department and Political Work"; "Work of the Lenin Room"; *Red Star Supplement, The International Line*, vols. 1-3; "The Experience and Lesson of the Soviet Civil War"; "The Nation and Revolution"; all issues of *Revolution and War; Political Work*; and "Regulations for Consolidation of the Work of the Political Commissar." To keep abreast of current events and daily developments in the war effort, students were also to read *Hung-se Chung-hua [Red China]* and *Chün-shih t'ung-pao [Military Notice]*. See Kung-nung Hung-chün ta-hsüeh (WPRA Red Army Academy), "Cheng-chih kung-tso chiang-i" [Lectures on Political Work], June 6, 1934, Shih-sou Collection, reel 8, pp. 1-24. See also "Hung-chün ta-hsüeh shang-chi cheng-chih k'o," p. 9; and Liu Tao-sheng, p. 46.

[59] Kung-nung Hung-chün ta-hsüeh cheng-chih ch'u (WPRA Red Army Academy Political Office), "Chung-kuo ko-ming wen-t'i cheng-chih ch'ang-shih chiang-i" [Lectures on Political Common Knowledge of the Problems of the Chinese Revolution], March 28, 1934, Shih-sou Collection, reel 8, pp. 8-53.

[60] Liu Tao-sheng, pp. 48-49; Hsü Meng-ch'iu, p. 33; "Hui-i Hung-ta," *Kuang-ming jih-pao*, September 15, 1957, p. 3.

[61] "Hui-i Hung-ta," p. 3.

[62] Among the Red Army Academy graduates known to have specialized in commissar functions were Sung Jen-ch'iung, Liu Tao-sheng, Hsieh Fu-min, and Ch'eng Tzu-hua. Those known to have specialized in military work included Sung Shih-lun, Ch'en Man-yün, and Chang Tsung-hsün. Yang Yung, Yang Te-chih, Huang Yung-sheng, P'eng Hsüeh-feng, and Chang Ai-p'ing remained as students in the Red Army Academy when it moved to Shensi and thus formed part of the first K'ang-ta class. They are discussed further in the next chapter. Sung Jen-ch'iung, Sung Shih-lun, Ch'eng Tzu-hua, and Chang Tsung-hsün also had studied at Whampoa. Others known to have attended the Red Army Academy include Ch'iu Ch'uang-ch'eng, Kuo T'ien-min, Li T'ien-kuei, and Chou Tzu-k'un. Klein and Clark; Liu Tao-sheng; "Hui-i Hung-ta"; and the Union Research Institute *Who's Who* are sources of biographical information on these figures.

[63] See Bobrow, p. 248.

[64] Political education at higher-level Red Army schools also served as the model for the training of political cadres within the Red Army. See "Kan-pu cheng-chih chiao-yü chi-hua ts'ao-an" [Draft Plan for Political Education of Cadres] (1932?), Shih-sou Collection, reel 8.

[65] Harrison, *March*, p. 239; and Kim, *Politics*, pp. 200-201.

8   The Student City

Two Chinese visitors to Yenan observed in 1937:

> What one notices most in Yenan is not the Border Region
> Government nor the Eighth Route Army but the North
> Shensi [Public School] and Resistance University. The vital-
> ity of Yenan is sustained largely by the sons and daughters of
> North Shensi [Public School] and Resistance University.

> If Peking was a student city before its loss [to the enemy],
> then Yenan has been a student city since the loss of Peking
> and Tientsin.[1]

These accounts suggest that leadership education had a prominent
role in Chinese Communist activities during the Sino-Japanese
War. By 1942 there were over twenty full-time formal leadership
training institutions in the city of Yenan alone and numerous
others throughout the Communist base areas. Communist cadre
education at all levels was more extensive and systematic than it
was during the Kiangsi period.

The quality of military and political leadership was an important
factor in the Chinese Communists' phenomenal expansion during
the war years. In conditions more stable than they were before
the Long March, the Chinese Communist Party was able to broad-
en its application of the "cadre" concept and "mass line" work
style. Party membership soared from 20,000 in 1936 to
1,200,000 by 1945, supplying new waves of working cadres to
mobilize the rural areas.

Many of those recruited into the Chinese Communist movement at this time were non-Communist "intellectuals" attracted by the Chinese Communists' resistance activities against Japan. A massive influx of these types from outside the Communist bases during the late thirties gave Yenan much of its character as a "student city"; leadership training programs provided the critical medium for absorbing large numbers of them into the Chinese Communist movement. Part of the Chinese communist cadre training complex channeled these newcomers into the service of anti-Japanese resistance. Leadership training programs taught them skills for "united front" mobilization work in the countryside and attempted to transform their nationalism into a commitment to Chinese Communism.

Despite some problems, the Chinese Communists found their recruitment of the educated a decided advantage during the anti-Japanese war. "Intellectuals" were not a reliable leadership group in all respects and many were hostile to the Communists' programs for social revolution. The Party continued to rely on local peasant leadership to promote its agrarian reforms. Nevertheless, elites not hampered by illiteracy facilitated implementation of Communist policies and helped to staff the growing Communist power structure in base areas won from the Nationalists and Japanese.

Between 1936 and 1945 the areas under Communist control had mushroomed from five pockets totalling approximately 38,600 square miles with a population of 2 million to nineteen bases with a population of 96 million.[2] This meant that by 1945 the Chinese Communist Party had jurisdiction over a sizable portion of China—in effect, its own "nation." To revolutionary mobilization were added the challenges of modernization and political unification. Chinese Communist leadership models further diversified to undertake nation-building activities. Considerable institutional development took place in stable areas such as the Shen-Kan-Ning Border Region. There, most Party leadership resources were devoted to technical, educational, and administrative work that became the model for nation-building after 1949.

In less consolidated "guerrilla" bases such as those in east-central and south China, military requirements were the first priority. The Party, as during the Kiangsi years, relied heavily on armed units to open up new base areas. Outside of the central stronghold at Yenan, battles were to be fought against Japan and renewed Nationalist hostilities after 1939. Thus military work continued to dominate Chinese Communist leadership policy throughout the Yenan period.[3]

Leadership training programs supplied most of the command structure for forces that grew from 22,000 around 1936 to 880,000 regulars less than ten years later. The programs implemented new refinements in the system of commissars and political workers needed to coordinate dispersed military units that were larger in size than those before the Long March. They continued to check "mountaintopism" and made the military a more obedient servant of civilian needs. By the end of the Sino-Japanese War, clearcut Party and government hierarchies had emerged in many areas that were former military preserves. All were part of a strong Communist infrastructure that became the springboard to the rest of China.

K'ANG-TA, THE "REVOLUTIONARY CRUCIBLE"

Formal leadership training institutions in Yenan were classified in two different ways: as "united front schools" training both Party and non-Party cadres for the War of Resistance and as "Party schools" exclusively for Chinese Communist Party members.[4] Administratively the schools fell under the jurisdiction of the military, Party, or border region government. Ultimately, however, all cadre education was supervised by the Chinese Communist Party Central Committee, and training guidelines were formulated by the Central Propaganda Bureau.

The Anti-Japanese Military and Political University *(K'ang-Jih chün-cheng ta-hsueh)*, commonly called K'ang-ta, belonged to the "united front" category. In number of graduates and impact on Chinese Communist movement-building, it was the most influential leadership training institution during the Yenan period. It produced military commanders, political commissars, and political workers for military-related mobilization activities. Graduates of the main campus at Yenan and its twelve outlying branches furnished much of the leadership for the Eighth Route and New Fourth Armies and the expanding Chinese Communist network in the base areas. The university operated until the end of the Sino-Japanese War and trained 100,000 students.

K'ang-ta retained many features of the educational model of Whampoa and the Soviet military schools and was the direct successor to the Red Army Academy in Juichin. The Red Army Academy made the Long March in the form of a "cadre corps" commanded by Ch'en Keng. After the Chinese Communist Party lodged in Wa-yao-pao in north Shensi, this group was renamed the Chinese People's Red Army Academy. When the Nationalists captured Wa-yao-pao the academy moved to Pao-an. In December

1936 the academy merged with the Red Army College of the Red Fourth Army and moved again to Yenan. On January 20, 1937, the academy was renamed the Chinese People's Anti-Japanese Military and Political University.[5]

Originally K'ang-ta trained only military-political cadres for the Chinese Communist armed forces, but after the outbreak of war with Japan it became oriented toward united front mobilization work and began to add non-Communist intellectuals and border region peasant cadres to its student body. The school's first session took place in Pao-an, while K'ang-ta was still the Red Army Academy. This class numbered around 240 students, mostly high-level military cadres.[6] The school's principal, Lin Piao, and its education director, Lo Jui-ch'ing, both Whampoa graduates, were concurrently students and teachers.

With the move to Yenan and reorganization into the Anti-Japanese Military and Political Academy, the second class enrollment jumped to 1,200. Eighty percent were cadres from the Second and Fourth Front Armies,[7] but the remainder included veteran local Communists from the northwest and a smattering of students from outside the border region. The class graduated in July 1937 and immediately left for the front.

The third class, in residence from September 1937 to April 1938, was a product of the united front in action. Forty percent of the total enrollment of 1,800 had previously been students elsewhere. Their presence at K'ang-ta inspired major adaptations of curriculum and teaching methods. The fourth class, from April to October 1938, was dominated by students from the "white areas," who boosted the enrollment to 4,500. Students also accounted for the majority of the 8,000 registered in the fifth class, which ran from October 1938 to January 1940.[8]

Due to the tightening Nationalist blockade of the Communist base areas, the fifth class was the last one in which intellectuals predominated. The main K'ang-ta campus moved to Wu-hsiang, Shansi, just before the class graduated. By January 1941 the school had resettled in Tz'u hsien in the Shansi-Hopei-Shantung-Honan border region. The remaining K'ang-ta classes concentrated primarily on training Eighth Route and New Fourth Army officers who had reached company level or above. There is some evidence that these officers were transferred to K'ang-ta towards the end of the Sino-Japanese War for rest and recuperation from war injuries.[9]

Some of the most outstanding Chinese Communist Party leaders headed the K'ang-ta instructional and administrative staff. Lin Piao was nominally principal of K'ang-ta but spent most of the

Sino-Japanese War years commanding the 115th division of the
Eighth Route Army or receiving medical treatment in Moscow.10
Under such circumstances daily management of the school fell to Lo
Jui-ch'ing, who became vice-principal and political commissar in 1938
and served as acting principal. Mao Tse-tung assumed chairmanship
of the education department during the first half of 1937. He was
assisted by Chang Wen-t'ien, Ch'en Po-ta, Ch'eng Fang-wu, Ho
Kan-chih, and Ai Szu-ch'i. Tung Pi-wu served as political commissar
for students from the "white areas," who were under daily supervision by Nieh Ho-t'ing.11

In curriculum K'ang-ta placed priority on united front issues and
basic military knowledge. All students took both military and
political courses, but the ratio of military to political subjects was
determined by each student's future work assignment. Military
cadres who entered K'ang-ta from the army or faced military assignments upon graduation devoted seventy percent of their time to
military subjects and thirty percent to political and cultural subjects.
The ratio of military to political subjects was reversed for political
cadres that would work in the army, mass organizations, or official
administrative positions.

Although to date there are no detailed descriptions of the content
of K'ang-ta courses, their titles were similar to those employed at
earlier leadership training schools such as the Red Army Academy
in Juichin. There was more emphasis on united front matters at
K'ang-ta and considerable attention to guerrilla warfare. The Wuhan
Mobilization Society's report on *The Situation at K'ang-ta* described courses that fell into three categories. Political courses consisted of Chinese Problems, General Discussion of Social Science,
General Discussion of the Three People's Principles, Political Common Knowledge, and Philosophy. Military courses involved Guerrilla Warfare, Strategy and Infantry Tactics, and Drill and Deport-
ment. Cultural courses included Common Knowledge of History
and Geography, Basic Natural Science, Arithmetic, and Japanese
Language.12

A wartime Japanese source classified the K'ang-ta curriculum into
courses for cadres in the Red Army and other Chinese Communist
organizations and courses for students working in the "white"
Nationalist or Japanese-occupied areas. Both categories of course
work show considerable overlap in content and teaching person-
nel.13

Many of Mao-Tse-tung's basic works were originally delivered as
lectures to K'ang-ta students. "On Contradictions" was presented
in August 1937 to introduce trainees to Marxist dialectics. "Strategic Problems of China's Revolutionary War," written as a series

TABLE 2

K'ang-ta Curriculum

Course	Instructor
For Cadre Companies	
Strategy and Tactics of the Red Army	Mao Tse-tung
Dialectical Materialism	Mao Tse-tung
History of the Founding of the Red Army	Chu Te and Lin Piao
History of the Chinese Revolution	Chu Te and Chang Wen-t'ien
Tactics and Strategy of the Chinese Revolution	Chang Wen-t'ien and Ch'in Pang-hsien
Leninism	Chang Wen-t'ien
Materialism	Ch'in Pang-hsien
Study of Political Economy	Chang Ju-hsin and Chang Hao
Guerrilla Warfare	Lin Piao and Lo Jui-ch'ing
Military Affairs	Wang Li and Chang Chen-han
For White Area Companies	
Dialectics	Mao Tse-tung, Ai Szu-ch'i, and Chang Wen-t'ien
History of the Chinese Revolution	Wu Liang-p'ing and Chang Ju-hsin
Study of Political Economy	Ai Szu-ch'i, Liu Ting, and Chang Wu-yüan
Leninism	Wu Hsin-hsien and Ch'in Pang-hsien
Guerrilla Warfare	Lin Piao
Military Affairs	Li T'e and Chang Chen-han

of lectures in 1936 while K'ang-ta was still the Red Army Academy, stressed the necessity of understanding the specific problems of the Chinese revolution as a basis for appropriate military strategy. Mao's essay "On Practice," delivered at K'ang-ta in July 1937, took the position that "knowledge starts with practice."[14] This had already been reflected in leadership training methods and became a major theme in Chinese Communist educational philosophy. In addition to works by Mao, K'ang-ta employed texts edited by its Education Committee and selected Russian works.[15]

While much of the course content and study materials dealt with Chinese problems, there was considerable treatment of Marxist-Leninist theoretical issues. This aspect of the K'ang-ta curriculum may have been aimed at the non-Communist intellectuals in the student body. Courses on political economy, dialectical materialism, and the Marxist theory of history, as related to Chinese concerns, furnished an intellectual framework for translating nationalism into commitment to Communism.

In descriptions of the course work on social science, Chinese problems, and the united front, one can see how this conversion process might have operated. The course on Chinese problems covered the "semifeudal, semicolonial" nature of Chinese society. Instructors presented the "correct" revolutionary viewpoint as "antifeudal and anti-imperialist" and enjoined students to fight Japanese imperialism to achieve national independence. The course attempted to show the historical roots of the Three People's Principles and their realization through the Anti-Japanese united front. Along similar lines, the social science course tried to demonstrate the theoretical basis for the eventual collapse of Japanese imperialism and the success of the National Revolution in China.[16]

A former student, later hostile to the Chinese Communist Party, described his class on the united front. The course consisted of a series of lectures reproduced in a ninety-page booklet. The first sections described China's state of crisis in the nineteenth century and her decline to a semi-colony. There followed a discussion of the formation of the anti-Japanese united front, giving the impression that the Chinese Communist Party steadfastly resisted Japan while the Nationalists stood on the sidelines. The same student found the attitude at K'ang-ta toward the Three People's Principles to be highly critical. His instructor characterized the principles as "part revolutionary, part reactionary," progressive in calling for the equalization of political and economic rights but not equivalent—contrary to the claim of Sun Yat-sen—to socialism. K'ang-ta instruction pictured the Kuomintang as representing the Chinese capitalist class and argued for class struggle as the ultimate solution to China's problems.[17]

Other courses on wartime political work and guerrilla warfare introduced Communist organizational principles and Maoist military
strategy. Students of wartime political work were to learn the importance of political work among regular army units and guerrilla bands,
how to inspire troops for both offensive and defensive combat, how
to plan retreats, and how to conduct political work among local
inhabitants and enemy troops. The guerrilla warfare course defined
guerrilla activity as a positive, offensive form of combat involving
unity with the common people. Students were to master the "Sixteen Character Formula for Guerrilla Warfare" attributed to Mao
Tse-tung.[18]

Actual military classes at K'ang-ta were conducted in the open air.
To bring training as close as possible to actual combat, the school frequently staged large-scale maneuvers. Every company simulated military operations on a regular basis by drawing them up in a sandpan—
a technique employed at the Whampoa Military Academy by Soviet
advisers. Among the military lessons at K'ang-ta were night combat,
close-range combat, bayonet fighting, and hurling grenades.[19]

The military as a source of organizational inspiration pervaded many
aspects of student life at K'ang-ta. Student conduct was regulated by
military codes of behavior to develop qualities such as discipline,
efficiency, and endurance in a crisis environment. The student body
was divided in a military fashion, breaking down into "battalions"
(*ta-tui*), companies" (*tui*), "district companies" (*ch'ü-tui*), and "small
groups" (*hsiao-tsu*). Although the size of each division changed periodically, the small groups remained constant at ten persons each. An
instructor for military and political education was assigned to each
battalion and company. Some of the companies also had cultural
instructors.[20]

Qualities nurtured through the militarization of student life were
considered part of a distinct "school style," articulated at K'ang-ta
as "unified, tense, lively and serious."[21] Procedures for developing
these characteristics drew on earlier Chinese Communist experiences
in leadership education, especially at Whampoa, the Peasant Movement Training Institute, and the Red Army Academy in Juichin.
However, K'ang-ta stressed these objectives in character development
more than any other leadership training institution had in the past.

K'ang-ta authorities traced the evolution of their "school style" to
the school's "ability to overcome difficulties in the face of immense
hardships" and "turn liabilities into assets." From its inception
K'ang-ta constantly struggled against a hostile environment. The
first class had only three full-time instructors and a staff largely inex-
perienced in educational work. To compensate, students turned to
teaching themselves. They used their knees as desks and dug classrooms and sleeping quarters out of caves in the hills outside Yenan.

The second class also found severe shortages of facilities, books, and teaching materials. The student mix—Red Army fighters, local peas- and cadres, and non-border region students—posed certain social and pedagogical problems. School authorities, however, came to view the disparity in knowledge and experience as potentially beneficial. Accentuating the positive, they encouraged former students, soldiers, and peasants to pool their experiences and learn from each other. It is likely that this policy was inspired by similar experiments at the Red Army Academy in Juichin.

In the third K'ang-ta class this trend continued. Students pooled their books into a "circulating library." Between November 1 and November 15, 1937, students, faculty, and administration dug over 170 caves in the loess cliffs outside Yenan. One participant observed:

> The work was not heavy, but it was a stern test to the majority of the young students who had never worked with a pick before. After a day of work, we were all sweaty and our two hands were studded with blisters. Everybody had sore legs and an aching back. However, it was precisely such labor which steeled and educated us and transformed our way of thinking. It gave us even greater courage and strength to overcome difficulties.[22]

The educational value of physical labor took on a new dimension in the fourth K'ang-ta class. Its students began to participate actively in production campaigns,[23] which marked the beginning of a regular program of combined work and study in Chinese Communist leadership training schools. These campaigns helped K'ang-ta to become self-sufficient in food. They introduced students to basic-level economic life and the dignity of manual labor. Production activities were conducted with local peasants and instructed students from former elite backgrounds how to relate to the common people—an important mobilization skill for "mass line" operations.

At K'ang-ta educational thinking on physical labor went one step further than at the earlier Chinese Communist leadership training schools. Before the Long March physical labor was recognized as useful for revolutionary consciousness-raising and for breaking down barriers between elite and commoner. K'ang-ta regarded physical hardship in an even more positive light as a mandatory requirement for character-building: daily trials steeled cadres for future hardships on the revolutionary battleground. The extent to which K'ang-ta succeeded despite physical hardships helped to demonstrate the value of thinking dialectically, of seeing phenomena in terms of their opposites. It also reinforced voluntaristic attitudes among potential Communist leaders and bolstered confidence in the human will as a revolutionary instrument.

Other pedagogical principles articulated at K'ang-ta took inspiration

from the Chinese Communists' material shortages and crisis environment. These principles likewise had roots in schools such as Whampoa, the Peasant Movement Training Institute, and the Red Army
Academy. However, at K'ang-ta, they were more systematically defined and conscientiously implemented.

One cardinal principle, called the *ch'i-fa* ("mind-opening") method,
was first mentioned in Chinese Communist discussions on education
during the Kiangsi period. At K'ang-ta the *ch'i-fa* method was contrasted to the traditional lecture format, rote memorization, and
simple questions and answers. It was defined as "a method of investigation moving from induction to deduction." A practitioner of *ch'i-
fa* proceeded "from near to far, from concrete to abstract, from part
to whole," thereby grasping from one incident or example the law of
development of a complex phenomenon.

Employing *ch'i-fa*, a topic would be first dissected into its main
points. Then, through questions and answers, each major point
would be broken down into minor points that illustrated facets of
the main issue. For example,

> in discussing how feudal society was able to develop into capitalist society,
> the internal contradictions of feudal society and the process and outcome
> of their development must be explained, which leads to an investigation
> of the laws of development of society based on private ownership as well
> as speculation on its future.[24]

This learning method had ideological as well as pedagogical value.
It, too, encouraged dialectical thinking supportive of Marxist-Leninist analysis and was another means of bringing K'ang-ta trainees
closer to Chinese Communist beliefs.

Another anticipated outcome of the *ch'i-fa* procedure was the ability
to apply abstract principles to situations in real life. Students who
had mastered this technique were expected to use it in the future
when lacking specific instructions from higher authorities. K'ang-ta
education constantly underlined the "unity of theory and practice."
In the words of former student Niu K'o-lun:

> Whatever was taught was done. When the lesson dealt with weapons, we
> promptly dismantled a rifle and learned to shoot. When the lesson dealt
> with attack or defense by a battalion or company, a field exercise was
> held. Things were studied for application.[25]

To prevent both teachers and students from digressing from the key
points of each lesson, the *hsiao-erh-ching* ("small-but-essential")
principle governed curriculum and course content. This principle was
very much like the procedure for developing lessons at the Red Army

Academy in Juichin. At K'ang-ta, too, one can see military imperatives influencing educational philosophy. Instructors conscientiously planned to teach students essential points in a minimum
amount of time. They tailored lecture and discussion topics to the
time limit of each class period and each student's span of thought.
Students were taught to evaluate the essential points of reading
materials.

Streamlined curriculum and pedagogical practices at K'ang-ta were
spurred on by the dictates of revolution and war and by perennial
shortages of qualified teachers. Top Party leaders, responsible for
many of the lectures, were often too pressed by other duties to
adhere to a regular class schedule. Through careful planning, the principles of *ch'i-fa* and *hsiao-erh-ching* were combined with group study
so that students under supervision could largely educate themselves.
The school began to rely on a corps of paraprofessionals called the
"education staff."

The education staff qualified for their assignments by spending a
great deal of time auditing classes, participating in instructors'
discussion sessions, writing supplementary educational reports, and
leading relatively simple class sessions such as those on cultural matters. They received instructions from a weekly "education preparation meeting" for each military and political course. Led by
training department representatives, these meetings focused on the
essential points that students in each course were expected to master.
Previous lessons were evaluated to ascertain areas for improvement.
The meetings also anticipated questions that might arise in class and
discussion sessions and suggested appropriate answers. Lists of basic
reference materials, instruction outlines, topics for small group discussions, and examples to illustrate major points were distributed.

Before classes began, the education staff assembled students and explained how to listen to lectures, take notes, prepare assignments,
participate in discussion meetings and group reading sessions, and
find reference materials. About once a week the education staff and
instructors for each company sat in on the students' small-group
study sessions to insure that the group members comprehended their
lessons. At fixed intervals company instructors also called meetings
of the heads of the small groups to elicit student criticism of the
teaching program.

Besides alleviating the burdens of regular instructors, the education
staff served as another mechanism at K'ang-ta to break down hierarchical social barriers and inculcate revolutionary values. Education staff members were expected to fraternize with students as if
equals, and they shared the same living quarters and food allotment.

Students at K'ang-ta first encountered new material in lectures, at which they were advised to take notes only on important points. Afterwards, they broke down into small groups of five to ten for a collective "book reading session" (*tu-shu hui*) with staff members. As with lectures, the readings were analyzed for important points. Students also did some independent reading, and kept records of their assignments, and submitted their opinions for later discussion. A "discussion meeting" (*t'ao-lun hui*) following the reading session probed students' comprehension of lectures and readings. These meetings were highly structured and followed outlines composed by the education staff. Leading the talks were either the head of a district company, the Chinese Communist Party political director attached to a company, or a discussion leader. All participants were required to voice an opinion, with meetings expected to end in consensus. For each meeting school authorities received an evaluation report.

School authorities believed group discussions were superior to individual study for conveying all facets of a problem and for educating students of "low cultural and educational level." The verbal exchanges helped to develop students' speaking abilities—another important skill for working cadres. One can also view discussion meetings as promoting ideological unity and group solidarity.

The standard discussion sessions were supplemented by "sit-and-talk" meetings (*tso-t'an hui*) and "current-events-discussion" meetings (*shih-shih t'ao-lun hui*). Sit-and-talk meetings were less formal than discussion meetings and took place on a less regular basis. Only the subject of discussion was predetermined by the K'ang-ta political department. Sit-and-talk meetings were frequently employed as preliminary "struggle" sessions prior to regular discussion meetings. Current-events-discussion meetings helped to keep students abreast of the news while developing oral skills and group cohesion.

Although teaching methods were essentially the same for all companies at K'ang-ta, there was some adjustment for variations in students' "social background, war experience, political and cultural level and theoretical experience." For example, in the fourth K'ang-ta class, the first battalion's second district company consisted of middle and lower-level Eighth Route Army cadres, and the fourth battalion's sixth company was composed of "worker-peasant elements with rich struggle experience but low theoretical and cultural level." For these groups instruction concentrated on the *ch'i-fa* method and discussion format plus supplementary "cultural classes." Students with middle school or university backgrounds had more lectures, in combination with *ch'i-fa*.26

K'ang-ta authorities found written examinations useful for motivating students and measuring the efficacy of the instructional program. However, the testing system discouraged "championism" and "insidious gradations." Before each examination the teacher announced examination questions and suggested relevant reading materials. Students then took about a week to research the questions in consultation with members of the education staff. They answered the questions individually in writing, and then exchanged papers with other students for grading against a standard set of answers issued by school authorities. Criteria for grading were, first, errors in principle; second, substantive detail; and third, sentence structure and composition.

Such testing methods tried to discourage selfish work motivations and "unify" students' thinking on a given subject. Kang-ta's examination procedures also helped to reduce instructors' duties. It is unknown whether Mao Tse-tung as chairman of the education department instituted this testing system, but it does resemble that of his sixth class at the Peasant Movement Training Institute.[27]

These features of K'ang-ta study life indicate that "mutual help and collective study" was another school ideal. Each company selected several students to tutor illiterate and semiliterate students of worker-peasant background. The educationally disadvantaged were also encouraged to participate actively in discussion meetings to clarify anything they could not understand. Group study and tutoring upgraded the general level of student performance while developing human relations skills for future mobilization work.

The only kind of competition fostered at K'ang-ta was "revolutionary competition," very much like the contests at the Red Army Academy in Juichin. Those in charge of the school considered "revolutionary competition" and collective learning practices the chief factors in the progress of students of so many varied backgrounds. School authorities believed the group setting encouraged students to perform at maximum capacity. They reported that the scores of students tested according to the same standards varied as little as ten percent.[28]

The center for student activities outside the classroom was the "salvation room." Salvation rooms were equivalent to the Soviet-inspired culture and entertainment centers known as Lenin Clubs in the Kiangsi period. There was one salvation room for each company under the supervision of the company political director and the general jurisdiction of the K'ang-ta political department. The informal, participatory setting of the salvation room was supposed to help students "develop activism, creativity, and revolutionary friendship."[29]

Salvation rooms sponsored wall newspapers, similar in content and function to those at the Red Army School in Juichin. They also staged dramatic productions designed to heighten group participation. These took the form of "living newspapers," where participants acted out news events, musical productions, short "word plays," and "shadow plays."

The salvation room was also the site of "livelihood self-examination meetings" (*sheng-huo chien-t'ao hui*). As distinguished from regular discussion sessions, the livelihood self-examination meetings investigated the activities and histories of individual students. Their procedures were similar to "criticism and self-criticism" methods at earlier Chinese Communist and Soviet Party schools. Participants probed an individual's entire life history in order to measure his or her conduct against school principles. These meetings were the most heavy-handed method for curbing potentially deviant behavior and beliefs. One observer described the course of a meeting:

> One named Chang criticized himself and as soon as he stopped talking another asked to speak. I noticed he was only fourteen or fifteen years old.... "Comrade Chang, I have an opinion about you. For the past several days your work and study, I feel, have regressed compared to the week before. For example, one day you did not go to work voluntarily and had others divide it up and also did not read or speak with us.... Comrade Chang, you have just criticized yourself but failed to mention these shortcomings of yours.... If you don't recognize your mistakes you are not being responsible to yourself. I realize this is not a good situation and therefore have this opinion about Comrade Chang."...
>
> Although Chang felt very ashamed his expression was unmoved and he said slowly, "It's true. I last week because.... It's true. I certainly made a mistake. You have pointed it out and I am very grateful. From now on I hope that comrades upon seeing my mistakes will point them out right away."[30]

This picture of K'ang-ta should not be construed to suggest that the school lived up to all of its ideals and promises. School authorities themselves did not refrain from pointing out shortcomings. Lo Jui-ch'ing believed that despite impressive gains in the size and quality of his staff, some cadres remained weak in teaching and leadership skills. Lo found that the coordination of work and study did not always proceed smoothly and that funds for operating expenses were perenially scarce.[31]

It would appear that the students from non-Communist areas were the most disappointed in K'ang-ta education. The K'ang-ta setting exposed the tensions generated by the absorption of large numbers of outside intellectuals into the Chinese Communist movement. Youthful emigres to Yenan displayed a number of motives for attending K'ang-ta besides the call of pure patriotism. Many fled to Yenan in pursuit of a "university" diploma and release from the strictures of traditional family life. Hostile accounts of K'ang-ta are replete with vignettes of "free love between the sexes" and condemnations of the school's socially permissive atmosphere. Some found the life of recurrent hardship too much to bear. Others resented restraints on individual self-expression in study groups and the steady diet of Marxist-Leninist analysis. Still others were disappointed in the quality of military and political instruction at the school. One senses that a number of intellectuals became disenchanted with the Chinese Communists' commitment to relentless class struggle and feared its threat to national unity.[32]

This did not mean that all K'ang-ta students had a negative reaction. Many of the thousands who flocked to Yenan stayed on as political workers for units of the New Fourth and Eighth Route Armies or as leaders for united front mobilization activities behind the lines. Propaganda teams prepared at K'ang-ta moved into villages, challenged local gentry, and organized mobilization committees to funnel manpower and resources to the front. K'ang-ta alumni were among those supervising village-level guerrilla, logistical, and personnel replacement groups that stood in for regular Communist army units.[33]

The bulk of united front workers and lower-level cadres attached to military units were K'ang-ta alumni. Their input into the Chinese Communist Party's leadership resources proved decisive in mobilizing large numbers of people of diverse backgrounds to support the Chinese Communist movement during the Sino-Japanese War. These leadership types also staffed important positions in the expanding Chinese Communist infrastructure throughout the base areas. They brought law, order, and organizational coordination to the power vacuum created in the Chinese countryside by wartime hostilities. This counterelite enabled the Chinese Communist Party to develop an infrastructure more powerful and effective than that of any of its challengers.[34] Little is known, however, about the activities of this type of K'ang-ta graduate after 1949 or his long-term effect on the Chinese Communist leadership structure.

Most K'ang-ta graduates with biographical records were well-established military figures, many from the first class of high-level cadres.[35] For the military, K'ang-ta performed functions similar to those of the Red Army Academy in Juichin. The main K'ang-ta campus and its outlying branches upgraded the skills of commanders and commissars while preparing new leaders for the rapidly expanding Chinese Communist forces during the Sino-Japanese War. The pool of skilled military personnel was a factor in Chinese Communist victories between 1937 and 1949. Commissars and political workers helped to keep military work in line with the objectives of the Party center.

K'ang-ta provided a forum for sounding out and refining policies for peasant revolution and united front mobilization work. Courses on the united front, guerrilla warfare, and Chinese problems; glorification of group life, manual labor, and military discipline; and efforts to bridge gaps between intellectuals, peasants, and soldiers were valuable for "mass line" operations. One can credit K'ang-ta with the dissemination of "mass line" principles among broad segments of the Chinese Communist leadership.

K'ang-ta education is also of interest for its synthesis of a number of earlier Chinese Communist training techniques. It applied learning and teaching methods such as *ch'i-fa* and *hsiao-erh-ching* as well as "battlefield" methodology to the preparation of both nonmilitary and military leadership. Practices inspired by the Communist military model were infused from K'ang-ta into Chinese Communist organizational life. Other aspects of the K'ang-ta study experience, such as revolutionary competition, group study, the discussion method, criticism and self-criticism, wall newspapers, salvation rooms, education staff, and political directors, all derived from earlier leadership training programs, were also applied to a wider range of leadership types than they had been in the past. The educational "theory and practice" developed at K'ang-ta remains at the heart of Chinese Communist Party-political education today.

OTHER UNITED FRONT SCHOOLS

Other leadership training institutions that produced personnel for mobilization work tried to emulate the K'ang-ta model. The North Shensi Public School *(Shen-pei kung-hsüeh),* which maintained close ties to K'ang-ta, opened in the summer of 1937 to help to prepare patriotic intellectuals for national salvation work. Situated in the foothills east of Yenan, Shen-pei was headed by Ch'eng Fang-wu; Shao Shih-p'ing was director of the education department. The school offered at first a two-month course and later a three-month course of study specifically geared to "intellectuals" from outside the border regions.[36]

Most of the students at Shen-pei had received a middle-school to university-level education. They included writers, painters, musicians, military men, and self-employed individuals between seventeen and forty years of age. An entrance examination, consisting of ten simple questions, favored enthusiasm and commitment to the anti-Japanese united front over educational achievement or political persuasion as criteria for admission.[37]

Once enrolled, students spent seventy percent of their time on political subjects. There were four basic courses: (1) General Introduction to the Social Sciences; (2) United Front and People's Movement Work; (3) Guerrilla Warfare and Basic Military Knowledge; and (4) Lectures on Current Events. The teaching staff, described as "experienced revolutionary fighters," included Mao Tse-tung, Chang Wen-t'ien, K'ang Sheng, Li Fu-ch'un, Ho Kan-chih, Wang Jo-fei, Li Fan-fu, Hsü Ping, Yang Sung, Ai Szu-ch'i, Ho Ting-huai, Li Wei-i, principal Ch'eng Fang-wu, Lo Mai (Li Wei-han), Chou Ch'ün-ch'uan, Ch'en Ch'ang-hao, and Wu Liang-p'ing. Since quite a few of these individuals also lectured at K'ang-ta, one can assume some overlap in course content between the two institutions.[38]

Suffering from the same teacher and material shortages as K'ang-ta, Shen-pei tried to emulate K'ang-ta's organizational and study principles. Students were arranged in companies, platoons, and sections, with each section numbering ten to twelve persons. "Study representatives" for each subject supervised the study life of every company. Study plans issued by school authorities were developed through a series of discussion meetings of students and instructors.

As at K'ang-ta, most of the study life at Shen-pei was governed by the group discussion format and the "educational principles" of (1) the "unity of theory and practice," (2) *hsiao-erh-ching*, and (3) the "unity of students and teachers." Shen-pei likewise boasted a slogan for its "school style"—"Devotion and unity, tenseness and liveliness"—and valued material hardship as "a compulsory course for participating in the front line resistance war or people's movement work."[39] Other aspects of school life, including revolutionary competition and criticism and self-criticism followed the K'ang-ta pattern.[40]

By June 1938 Shen-pei had produced five classes totalling three thousand graduates. Upon termination of studies males were usually dispatched to the front lines to organize guerrilla bands or mass agitation activities. Female graduates generally took charge of mobilization work behind the lines. Some outstanding students were sent on to K'ang-ta or another Chinese Communist Party school for further training.[41]

Some united front schools catered to particular mobilization needs. Chinese Women's University *(Chung-kuo nü-tzu ta-hsüeh)* in Yenan, set up in March 1939, trained only female cadres to head mobilization work involving other women. Much of its top staff came from the former "Twenty-eight Bolshevik" faction of the Chinese Communist Party. Under principal Ch'en Shao-yü and vice-principal Hsün Li-chih, ex-"Bolsheviks" Ch'en Ch'ang-hao headed the instructional affairs office and Meng Ch'ing-shu directed general affairs.[42]

Although Chinese Women's University gave preference to "worker-peasant women," anti-Japanese activists, and students from military-political training schools behind Japanese lines, the majority of those enrolled were non-Communist intellectuals. Students from proletarian backgrounds constituted only ten percent of the enrollment; peasants, six percent; and "others," four percent. Trainees ranged in age from fourteen to forty-one years, with the average around twenty. Most were unmarried. In the first class students came from twenty-one provinces, with the largest contingents from Honan, Szechuan, Kiangsu, and Hupei.[43]

On the basis of preliminary examinations students were assigned either to one of six general classes, one high-level research class, or one "special class." The research class trained "theoretical cadres" who had a university education (or its equivalent) or two years of study in other Communist institutions. Graduates were assigned to lead war work, political work in enemy areas, teaching, medical work, propaganda work, or cooperative organizing. The special class furnished basic literacy skills to worker-peasant students with some experience in the women's movement.[44]

The curriculum varied with each type of class but all students took required courses in (1) History of Social Evolution (Historical Materialism); (2) Political Economy; (3) Marxism-Leninism; (4) Philosophy; (5) Problems of the Chinese Revolution; (6) Problems of the Chinese Communist Party; (7) Three People's Principles; (8) Women's Movement; (9) Military Education; and (10) Health Education. Students also chose among electives in vocational education, shorthand, news reporting, music, library science, dramatics, literature, bookkeeping, English, Japanese, and accounting[45].

As this description of courses reveals, very little study time was allocated to issues concerning the Chinese women's movement alone. Instead, the university, in accord with the Chinese Communist Party's position on women, tried to tie in female emancipation with more general revolutionary goals. The Chinese Communist Party continued to argue that the interests of women could be best served through measures to eliminate an exploitative social and economic system. Feminist concerns were thus subordinated to the Chinese Communists' general mobilization strategy during the Sino-Japanese War period. In his address at the university's opening ceremony, principal Ch'en Shao-yü cautioned his students to remain "steadfast wives, good mothers and filial daughters" for the sake of maximizing support for the Chinese Communist Party in its conservative peasant milieu. The curriculum and other aspects of the university thus attempted to acclimate independent-minded women intellectuals to conditions in the base areas and to convert their feminism into Marxism.

Like K'ang-ta and Shen-pei, Chinese Women's University embraced the educational philosophy of the "unity of theory and practice" and the combination of collective and independent study. An observer described all of the courses as "salted with Marxist philosophy, including the Chinese Communist Party's own interpretation of the Three People's Principles."[46] Students also participated in production campaigns. The majority of the university's graduates went into rural education work; a portion returned to their homes in guerrilla districts to lead mass organizations; and a few pursued further military training at K'ang-ta.[47]

United front schools emulating K'ang-ta proliferated outside of Yenan. The most notable was the People's Revolutionary University *(Min-tsu ko-ming ta-hsüeh)* headed by K'ang-ta graduate P'eng Hsüeh-feng in Lin-feng Shansi. This school was operated by the Eighth Route Army to produce "national salvation" cadres for Yen Hsi-shan's New Army. Like other united front schools, it developed military and mobilization skills that linked "theory and practice" and utilized the *ch'i-fa* learning technique. Its graduates served as military or political cadres with the New Army or as specialized "people's movement" cadres that set up mass organizations in the countryside.[48]

On the whole most united front schools, such as Chinese Women's University and Shen-pei, were as short-lived as the united front itself. They flourished only before relations between the Chinese Communist Party and the National Government deteriorated. After the Nationalists cut off access to the Communist areas in mid-1939, these schools found potential students in short supply, especially the "intellectuals." Both Chinese Women's University and Shen-pei came under fire from the Chinese Communist educational authorities for course content judged "too abstract" and remote from the daily problems of cadre work. These schools continued to suffer from shortages of teachers and texts, especially introductory theoretical materials, and from the pressure of limited matriculation periods.

It is likely that the struggle between Mao Tse-tung and Ch'en Shao-yü during the *cheng-feng* movement contributed to the closing of Chinese Women's University. The university merged with the Tse-tung Youth Cadre School and parts of other schools to form Yenan University in September 1941. Shen-pei combined with the Youth Training Class and the Work School of the Lu Hsün Academy of Arts in 1939 to form North China Associated University.

SPECIALIST SCHOOLS

"Specialist schools" that provided training in specific skills to non-

Communist intellectuals, peasants, and Chinese Communist Party members multiplied in Yenan and the base areas during the Sino-Japanese War. They produced revolutionary bureaucrats, scientists, technicians, teachers, physicians, and propagandists for the Communists' new institutions in their base areas. These leadership types were part of a systematic approach to nation-building formulated during the Yenan period. It enabled the Chinese Communists to consolidate large areas of territory that supported massive military campaigns during the civil war. The leadership and organizational structure developed for the Communist bases was extended throughout China in 1949. Communist cadres skilled in administration, institution-building, and mobilization work thus became the leadership core for the reunification of China.

Specialist schools appear to have been less influenced by the K'ang-ta model than were schools preparing mobilization workers. The Natural Sciences Research Institute, founded in Yenan in July 1939, trained scientific and technical personnel and operated a scientific research center. Under principal Hsü T'e-li and vice-principal Ch'en K'ang-po, the institute consisted of two departments, each with a two-year course of study. The "standard" department concentrated on pure research and offered courses in chemistry, biology, physics, and geology. In the "preparatory department," courses were more elementary (mechanical drawing, basic physics, mathematics, and chemistry) and included subjects such as history, geography, Chinese problems, Marxism-Leninism, political economy, and Russian and English language.

In early 1943 it was reported that 180 students had enrolled in the preparatory department and 80 in the standard department. The institute experienced some difficulty adjusting its "theoretical" orientation to the realities of border region life and Communist movement-building requirements. Students were said to have found available facilities inadequate for their research objectives and their texts—usually adapted from those of the United States or Europe—ill suited to border region problems. However, the institute did try to link scientific theory to practical border region problems and met operating expenses by running three factories—a "machine" factory, manufacturing tools, looms, carts, and agricultural implements; a glass factory; and an alcohol factory.[50]

Workers' University on the outskirts of Yenan trained middle-level technicians and was organized from the worker and staff company of K'ang-ta. In 1939 this university had more than seven hundred students, most from enemy-occupied areas. The students were organized into six battalions according to area of specialization and educational background. The first and second battalions were high-level classes; the third and sixth were preparatory classes; and the fourth a women's section. Handicraft and technical workers such as steelworkers, woodworkers, cobblers, haircutters, tailors, and masons made up the fifth, or "construction" battalion.

Curriculum for the first and second battalions consisted of courses on leadership of people's movements, political work, political economy, guerrilla tactics, and Party construction. Students in the third, fifth, and sixth battalions took courses on national language, natural science, arithmetic, history-geography, mobilization of national spirit, and protracted war. Outside of formal classes students participated in small group discussions, mountain-climbing, and land reclamation projects.[51]

Motor University *(Mo-t'o ta-hsüeh),* founded on June 1, 1937, prepared cadres for motorized transport and communications work for the Chinese Communist armed forces. Liu Ting, its principal, supervised more than sixty students, organized into two companies. Most were low-level Red Army cadres of predominantly worker-peasant background and uneven educational level. At first instruction centered on automobile driving, but it later branched out to include work with military vehicles, air raid protection, and mechanics. There were also remedial courses in arithmetic, physics, politics, national language, and English.

Specialists in artistic and cultural work were nurtured at the Lu Hsün Academy of Arts,[53] founded in Yenan in February 1938. The school originally had three departments—drama, art, and music—but added a literature department and experimental drama troupe in September 1938. "Shakov," or Wu Yü-chang, has been identified as the Academy's principal, and Chou Yang as its vice-principal.

During a six-month training period academy students could choose from an array of offerings in language, dancing, phonetics, singing, musical instruments, folk music, famous compositions, rehearsal and practice, folk drama, famous plays, composition and study, the present situation of music and drama movements; drawing, calligraphy, Chinese folk art, famous world paintings, creation and study, the present situation of the art movement, Chinese literature, practical writing, the present situation in literature, writing and practice, journalism, border region education, and selections from world literature. They were required to take general courses in the theory of art and contemporary political theory.

The students, most of them from the "white areas," numbered over fifty in the first class, two hundred in the second, and three to four hundred in 1939. Graduates were expected to function as revolutionary artists promoting "a New Democratic art and culture" from "the standpoint of Marxist-Leninist theory."

Schools to train specialists in Party work also operated in Yenan
and the base areas. The most prominent was the Central Party
School in Yenan, which had a branch in Central China. It was modelled after the Academy of Marxian Communism in Juichin and
had been set up initially after the Long March at Wa-yao-pao. The
school then moved with the central Party leadership to Pao-an and
eventually Yenan. During this period its principal was Tung Pi-wu,
who had headed the Juichin Academy of Marxian Communism. In
late 1937 Tung was succeeded by Li Wei-han, who retained the post
until 1940. Between 1940 and 1942 the principal was Teng Fa,
with Hsieh Chüeh-tsai as vice-principal, P'eng Chen as director of
political education, and Lin Piao as director of military education.
In the wake of difficulties encountered during the early phase of
the *cheng-feng* movement, Mao Tse-tung served temporarily as principal and Lin Piao and P'eng Chen as vice-principals. P'eng was
named principal in 1944.[54]

The student body, which grew from approximately three hundred
around 1938 to about five thousand in 1944, was composed almost
exclusively of high- and middle-level Chinese Communist Party
cadres. Most were either peasants or former students.[55] A sizable
contingent from the "white areas" was enrolled in a short-term program. Visitors to the Central Party School also observed national
minorities receiving basic literacy training and administrators and
other experts undergoing remedial political education.[56]

In its early years the Central Party School offered a three-month
program of study involving courses in (1) Political Economy; (2)
History of the Communist Party of the Soviet Union; (3) Leninism;
(4) Chinese Problems; (5) World Politics (6) Philosophy; (7) Dialectical Materialism; (8) Communist Party Work with the Masses; and
(9) Military Training (practical military work, partisan warfare, and
tactics and strategy).[57] However, much of this curriculum was considered too abstract and unsuitable for a short training period. After
reorganization in 1941 the school directed its curriculum towards
the practical concerns of Party workers and extended its training
period to two years. Thereafter, twenty-five percent of the students' total study time was devoted to problems of current events;
seventeen percent to the Chinese situation and Chinese revolutionary strategy; thirty percent to Party construction; twenty-three percent to Marxism-Leninism; and five percent to group research. Mao
Tse-tung was principal lecturer in the areas of "philosophy," "history of the modern Chinese revolution," and the "theory of New
Democracy." Other instructors included Fan Wen-lan, Ai Szu-ch'i,
Ch'en Po-ta, and various Central Committee members and scholar
specialists.[58]

After the Central Party School underwent reorganization, *The*

History of the Communist Party of the Soviet Union became the basis for theoretical work in Marxism-Leninism. This book, edited by a commission of the Central Committee of the CPSU under the guidance of Stalin, was an effort to rewrite Soviet party history to legitimate the Stalinist leadership.[59] It traces the history of the Bolshevik Party and the politics of the CPSU in the twenties and thirties, and gives attention to distinguishing orthodox revolutionary practice from other erroneous "lines"—Narodism, Legal Marxism, Economism, Menshevism, and Trotskyism. Many of the theoretical issues discussed in *The History* deal with revolutionary strategy and are introduced through synopses of Lenin's writings, such as "What is to Be Done?", "One Step Forward, Two Steps Backward," and "Two Tactics of Social Democracy in the Democratic Revolution." The book also includes a short summary of Lenin's "Materialism and Empiro-Criticism" to acquaint the reader with the basic principles of dialectical and historical materialism.

Although the book does not limit itself to the Russian revolutionary experience, it contains little material on the peasant problem or the appropriate strategy for rural-based revolution—concerns of immediate relevance to the Chinese Communist Party. However, the synopses of Lenin's writings and the history of the Russian Revolution provide a concise introduction to Marxism-Leninism as developed in the Soviet Union and its application to an actual revolutionary situation.

Some statements in *The History*'s "Conclusion" also lend themselves to legitimating "mass line" policies and the thrust of Chinese Communism under Maoist leadership during the Yenan period. For example:

> It may seem that all that is required for mastering the Marxist-Leninist theory is diligently to learn by heart isolated conclusions and propositions from the works of Marx, Engels and Lenin, learn to quote them at opportune times and rest at that.... But such an approach to the Marxist-Leninist theory is altogether wrong. The Marxist-Leninist theory is a science of the development of society.... and as a science it does not and cannot stand still, but develops and perfects itself. Clearly, in its development it is bound to become enriched by new experience and new knowledge, and some of its propositions and conclusions are bound to change in the course of time, are bound to be replaced by new conclusions and propositions corresponding to the new historical conditions.... Mastering the Marxist-Leninist theory means assimilating THE SUBSTANCE of this theory and learning to use it in the solution of the practical problems of the revolutionary movement under the varying conditions of the class struggle of the proletariat.... Mastering the Marxist-Leninist theory means being able to enrich this theory with the new experience of the revolutionary movement, with new propositions and conclusions, it means being

able to DEVELOP IT AND ADVANCE IT without hesitating to replace—
in accordance with the substance of the theory—such of its propositions
and conclusions as have become antiquated by new ones corresponding to
the new historical situation.

Moreover,

> the history of the Party teaches us that unless it has wide connections with
> the masses, unless it knows how to hearken to the voice of the masses and
> understand their urgent needs, unless it is prepared not only to teach the
> masses but to learn from the masses, a party of the working class cannot
> be a real mass party.....60

There is some evidence of K'ang-ta's influence on learning practices
at the Central Party School. The program combined independent
study with group discussion. Students from diverse backgrounds
traded knowledge and experiences. Each student tried to supplement
his area of expertise with a general understanding of basic problems
and the manner in which they were solved in other fields.61

Unfortunately, little else is known about the Central Party School or
the disposition of its graduates. Because many of its students engaged
in "white area" work in hostile territory, its activities were not made
public. The Chinese Communist Party center used the school as a
common training center for ranking leadership personnel, and it
was thus able to coordinate cadre activities in scattered base areas:
high-level Chinese Communist Party cadres from various border
regions underwent periodic education at the school, especially during
the *cheng-feng* movement. As a centralizing instrument for Party
operations the Central Party School became the main staging ground
for rectification activities in 1942-1944.

Concurrent with the Central Party School, the Border Region Party
School was set up in Wa-yao-pao. It likewise moved to Yenan in
1937. Kao Kang, head of the Border Region Party Committee, served
as principal. This institution trained Party personnel with special
competence in the problems of the Shensi-Kansu-Ningsia border
region. Its curriculum contained fewer theoretical courses than that
of the Central Party School and placed greater emphasis on border
region issues and remedial education. This school appears to have
prepared party leaders of a lower level than those of the Central
Party School. Its graduates were dispatched to various *hsien* as local
border region cadres or Party operatives. In 1941 the school was
placed under the jurisdiction of the Chinese Communist Party
Northwest Bureau and changed its name to the Northwest Party
School.

For high-level theoretical work the Chinese Communist Party operated the Central Research Institute. It had been founded in 1938 in Yenan and was called the Academy of Marxism-Leninism before its reorganization in late 1941. Under the jurisdiction of the Central Propaganda Department, the institute trained specialized theoretical cadres recruited through a highly selective admissions policy. The institute was strictly research-oriented and included some of the Party's most outstanding theorists on its staff. Chang Wen-t'ien was head of the institute in 1940, followed by Lo Mai (Li Wei-han) in 1943. Fan Wen-lan served as assistant director, and chief Party theoretician Ai Szu-ch'i headed the institute's Cultural Research Office. There were three departments at the institute—philospophy, political economy, and research on Chinese problems. Graduates were usually sent to staff various levels of Chinese Communist Party schools or high-level Party posts.[63]

The trend towards specialization in Chinese Communist leadership education received impetus from the Party Central Committee's evaluation of leadership policy in 1941: The Committee's "Resolution on the Yenan Cadre Schools," dated December 17, strengthened the position of education specialists relative to that of Party branches at the major cadre schools.[64] Especially in the united front specialist schools open to non-Communists, policy shifted away from political studies in favor of technical pursuits.

This did not mean, however, that the Chinese Communist leadership wished technical specialization to be divorced from political objectives. To prevent specialized education from becoming an end in itself, the resolution on Yenan cadre schools also called for increased study of Chinese history, local conditions, and Party history and policy. Foreshadowing a major *cheng-feng* theme, the resolution denounced excessive attention to Marxist-Leninist theory without regard for its application to Chinese problems. It upheld *The History of the Communist Party of the Soviet Union* as the principal source for middle- and high-level cadres' theoretical education.[65]

The most well-known specialized training institution to emerge after the 1941 reforms was Yenan University.[66] After its opening in September 1941 it underwent two reorganizations in April 1943 and May 1944. In the process the university absorbed other ranking specialist schools, such as the Natural Sciences Research Institute, the Lu Hsün Academy of Arts, and the Administration Academy.[67] Yenan University aimed at developing skilled personnel to deal with specific border region problems.

Prior to its reorganization Yenan University was headed by Wu Yü-chang with Wang Tzu-yi as vice-principal and Sung Kan-fu as secretary. Chou Yang became principal in April 1943.[68] Along with staff personnel, the number of departments, the curriculum, and the student composition changed with each reorganization. These changes at the university were in line with the trend in Chinese Communist leadership education after 1941 toward increased specialization and concentration on local border region problems.

After 1943 most of the students and teachers were border region locals, especially those active in war and production work. The statistics on university staff and students in 1944 show that, of a total of 1,302 students in 1944, most came from Shensi, Shansi, Honan, Hopei, and Shantung. Very few hailed from proletarian and poor peasant backgrounds and sixty percent had acquired at least a middle-school education. Yenan University appears to have continued in the tradition of the united front schools in processing intellectuals for leadership positions in the Chinese Communist movement. The 1944 statistics show that over half the students were being trained for administrative positions in the border regions.[69]

Following reorganization in 1944 Yenan University consisted of five major divisions: (1) the Administration Academy; (2) the Lu Hsün Arts Academy; (3) the Natural Sciences Academy; (4) a Medical Department; and (5) a special "Female Section," probably meeting the same leadership requirements as the Chinese Women's University. Each division offered general and specialized courses in its field. Matriculation periods ranged between one to two years at the Medical School, two years at the Administration and Lu Hsün Arts Academies, and three years at the Natural Sciences Academy. From the breakdown of courses and departments at Yenan University one can see the growth of specialization in Chinese Communist leadership education:

I. College of Administration
    A. General course for the whole college: present policies in Border Region construction

    B. Department of Administration
        1. Administrative class
            a. 3:3 system and democratic centralism
            b. work of village government power
            c. cadre work

        2. Police class
            a. police methods
            b. general social knowledge

        3. Department of Law
            a. Border Region laws
            b. investigation of precedents
            c. legal practice

       d. arbitration among the people
       e. general theory of law
       f. investigation of present laws

  4. Department of Education
       a. general situation of education and culture in the Border Region
       b. primary school education
       c. middle-level education
       d. social education
       e. investigation of teaching materials
       f. investigation of educational thought in present-day China

  5. Department of Finance and Economics
       a. For the whole department:
         (1) general economic situation of Border Region
         (2) accounting, office methods and statistics
       b. For the economic reconstruction class:
         (1) Border Region agriculture
         (2) Border Region industry
         (3) cooperative problems
         (4) communications and transport
       c. For the finance class:
         (1) finance
         (2) tax collection
         (3) banking
         (4) trade

C. College of Natural Science
  1. General courses for the whole college:
       a. mathematics
       b. physics
       c. general chemistry
       d. graphic methods
       e. foreign languages

  2. Department of Engineering
       a. dynamics
       b. theory of structures
       c. theory of engineering materials
       d. engineering art
       e. principles and fundamentals of machinery
       f. prime movers
       g. architecture
       h. mechanical design
       i. electrical engineering
       j. factory management

3. Department of Chemistry
    a. organic chemistry
    b. industrial chemistry
    c. theoretical chemistry
    d. qualitative analysis
    e. quantitative analysis
    f. industrial analysis
    g. chemical engineering
    h. general geology
    i. factory management

4. Department of Agriculture
    a. agricultural botany
    b. agricultural chemistry
    c. soils and fertilizers
    d. genetics
    e. plant diseases and insect pests
    f. general theory of Border Region agriculture
    g. organization and management of agricultural production
    h. theory of plants
    i. theory of animals
    j. forestry
    k. gardening

D. Lu Hsün Art School
    1. Course for the whole college; discussion of literature and art (including all questions of the history, present situation and theory of art and literature)

    2. Department of Drama and Music
        a. language
        b. dancing
        c. phonetics and singing
        d. musical instruments
        e. folk music
        f. study of famous compositions
        g. rehearsal and practice
        h. folk drama
        i. readings of famous plays
        j. present situation of the drama movement
        k. present situation of the music movement
        l. composition and study

    3. Department of Art
        a. drawing
        b. calligraphy
        c. study of Chinese folk art
        d. study of famous world paintings

  e. the present situation of the art movement
  f. creation and study

 4. Department of Literature
  a. Chinese literature
  b. practical writing
  c. study of the present situation in literature
  d. selected readings in famous world literature
  e. writing and practice
  f. journalism
  g. Border Region education

E. Medical Department (courses not listed)[70]

Students in all divisions were required to study a core curriculum, which accounted for thirty percent of the total study time. Everyone took courses in (1) General Principles of Border Region Construction; (2) History of the Chinese Revolution; (3) Revolutionary Philosophy; (4) Methods of Thought; and (5) Current Events.

Features of study life evocative of K'ang-ta contributed to the development of the students' political consciousness. Both faculty and students were exhorted to "join in every kind of relevant practical work and research into every kind of practical question." Each course tied in to the administrative or production organs of the border region dealing with the problem under study. A considerable portion of course content dealt with the policies, directives, and operations of these organs. In many instances students divided their activities at Yenan University between the classroom and on-the-job training. Students also spent twenty percent of their time in physical labor and tried to "go to the people" through dramatic, educational, or medical work with local inhabitants.

The main standard for grading was "the ability to apply study to use and knowledge to action." As at K'ang-ta, students engaged in both independent study and group discussion; the instructors confined themselves to introducing key points and summarizing the results of discussion and research.[71] It appears that Yenan University did break with the K'ang-ta model in minimizing military training, probably because of the university's highly technical orientation and the relatively stable situation in the Shensi-Kansu-Ningsia border region.

Schools such as Yenan University represented only the tip of the iceberg in the Chinese Communists' leadership training system. Programs to prepare military, mobilization, and specialized cadres were not confined to Yenan alone. Though the most well-developed system of leadership education was to be found in the Chinese

Communists central base, the Shensi-Kansu-Ningsia border region, cadre training programs of all types—formal Party schools, short-term training programs, and in-service training programs—continued to grow throughout most of the Communist base areas. Not all Chinese Communist cadres had access to formal training, but the number of those who did rose throughout the Yenan period. Leadership education did not solve all of the problems of Chinese Communism and it exacerbated certain forms of tension in the Communist leadership structure. Nevertheless, its contributions to the Chinese Communists' leadership capacity made possible the flowering of Yenan Communism.

NOTES

[1] Wang Chien-min, vol. 3, citing Yüan Chin-hsing ("Impressions of North Shensi, July 1937") and Ma Chün ("North Shensi During the Resistance War, December 1937"), p. 270.

[2] These figures are from Harrison, *March*, p. 271; and Jerome Ch'en, p. 255.

[3] A Japanese intelligence map shows almost one hundred schools in the Chinese Communist base areas in 1941. Over half of those classified as higher institutions were for the training of military leadership. See Tada butai sambō bu (Tada Corps, Chief of Staff), *Chūgoku kyōsantō undō no kaisetsu* [Explanation of the Chinese Communist Party Movement] (Peking: February 17, 1941), chart on pp. 101-104.

[4] This classification of Party and non-Party institutions was similar to, and perhaps borrowed from, the divisions among institutions of higher learning during the 1920s in the Soviet Union. See Joravsky, pp. 65-68. For additional details on the jurisdictional breakdown of the Chinese Communist cadre school system, see T'ung-i ch'u-pan she, ed. *Chung-kung chih chiao-yü* (Chinese Communist Education] (n.p., 1943), pp. 16-17. The Revolutionary Military Council General Staff was in charge of K'ang-ta and its branches, other schools for military cadres, and all military cadre training classes. The Central Propaganda Bureau supervised the Central Research Institute, a high-level research organization, while a special Central Party School Management Committee under the CCP Central Committee oversaw the Central Party School. Specialized cadre schools such as Yenan University, North China Associated University, the Natural Sciences Research Institute, and Lu Hsün Academy of Arts were under the jurisdiction of the CCP Central Committee's Central Cultural Committee. All other cadre training organs in the Party and government and all levels of in-service cadre training were supervised by the Central Cadre Education Bureau of the Central Committee.

[5] On the origins of K'ang-ta see *Chung-kung chih chiao-yü*, p. 3; Warren Kuo, *Analytical History*, vol. 3, pp. 6, 232; Wang Hsüeh-wen, p. 19; and the biography of Sung Jen-ch'iung in Klein and Clark.

[6] Among the members of the first class were T'an Cheng, Ch'en Kuang, Chou Chien-p'ing, Mo Wen-hua, Lo Jung-huan, Yang Ch'eng-wu, Chao Erh-lu, Li T'ao, Yang Li-san, Liu Ya-lou, Chang Ai-p'ing, P'eng Hsüeh-feng, Yang Yung, Yang Te-chih, Huang Yung-sheng, Su Chen-hua, Li Tso-p'eng, Chang Ta-chih, and P'eng Shao-hui. See Tung-yüan she, ed., *K'ang-ta tung-t'tai* [The Situation at K'ang-ta] (Hankow: 1939), p. 37. See also *Chung-kung chih chiao-yü*, p. 3; "Hui-i Hung-ta," *Kuang-ming jih-pao*, September 15, 1957, p. 3; and Whitson, pp. 115-117, 296-297.

[7] According to William Whitson's study the Second and Fourth Front Army cadres were sent to K'ang-ta for indoctrination. One hundred were officers formerly enrolled at the Fourth Front Army Red Army College at Mou-kung (headed by Liu Po-ch'eng). Altogether four hundred Fourth Front Army cadres were reported in the second K'ang-ta class. See Whitson, pp. 149, 152, 154.

[8]On the various K'ang-ta classes see Wang Chien-min, vol. 3, p. 278; and *Chung-kung chih chiao-yü*, pp. 50-51. Several sources mention a sixth class in P'an-lung in Wu *hsien*, Shansi, that ran between April and December 1939 and a seventh class in Tz'u *hsien*, Hopei, between January and August 1941. See also Hua-tung chün-shih ta-hsüeh chieh-shao, in *Ta shih-tai ti yung-lu* (Hua-tung chün-shih cheng-chih ta-hsüeh cheng-chih pu, 1950), p. 6.

[9]Accounts differ on the number of branches K'ang-ta established, with most agreeing on a total of twelve. Many of the branches were set up by the Eighth Route or New Fourth Army units in various military regions under Communist control during the Sino-Japanese War. The first K'ang-ta branch, originally set up in southeastern Shansi, was reported to have moved eastward to Shantung. It was headed by Ho Ch'ang-kung, assisted by Chou Ch'un-ch'uan. The school was divided into five battalions, which trained Party, government, and army cadres from Shantung. Training lasted three months and many of the thousand students were illiterate. A second K'ang-ta branch in Ling-shou, Hopei, was headed by Ch'en Po-chün. It had originally separated from the main Yenan campus in the winter of 1938 and located in Wu-t'ai before moving to Ling-shou. This branch boasted two thousand students and a set-up similar to the main K'ang-ta school. The third K'ang-ta branch was in Yenan and headed by Hsü Kuang-ta. It occupied the former site of the main school and trained two battalions of students. The first battalion was composed of Long March veterans and the second of recent young émigrés from "white areas." In 1942 this branch school merged with the Military-Political Academy to form the Military Academy. P'eng Hsüeh-feng headed a fourth K'ang-ta branch in Szu *hsien* in northern Anhwei. Initially the school had been located at Wo-yang but moved eastward after Communist forces retreated from Ching-p'u. This branch was the school for the Fourth Division of the New Fourth Army after its battalion school had been reorganized. Founded in July 1940, it ran altogether three classes and featured courses on warfare, politics, and "people's movements."
Sources differ slightly on the location of the fifth branch. One report places this branch in Fou-ning, Kiangsu, headed by Ch'en I and Feng Ting. It was founded in September 1940 and originally situated in Yen-ch'eng. The branch had four divisions—military, political, military-official, and student—and altogether five hundred students. However, Chalmers Johnson, employing a report by the Japanese Asia Development Board entitled "Investigation and Report on the Current Situation in the North Kiangsu Communist Region" (Shanghai: June 16, 1941), describes the fifth branch as situated at Yen-ch'eng, Kiangsu, and founded in November 1940. This report lists Ch'en I and New Fourth Army chief-of-staff Lai Ch'uan-chu as school heads and describes the fifth branch as an amalgamation of the two older New Fourth Army schools—the former North Yangtze Command School at Hsüi and cadres' school attached to Ch'en I's North Kiangsu command, plus a training unit from Huang K'o-ch'eng's Fifth Column of the Eighth Route Army. Entrance requirements for the fifth K'ang-ta branch were the equivalent of a lower middle-school education and courses lasted six months. Military subjects included guerrilla tactics, infantry tactics, artillery, and strategy. Some subjects, such as education, dramatics, journalism, public administration, and politics (Three People's Principles, united front, Chinese revolutionary history) were useful for administrative and mass movement work.
Liu Yen-ming headed the sixth K'ang-ta branch in Wu-hsiang, Shansi. Established in November 1940, the school resulted from the merger of the fourth regiment of the main school and the 129th Division battalion school. The seventh K'ang-ta branch was reported to have been set up in March 1941 in northwest Shansi with over seven hundred students. The eighth was headed by Chang Yün-i and vice-principal Lo Ping-hui and was situated in T'ien-chang, Anhwei. A ninth K'ang-ta branch was reported in central Hopei and the tenth was located in Hsin-yang, Honan, headed by Li Hsien-nien and vice-principal Hsiao Yüan-chiu. This branch was run by the Fifth Division of the New Fourth Army and featured a six-month training period. Over one thousand students were organized into a special affairs regiment, subdivided into three battalions and a supplementary youth company. The branch moved from An-lu in northern Hupei to southern Honan in January 1943.
One report stated that at the end of 1942 the main school was ordered to return to the SKN border region along with its branches in Shansi-Chahar-Hopei and Shansi-Suiyuan.
Lin Piao, although rarely in Yenan, remained nominal principal, but Lo Jui-ch'ing was replaced by T'eng Tai-yüan on June 1, 1940. T'eng in turn was succeeded in August 1942

by Ho Ch'ang-kung, who retained the post after the main school was reconstituted in Yenan. By then Hsü Hsiang-ch'ien was named acting principal and Li Ching-ch'üan political commissar. The entire school underwent rectification from 1943 to the late summer of 1944. At the end of the Sino-Japanese War the main school and branches of K'ang-ta were transformed into the Chinese People's Liberation Army Political University.
On the fourth and fifth K'ang-ta branches see Johnson, *Peasant Nationalism*, pp. 153, 233. For lists of various K'ang-ta branches see also *Chung-kung chih chiao-yü*, pp. 47, 54-55; *Ta shih-tai*, pp. 6-8; and Chung-kuo jen-min ko-ming chün-shih po-wu-kuan [Chinese People's Revolutionary Military Museum], ed., *K'ang-ta* (n.p., K'ang-ta hsiao-shih chan-chien Kwangtung sheng Kuang-chou shih chan ch'u-pan kung-shih, 1966), p. 9. Hsieh Fu-chih was identified as head of a Tai-yüeh branch of K'ang-ta and Shao Shih-p'ing the head of the second K'ang-ta branch. Their biographies can be found in Klein and Clark.

10According to Thomas W. Robinson, Mao Tse-tung assigned Lin Piao to K'ang-ta because of the defeats suffered by the First Army Corps between February and May 1936. Lin remained nominal head of the corps but spent his time at K'ang-ta until July 1937 and supposedly used his position there to win back Mao's favor by training competent military and political cadres. See Thomas W. Robinson, "Lin Piao As An Elite Type," in *Elites in the People's Republic of China*, pp. 185-186. Lo Jui-ch'ing, a Whampoa graduate, was political commissar for the Eleventh Division of the Fourth Red Army under Lin Piao and Lo Jung-huan. There are unconfirmed reports that he received training in political security work in the USSR in 1932, and from 1933 through the Long March Lo directed the Political Security Bureau for Lin's First Army Corps. See Whitson, pp. 344-345, and the biographies of Lo and Lin in Klein and Clark.

11Other members of the K'ang-ta staff included Wang Chia-hsiang, who served in both administrative and teaching positions. He conducted an officer training class and published a book for cadets entitled *Chung-kuo kung-ch'an-tang yü ko-ming chan-cheng* [The Chinese Communist Party and Revolutionary War] in 1941. Ting Ling, the leftist writer, both taught at K'ang-ta and served as deputy-director of a regimental political department. Lo Jung-huan in 1937 was a political instructor and Liu Ya-lou, a graduate of the first K'ang-ta class, headed the training department. Lo later became dean of education. Keng Piao, another early alumnus, continued on as an instructor. Chang Chi-ch'ien, an instructor from early 1937 on, rose by 1939 to direct the school's political department. Before leaving the CCP Chang Kuo-t'ao taught political and economics courses. Other K'ang-ta instructors were Chang Ai-p'ing, Li Wen-ling, Ch'eng Fang-wu, Tung Pi-wu, Wu Hsi-ju, Chang Hsiang-fu, K'ai Feng, Ts'ai Shu-fan and Wu Hsi-kung. See the biographies of these figures in Klein and Clark. See also Nym Wales, *My Yenan Notebooks* (Madison, Conn.: Helen F. Snow, 1961), p. 39; Agnes Smedley, *The Great Road*, p. 243; and Kang P'ing, "K'ang-Jih ta-hsüeh hsün-li" [Inspection of the Anti-Japanese Academy], in *K'ang-chan chiao-yü tsai Shen-pei* [Education for the Resistance War in North Shensi], ed. T'ien Chia-ku (Hankow: Ming-jih ch'u-pan she, 1938), pp. 43, 46.

12*K'ang-ta tung-t'ai*, pp. 96-97. For course lists with slightly different terminology see *Chung-kung chih chiao-yü*, p. 49; and Wang Chien-min, vol. 3, p. 280. The curriculum for the first K'ang-ta class is described in Snow, *Red Star*, p. 107.

13Kusano Fumio, *Shina henku no kenkyū* [Study of the Chinese Border Regions] (Tokyo: Kokuminsha, 1944), pp. 81-82.

14It was reported that Mao's essays "On Tactics Against Japanese Imperialism" (December 17, 1935), "The Chinese Revolution and the Chinese Communist Party" (written with others as a text in December 1939), "On New Democracy" (January 1940), "Combat Liberalism" (September 7, 1937), "On Protracted War" (May 1938), "Problems of Strategy in Guerrilla War Against Japan" (May 1938), and "Reform Our Study" (May 1941) were all basic study materials at K'ang-ta. Mao also edited some texts for the school entitled *Guerrilla Warfare, On Contradictions, On Practice,* and *Strategy of the Chinese Revolution.* Numerous teaching materials of Maoist authorship would tend to support William Whitson's contention that K'ang-ta was employed as a forum for attacks on military "professionals" who had traditionally opposed Mao's ideas on guerrilla warfare and mass mobilization for movement-building. Available information on K'ang-ta makes it difficult to determine whether the school actually was a strong Maoist bastion. Many aspects of K'ang-ta's "educational line" can be traced to earlier CCP leadership training schools that were heavily influenced by Russian models. Also a number of K'ang-ta faculty were former "Bolsheviks" from Sun Yat-sen University. K'ang-ta did serve as a Maoist instrument in the campaign against Chang Kuo-t'ao and the reindoctrination of Chang's former Fourth Front Army officers. See Whitson, pp. 66-67, 289, 154-155. Of course K'ang-ta training placed more emphasis on popular mobilization work because of the large proportion of prospective political workers in its student body relative to earlier CCP schools. On the use of Maoist works at K'ang-ta, see *K'ang-ta*, p. 4; and Phyllis Andors, "K'ang-ta University" (unpublished East Asian Institute essay, Columbia University, 1972), pp. 11-12.

[15] The principal study materials for political and economic subjects were *Political Common Knowledge* (a Soviet translation), *Outline of Politics* by Lin Po-ch'ü, *Political Economy* by Ch'en Chih-yüan, *The February Revolution and the October Revolution* (a Soviet translation), *History of the Development of Human Society* (edited by the Education Committee), *People's United Front* (edited by the Education Committee), Lenin's *Left-wing Communism, an Infantile Disorder: Inevitability of Proletarian Revolution* (a Soviet translation), *Imperialism* (edited by the Education Committee), and *Party Principles* by Chang Wen-t'ien. For philosophy, materials consisted of a piece attributed to Marx on *Dialectical Materialism* (a term never used by Marx but first employed by Plekhanov), and one by Mao called *Outline of the New Philosophy*. The texts for military studies were called *Problems of Military Strategy, Basic Military Tactics,* and *Guerrilla Tactics,* all edited by the Education Office.

[16] *K'ang-ta tung-tai*, pp. 102-103.

[17] See Hsü Shu-huai, *K'ang-ta kuei-lai* [Return from K'ang-ta] (Hangkow: Ch'iu-shih ch'u-pan she, 1939), pp. 37-39.

[18] *K'ang-ta tung-t'ai*, p. 103. The "Sixteen-Character Formula" was issued at Chingkang-shan in 1929 ("If the enemy advances, we retreat; if the enemy halts, we harrass; if the enemy tires, we attack; if the enemy retreats, we persevere.") Kung Ch'u claimed he and Chu Te were the actual authors of the formula rather than Mao. See Whitson, pp. 136, 420, and n. 38, p. 572.

[19] *K'ang-ta tung-t'ai*, p. 85; *K'ang-ta*, p. 7.

[20] The Education Committee selected the heads of the battalions, companies, and district companies, but members of the small groups chose their own leaders (subject to approval by school authorities). Wang Chien-min, vol. 3, p. 280; and *K'ang-ta tung-t'ai*, p. 96. The proper Chinese words for battalion and company are *ying* and *lien*, respectively. However, this study will employ the terms "battalion," "company," and "district company" to distinguish various student groupings. *Tui* is a general term for unit, group, or corps.

[21] *K'ang-ta tung-t'ai*, p. 124.

[22] Niu K'o-lun, "The Smelting Furnace," translated and reprinted from *Jen-min jih-pao*, August 23, 1965, in *Current Background*, no. 777 (November 18, 1965), p. 32.

[23] Production campaigns were a response of the border regions to the reimposition of the Nationalist blockade in May 1939 and the Japanese "Three-All" campaigns launched in 1941. See Harrison, *March*, pp. 316-317. On the trials of the various K'ang-ta classes see *K'ang-ta tung-t'ai*, pp. 18-22, 40-42.

[24] *K'ang-ta tung-tai*, pp. 88-90.

[25] Illustrating the length to which this principle was carried, Niu K'o-lun recalled a class by Liu Ya-lou on the element of surprise in guerrilla warfare and night attacks. In the middle of the next night students were mustered out of bed to take up positions on a ridge outside the city. Niu K'o-lun, p. 34.

[26] This discussion of learning methods and the "educational staff" is based on *K'ang-ta tung-t'ai*, pp. 54, 84-96, 100-114; *Chung-kung chih chiao-yü*, p. 51; and Hsü Shu-huai, p. 50.

[27] *K'ang-ta tung-t'ai*, pp. 92-93.

28Ibid., pp. 206-213; and Andors, p. 17. See also Seybolt, p. 66.

29*K'ang-ta tung-t'ai*, p. 122.

30Ibid., pp. 209-210.

31Ibid., p. 33. See also Agnes Smedley, *Battle Hymn of China* (New York: Alfred A. Knopf, 1943), p. 165.

32Hsü Shu-huai, pp. 21-26. See also Ch'en Lien-hua, *K'ang-ta yü ch'ing-nien* [K'ang-ta and Youth] (Chungking: 1940), pp. 5-8, 20-21, 27-29.

33See Whitson, pp. 157-159, on the role of K'ang-ta in supplying CCP political workers during the Sino-Japanese War.

34On the importance of outside cadres in Chinese Communist expansion during the Sino-Japanese War and their relationship to the Party's organizational effectiveness, see Kataoka, pp. 139-141, 230-232.

35Association with specific military units or leaders appears to have had some influence on the work assignments and career patterns of commanders and commissars who trained at K'ang-ta. A portion of K'ang-ta alumni had prior association with units under the command of principal Lin Piao. Many continued to serve under Lin in the 115th Division of the Eighth Route Army after graduation. In this group were Chao Erh-lu, Yang Te-chih, Ch'en Shih-ch'ü, Lo Jung-huan, Yang Ch'eng-wu, Liu Ya-lou (who remained at K'ang-ta as head of the training department and later dean of education and spent 1938-1942 at the Frunze Military Academy in the USSR), Keng Piao, T'an Cheng, Ch'en Kuang, and Li Tso-p'eng. Some K'ang-ta students orginally under other commanders appear to have developed ties to Lin that continued after graduation. They included Wang P'ing, Su Chen-hua, Yang Yung, Huang Yung-sheng, and Li T'ien-yu, all of whom joined units of the 115th Division after matriculation. Commanders in Chang Kuo-t'ao's Fourth Front Army known to have studied at K'ang-ta, such as Ch'en Hsi-lien, Hsü Li-ch'ing, Hsü Shih-yu, Li Hsien-nien, and Han Hsien-ch'u, appear to have been assigned to units in Liu Po-ch'eng's 129th Division of the Eighth Route Army upon graduation. The 129th Division was composed largely of former Fourth Front Army units. Among the K'ang-ta alumni who maintained a relationship with Ho Lung before or after their term of study were Hsü Kuang-ta, Peasant Movement Training Institute graduate Li Ching-ch'üan, Wang En-mao, and P'eng Shao-hui. Others who trained at K'ang-ta include Li T'ao, P'eng Hsüeh-feng (later head of the People's Revolutionary University in Shansi and fourth K'ang-ta branch in Szu *hsien* in northern Anhwei), Yang Li-san, Chang Ai-p'ing, Chang Ta-chih, Chang Chung-liang, Lo Ping-hui, Mo Wen-hua, Ch'en Wei-shan, Ho Wei, and Hu Yao-pang. Both Ho and Hu had been associated with the student movement or youth before matriculation. Biographies for most of these figures can be found in Klein and Clark. On Li Tso-p'eng, Ch'en Kuang, Ch'en Wei-shan, Wang En-mao, P'eng Shao-hui, Hsü Li-ch'ing, and Ch'en Wei-shan, see Whitson, pp. 115-119, 283, 290-297, 352. On Mo Wen-hua and Li T'ien-yu see the biographical listings in Union Research Institute, *Who's Who*. Nym Wales, *Inside Red China* (New York: Doubleday, Doran and Company, 1939), p. 124, lists Lo Ping-hui among K'ang-ta students. Others at K'ang-ta included Chou Chien-p'ing Liao Shih-kuang (Mme. K'ai Feng), and Chien Hsien-fo (Mme. Hsiao K'o). See Kang P'ing, p. 42; and Klein and Clark, p. 1055. Another source of ranking military cadres during the forties was the Military Academy in Yenan which primarily prepared cadres at the regimental level for military work.

36See Warren Kuo, *Analytical History*, vol. 3, p. 234; Wang Chien-min, vol. 3, p. 281; Seybolt, p. 153; and Lu P'ing, "Yenan ti szu-ko hsüeh-hsiao" [Four Yenan Schools], *Sheng-huo tsai Yen-an* [Life in Yenan], ed. Lu P'ing (n.p., 1938), p. 129.

37Hsü Hsing, "I-ko k'ang-chan ti hsüeh-hsiao" [A School for the Resistance War], in *K'ang-chan chiao-yü tsai Shen-pei*, p. 30.

38On courses and teachers see Shao Shih-p'ing, "Shen-pei kung-hsüeh shih-shih kuo-fang chiao-yü ti ching-yen yü chiao-hsün" [Experience and Lesson of North Shensi Public School Implementing National Defense Education], *Chih-fang* [Liberation], no. 37 (May 6, 1938), p. 13.

[39]On the organization of group study and curriculum at North Shensi Public School, see Hao Chung, "Tse-yang chin Shen-pei kung-hsüeh" [How to Enter the North Shensi Public School], in *Shen-pei ti ch'ing-nien hsüeh-sheng sheng-huo*, ed. Lo Jui-ch'ing and Ch'eng Fang-wu (Shanghai: Chien-she ch'u-pan she, 1940), pp. 5, 12.

[40]Shao Shih-p'ing, pp. 13-14; Lu P'ing, p. 129.

[41]Ma Chün, "Shen-kung, K'ang-ta ho tang-hsiao" [North Shensi Public School, K'ang-ta and the Party School], in *K'ang-chan chiao-yü tsai Shen-pei*, p. 18. Wang Chien-min, vol. 3, p. 281. There was a branch of Shen-pei in southeastern Shansi headed by Lo Mai. Two months after its opening on July 7, 1938 the branch had enrolled seventeen hundred students. See Lo Mai, "Shen-pei kung-hsüeh fen-hsiao ti ch'eng-ch'iu" [Attainments of the Branch School of the North Shensi Public School], *Chieh-fang*, no. 54 (October 15, 1938), p. 16.

[42]Chang Ch'in-ch'iu, another of the "Twenty-eight Bolsheviks," taught at Women's University as well as the North Shensi Public School. On the staff and organization of Women's University see Kusano Fumio, pp. 87-88; Ma Chi-ling, *Shen-pei niao-k'ao* [A Bird's-Eye View of North Shensi] (Chengtu: Cheng-chih, 1941), p. 91; Edgar Snow, *Scorched Earth*, vol. 2 (London: Victor Gollancz, 1941), p. 263; and Wang Chien-min, vol. 3, p. 283.

[43]Snow, *Scorched Earth*, vol. 2, pp. 263-264; and Ch'en Shao-yü, "Tsai Yen-an Chung-kuo nü-tzu ta-hsüeh tien-li ta-hui shang ti pao-kao" [Report on the Opening Ceremonies of Chinese Women's University in Yenan], in *Kung-fei fan-tung wen-chien hui-pien* [Collection of Reactionary Communist Bandit Documents], Yushodo Microfilms, reel 18, p. 128.

[44]Ch'en Shao-yü, p. 128; Wang Chien-min, vol. 3, p. 283; Snow, *Scorched Earth*, vol. 2, pp. 263-264.

[45]Those in the Special Class concentrated on (1) Chinese; (2) Social Problems; (3) Hygiene; (4) Political and Military Common Knowledge; and (5) a brief History of the CCP. The core courses for the high-level research class were (1) Political Economy; (2) Marxism-Leninism; (3) Philosophy; (4) History of World Revolution; and (5) one foreign language. On courses at Women's University see Ch'en Shao-yü, p. 129; Kusano Fumio, p. 87; and Snow, *Scorched Earth*, vol. 2, pp. 263-264.

[46]Snow, *Scorched Earth*, vol. 2, p. 264, is the source of the quotation describing the political orientation of the courses.

[47]On student life, see Ch'en Shao-yü, p. 129; Snow, *Scorched Earth*, vol. 2, pp. 262, 265; and Kusano Fumio, p. 89.

[48]On the People's Revolutionary University see T'ao Fen, "Ch'i-ta kuan-yü Min-tsu ko-ming ta-hsüeh" [Another concerning the People's Revolutionary University], in *K'ang-chan chiao-yü tsai Shen-pei*, pp. 92-105; Evans F. Carlson, *Twin Stars of China* (New York: Dodd, Mead and Co., 1940), pp. 61-63; and Donald Gillin, *Warlord: Yen Hsi-shan in Shansi Province, 1911-1949* (Princeton: Princeton University Press, 1967), p. 274. There were three other nearby branches of the university besides the main campus and the entire university boasted an enrollment of 4,500 in the late thirties.

[49]See *Chung-kung chih chiao-yü*, p. 68.

[50]On the institute, see ibid. Principal Hsü T'e-li, interviewed by journalists in 1961, described the institute as set up to accomodate university students who had emigrated to north Shensi. He estimated that the majority of those in the "standard" department, or "university section," were "advanced intellectual youths," many of whom came from "rather well-off families." See Klein and Clark, p. 364.

[51]On Workers' University, see *Chung-kung chih chiao-yü*, p. 69; and Wang Chien-min, vol. 3, p. 282.

[52]On Motor University, see Ma Chün, p. 22.

[53]On the Lu Hsün Academy of Arts, see *Chung-kung chih chiao-yü*, p. 70; Wang Chien-min, vol. 3, p. 283; Warren Kuo, *Analytical History*, vol. 3, pp. 234, 243, and vol. 4, p. 333; and the biographies of Chou Yang and Wu Yü-chang in Klein and Clark. There was also a central China branch of the academy founded in 1941 with Huang Yüan as

principal; Hsü Hsing-chih, head of the literature department; Ho Szu-te, head of the music department; Hsü Ching, head of the drama department; and Fang Hsiang, head of the fine arts department.

[54]Until the *cheng-feng* movement the Central Party School was under the jurisdiction of the CCP Central Committee (CC) Party School Management Committee. Thereafter it came under the direct control of the CCPCC Central Secretariat. Below the principal were offices for educational affairs, general affairs, and a self-defense force that supervised military training. Participation in military training was mandatory for all students except the ill. The Office for Educational Affairs also operated a research room for intensive study of political economy, world politics, Leninism, current affairs, and Chinese problems. On the leadership of the Central Party School see the biographies in Klein and Clark for Tung Pi-wu, Li Wei-han, and P'eng Chen. See also *Chung-kung chih chiao-yü*, p. 38; Warren Kuo, *Analytical History*, vol. 4, p. 576; Wales, *Red Dust*, p. 43; Ma Chün, p. 22; and Lu P'ing, p. 131.

[55]Warren Kuo, *Analytical History*, vol. 3, p. 233; *Chung-kung chih chiao-yü*, p. 38; Ma Chün, p. 22; Lu P'ing, p. 131.

[56]During her tour of the school Nym Wales observed four Tibetans, eleven Mongols, ten Moslems, and eight Lolos who had joined the Red Army or CCP. At the Central Party School they were receiving remedial education in Latinized Chinese, Chinese language, common political science, and basic natural science. The Chinese Communists also operated special schools for minority cadres such as the Islamic School (I-ssu-lan hsüeh-hsiao) and the Nationality School (Min-tsu hsüeh-hsiao). Other types of students at the Central Party School were given remedial political education to overcome their handicaps from "narrow expert knowledge." Gunther Stein cited among the students he met at the Central Party School an ex-manager of the border region bank, who saw the bank's function as earning income on interest rates rather than expanding credit facilities for the masses. The famous leftist writer and women's movement leader Ting Ling studied and taught writing at the Central Party School for two years after her censure during the *cheng-feng* movement. See Wales, *My Yenan Notebooks*, pp. 104, 106; and Gunther Stein, *The Challenge of Red China* (New York: Whittlesey House, 1945), pp. 152-153, 258.

A number of ranking CCP leaders such as Liu Tzu-chiu, Chang Ting-ch'eng, Sung Shih-lun, Sung Jen-ch'iung, Liang Pi-yeh, and Shao Shih-p'ing attended the Central Party School for rectification study between 1942 and 1944. Others reported to have trained there included Teng Ming-yüan, Ch'eng Yüeh-ch'ang, and Chiang Ch'ing. On Liang, a political commissar in the 685th Regiment of the 343rd Brigade, see Whitson, p. 298. On the others, see Klein and Clark.

[57]Wales, *My Yenan Notebooks*, p. 104.

[58]*Chung-kung chih chiao-yü*, p. 38.

[59]See Leonard Shapiro, *The Communist Party of the Soviet Union* (New York: Vintage Books, 1960), pp. 470-471.

[60]*History of the Communist Party of the Soviet Union (Bolsheviks): Short Course*, ed. Commission of the Central Committee of the CPSU (New York: International Publishers, 1939), pp. 355-362. My evaluation of the choice of this work as the basis for the CCP theoretical education in the Yenan period would be supported by Chinese Communist statements on this question. The CCPCC's "Resolution on the Yenan Cadre Schools" of December 17, 1941, enjoined cadres to "take the *History of the Communist Party of the Soviet Union* as the fundamental source in learning Marxism-Leninism and ... pay particular attention to learning the *actual application* of fundamental views of dialectical materialism (and not a mass of abstract principles) so they can overcome the extremely harmful errors of subjectivism and dogmatism." This document is reproduced in Boyd Compton, ed., *Mao's China* (Seattle: University of Washington Press, 1966), and this quotation is extracted from p. 75. That the "Conclusion" of the *History of the Communist Party of the Soviet Union* was included among the *cheng-feng* documents is another indication of the CCP view of the work as supportive of Maoist theory and practice. Other *cheng-feng* documents refer to the *History* as a "model for the union of theory and practice." Mao himself praised it for its advocacy of "savage struggle and merciless attack" against "enemies

and opposition thought" and "methods for criticism and self-criticism." He also found that "by observing the way in which Lenin and Stalin took the universal truths of Marxism and related them to the concrete reality of the Soviet Revolution and thereby developed Marxism, we can understand the manner in which we should carry out our work in China." See Compton, pp. 40, 68. A leading Soviet specialist has pointed out to me that with few elementary texts on Marxism-Leninism available in the USSR, the *History* was valued for its digest of theory and exposition of the "theory and practice of proletarian revolution." The Chinese Communists may have found the concise and simple description of historical materialism and other aspects of theory treated in the book useful for cadres with little education or exposure to Western philosophy. Conversation with Professor Loren Graham, Department of History, Columbia University, October 12, 1973.
In tone and choice of vocabulary the book puts forth an interpretation of Marxism-Leninism that complements the growing voluntarist elements in Chinese Communist thought. The triumph of dialectical materialists over the Mechanists in 1929 in Soviet intellectual circles and the requirements of rapid industrialization in the thirties nurtured a growing trend towards exalting the role of the individual in shaping his environment in Soviet thought. This development was encouraged by Stalin, who himself chose to stress the activist strain of Marxism. One of the purposes of the *History* was to depict individuals and the CPSU as agents capable of shaping history to their will. See the discussion of the *History* and Soviet educational and philosphical developments in Raymond A. Bauer, *The New Man in Soviet Psychology* (Cambridge, Mass.: Harvard University Press, 1952), pp. 15-29, 43-48, 76-80, 89, 117, 132-133, 192.
Gabriel Almond has analyzed the *History* in terms of its heavy use of military imagery. This aspect of the *History*, viewing political life as a form of combat, would also fit in well with the militarized political environment of Chinese Communism. See Almond, pp. 28-32. See also the discussion of Stalin's use of military imagery in Cohen, pp. 313-315.

[61]Stein, pp. 151-152. See also Lu P'ing, p. 131.

[62]*Chung-kung chih chiao-yü*, pp. 3, 38-39; *Hsüeh-hsi sheng-huo* [Study Life] , ed. Wen-hua chiao-yü yen-chiu hui (n.p., Wen-hua chiao-yü yen-chiu hui, 1941), pp. 129-130.

[63]On the Central Research Institute see *Chung-kung chih chiao-yü*, p. 39. Liu Shao-ch'i lectured at the Academy of Marxism-Leninism in 1939. In his address of August 7 concerning the "Training of the Communist Party Member," Liu mentioned a course at the academy on "the establishment of the Party." An entire section of this course was devoted to "self-criticism" and "thought struggle within the Party." Liu cited a book entitled *Political Parties* published by the China Publishing Company as a reference for academy students on these issues. See Compton, pp. 142-143. One of the students at the academy in 1940 was Jen Tso-min, also a graduate of Communist University of the Toilers of the East, who headed the CCP Northwest Bureau in 1941-1942. See Klein and Clark, p. 416.

[64]Party branch leaders, in other words, could no longer intervene directly in school administration as in the past. They were restricted to recommendations or criticisms within regular Party channels and an auxiliary role of aiding implementation of a school's educational plan.

[65]"Resolution of the Central Committee of the Chinese Communist Party on the Yenan Cadre Schools," December 17, 1941, reproduced in Compton, pp. 74-79. The resolution's stress on expertise also applied to policies concerning faculty and student recruitment and evaluation. "Cultural studies" won more attention for those in need of remedial work. With allowance for varying conditions among specialist schools, technical studies were to occupy fifty to eighty percent of the curriculum.

[66]Yenan University was formed in September 1941 from the merger of Chinese Women's University, the Tse-tung Youth Cadre School (founded in May 1940), and part of the North Shensi Public School. At that time the university was divided into departments of education, law, administration, finance, journalism, and foreign languages. An attached higher-middle school fed the university with local talent. The matriculation period ranged from two years for the middle school and law and education departments to one and one half years for other departments. There were special courses for each department as well as required subjects for all students. The basic curriculum did not include courses exclusively on Marxism-Leninism or revolutionary theory not directly applicable to China.

Core courses consisted of (1) Chinese History; (2) Chinese Politics; (3) Border Region Policies;(4) Chinese Economy; (5) Enemy and Puppet Operations; (6) International Problems; (7) The Three People's Principles; (8) Chinese; and (9) Methods of Thought. Yenan University was reorgainzed in April 1943 after combining with the Natural Sciences Research Institute; Lu Hsün Academy of Arts; Nationalities Academy (founded in July 1941); and the New Character Cadre School (founded in April 1941). It again underwent reorganization in May 1944, combining with the Administration Academy (founded in July 1940). These changes were inspired by the turn towards local problems promoted during the production campaigns. Yenan University began to cater increasingly to border region problems and it came under the jurisdiction of the border region government. Previously it had been under the jurisdiction of the CCPCC Cultural Committee. On the history of Yenan University, see *Yen-an ta-hsüeh kai-k'uang* [General Situation at Yenan University] , mimeographed (n.p., June 1944), p. 1.

[67] The Administration Academy was similar to the Public Administration Institute operated by the North Kiangsu Special Administrative Committee. The Public Administration Institute was founded in the autumn of 1940 to train cadres to run the new local governments set up by the New Fourth Army in central China. It was initially located at Tung-t'ai in North Kiangsu and moved in February 1941 to Yen-ch'eng. Kuan Wen-wei headed the institute and Chou P'ing, identified as a "former instructor at K'ang-ta in Yenan," was education director. The institute featured three months of training in basic public administration, economics, and mass operations, with the average size of each class around four hundred. Upon graduation trainees were dispatched to various *hsien* governments throughout North Kiangsu. See Johnson, *Peasant Nationalism*, pp. 153-154.

[68] Chou also headed the Education Office, assisted by Liu Ch'eng-yün; Wang headed the Cadre Office, also assisted by Liu and Chang Kuei-piao. See *Yen-an ta-hsüeh*, p. 4; and Stein, p. 265.

[69] Among the 532 staff members listed in 1944, only 43 were instructors. Eight taught in the Natural Sciences Academy; 30 in the Lu Hsün Arts Academy; and 5 in the Administration Academy. Most of the teaching staff of the Administration and Science Academies were also leaders in various work projects in the border region. Figures on the student enrollment at Yenan University in 1944 break down as follows—Geographic origin: Shensi, 180; Shansi, 165; Honan, 197; Hopei, 103; Shantung, 57; Kansu, 13. Family background: small property owners, 330; landlords, 270; rich peasants, 153; middle peasants, 303; poor peasants, 163; proletarian, 30. Educational background: middle school, 50%; upper elementary school, 10% and above; university, 10%. Work experience: one to three years, 50%; less than one year, 25%; over six years, 5%; Area of specialized study: Administration Academy, 773; Lu Hsün Arts Academy, 314; Medical Department, 72; Natural Sciences Academy, 49; Special "Female" Section, 74. These statistics are from *Yen-an ta-hsüeh*, pp. 13-14.

[70] Curriculum outlines from "Yenan University Educational Line and Temporary Regulations," May 21, 1944, translated and reproduced in Michael Lindsay, *Notes on Educational Problems in Communist China, 1941-47* (New York: Institute of Pacific Relations, 1950), pp. 133-139.

[71] On study methods and student life at Yenan University, see ibid.; Harrison Forman, *Report from Red China* (New York: Henry Holt and Co., 1945), p. 86; and Chao Ch'ao-kou, ed., *Yen-an i-yüeh* [One Month in Yenan] (Nanking: Hsin-min, 1946), pp. 149-150.

9 High-level Schools and the *Cheng-feng* Movement

In terms of effects on the Chinese Communist leadership structure, the educational system developed during the Yenan period proved both a blessing and a curse. Institutions for the training of various leadership types had upgraded the quality of tens of thousands of Communist leaders, enlarging the Chinese Communist movement's capacity to coordinate mobilization, military, and modernization activities. At the same time, however, continued production of specialized leadership types threatened to pit segments of the Communist movement at cross purposes—commanders versus commissars and Party representatives in the military; bureaucrats versus peasant organizers; Party theorists versus "practical workers." Some of these conflicts were early hints of the "red expert" controversy that has continued to haunt Chinese Communism.

As in the Kiangsi years there were fears of "mountaintopism" among military leaders in isolated base areas with slender ties to the Party center in Yenan. Party unity also suffered from the inability of united front schools to radicalize the rising proportion of intellectuals absorbed into the Chinese Communist movement. Those drawn to Communism through nationalism and the united front had not been reconciled to the outlook of peasant cadres committed to local interests served by the land revolution. All of the problems were exacerbated by intensified Nationalist and Japanese pressure on the Communist base areas.[1]

Education was again invoked as the principal corrective for these fragmenting tendencies, and Chinese Communist study programs went on the upsurge after 1939. The *cheng-feng* rectification movement of 1942-1944 can be seen as an effort to counter growing divisions in the Chinese Communist leadership structure. Launched officially on February 1, 1942, this study campaign defined clearly and comprehensively—for the first time in Party history—the basic goals of the Chinese Communist movement and presented a common denominator of actions, attitudes, and beliefs expected of all Communist leaders. It aimed at strengthening the Party chain of command—without sacrificing local flexibility—through a systematic educational program to remold Party members' ideological outlook and behavior.

To bridge the gaps between various leadership types, *cheng-feng* study materials set forth a basic core of knowledge to be mastered by every Chinese communist cadre, regardless of work specialty. The Party propaganda department issued a standard set of twenty-two documents[2] as the basis of rectification study for cadres of all levels. These documents dealt with three major questions: (1) intra-Party organizational behavior; (2) ideological tendencies; and (3) proper work style towards the non-Party community. A composite of desirable qualities from all three categories outlined the "ideal" leadership model for all Chinese Communists.

Guidelines for the conduct of Party members were suggested in documents such as "Training of the Communist Party Member" and "On the Intra-Party Struggle" written in 1939 and 1941, respectively, by Liu Shao-ch'i; "How to Be A Communist Party Member" (1939) by Ch'en Yün; and the Central Committee's "Resolution on Strengthening the Party Spirit" (July 1, 1941) and "Resolution on the Unification of Leadership in the Anti-Japanese War Bases" (September 1, 1942).

Liu's writings discussed intra-Party discipline. Liu did not expect prospective Party members to exhibit a thorough understanding of Communism; however, he did demand that the "individual interests" of Party members be "subordinated unconditionally to the interests of the Party." He upheld intra-Party struggle as a tool for enforcing organizational discipline and combating deviationist views. While opposed to "unprincipled," "mechanical" struggle and disputes based on factionalism or cliquism, Liu specified the legitimate area of struggle as "thought, which consists of divergencies and mutual opposition in ideological principles."[3]

Ch'en discussed the qualifications and procedures for admission into the Party and criteria for evaluating members in good standing. He measured a good Party cadre in terms of his or her "life-long struggle for communism" and "unlimited devotion to the revolution and the Party."[4]

Both Central Committee resolutions discussed the question of Party unity and centralization. They underlined the necessity of "unity and centralization of leadership in the War Bases." There were also instructions on the coordination of Party committees at all levels, the duties of Party representatives in military units, and the operation of the "three:three" system in governments and mass organizations.5

Proper work style for Communists dealing with people outside the Party was discussed in documents such as Mao Tse-tung's "Second Preface to Village Investigations" (March 17, 1941) and "Address to the Shen-Kan-Ning Border Region Assembly" (December 22, 1941); and the Central Committee's "Resolution on Methods of Leadership" (June 1, 1943) and "Resolution on Investigation and Research" (August 1, 1941). Mao defined the basis of "real leadership" as "correct and concrete understanding of the actual conditions of the various social classes of China" which in turn depended on the ability "to investigate society and the conditions of each class's livelihood."6 In his "Address to the Shen-Kan-Ning Border Region Assembly" he outlined the correct work style for united front activities under the "three:three" system as "democratic cooperation with men outside the Party" and "the attitude and spirit of discussing problems with others."7 The Central Committee resolutions detailed the procedures for "investigation and research" that promoted "correct relations between the leading nucleus and the broad masses."8

Maoist writings dominated the third category of rectification documents that were concerned with Party members' attitudes and ideological tendencies and the application of Marxist-Leninist theory to conditions in China.9 Mao singled out "subjectivism in study," "sectarianism in Party work," and "formalism" in propaganda work as "three evil winds" polluting Party members' work style. He distinguished two forms of "subjectivism": the "dogmatism" or doctrinairism characteristic of intellectuals and the "empiricism" exhibited by practical Party workers. Mao called for further Party centralization to extinguish vestiges of "sectarianism" which were the product of tensions "between the individual and the Party, between native cadres and cadres from the outside, between cadres in army service and cadres in civilian work."10

Mao attacked "formalism" in Party writings as manifested in empty, long-winded phrases, pretentiousness, rambling style, and lack of clarity, meaningful content, and popular appeal. He aimed this barb at the "Twenty-eight Bolsheviks," lashing out at Party leaders who "can only repeat quotes from Marx, Engels, Lenin and Stalin from memory" but "are unable to use the standpoints and methods of Marx, Engels, Lenin and Stalin....for concrete analyses of the problems of the Chinese Revolution."11

There were pressing reasons for Mao's attack on the "Twenty-eight Bolsheviks" during the rectification campaign. Some of those with

Soviet training had made important contributions to Chinese Communism in the past. But taken as a whole, the foreign-trained Chinese Communists appear to have been somewhat out of touch with the growing "native" or indigenous orientation of the Maoists during the Yenan period. For years after the Chinese Communist Party came under Maoist domination many "Bolsheviks" retained key Party positions, especially in the educational and propaganda apparatus. There they posed obstacles to the finalization of the Party's language of communication and work style for rural revolution. As leading educators and ideologues they continued to project their influence on the outlook and activities of Chinese Communists at all levels.

K'ai Feng remained director of the Central Committee Propaganda Department until 1943 or early 1944, after which Ch'in Pang-hsien filled the position for one year. Ch'in also served as the first director of the New China News Agency, established in 1941, and as editor-in-chief of the leading Party organ, *Liberation Daily (Chieh-fang jih-pao)*. Chang Wen-t'ien, who had been secretary-general of the Chinese Communist Party before the post was abolished in December, 1937, served as secretary of the Central Committee Press Committee and as director of the Academy of Marxism-Leninism—obviously critical positions of influence for theoretical matters and Party study life. Chang and Ch'in, along with Mao, Chou En-lai, and Ch'en Yün, also belonged to the powerful five-man Standing Committee of the Political Bureau. Mao's major "Bolshevik" adversary Ch'en Shao-yü had been secretary of the Chinese Communist Party South China Bureau in Chungking between 1938 and 1941, and between 1939 and 1941 he headed the Chinese Women's University in Yenan. All but one of the Chinese Communist Party research associations issuing educational materials for cadres were headed by theorists trained abroad.[12]

Among the documents supporting Mao's position on the deviant tendencies of Party members was Liu Shao-ch'i's discussion on "Liquidation of Menshevik Thought in the Party" (July 1943). Liu echoed Mao's call for a Chinese Communist political strategy based on the "Chinese revolutionary experience" and condemned "false Marxists" who "do not rely on experience and calculations drawn up from actual work but rely instead on books." He branded as "Mensheviks" both allegedly left and right deviationists such as "Ch'en Tu-hsiu, P'eng Shu-chih, and the Chinese Trotskyites; the Li Li-san line; the left opportunism of the Civil War period; and dogmatism."

As was Liu's article, the Soviet pieces included among the *cheng-feng* documents were selected to legitimate the Maoist revolutionary line—and using fire to fight fire, to support the attack on the Internationalists. An exerpt from Dimitrov's "Cadre Policy and Cadre Educational Policy" underlined the role of cadres in movement-building: "people, cadres decide everything." The Dimitrov piece also condemned "pernicious scholasticism" and "abstract theory," advocating "training in which mastering the fundamental principles of Marxism-Leninism is based on the key problems of the struggle of the proletariat in his own country." Its definition of "revolutionary theory" supported that of the Chinese rectification documents:

> Our theory is not dogma, but a guide to action.... Revolutionary theory is the *generalized, summarized experience* of the revolutionary movement. Communists must carefully utilize in their countries not only the experience of the past but also the experience of the present struggle.... However, correct utilization of experience does not by any means denote *mechanical transposition* of ready-made forms and methods of struggle from one set of conditions to another, from one country to another.... Bare imitation, simple copying of methods and forms of work, even of the Communist Party of the Soviet Union ... may with the best of intentions result in harm rather than good....13

Similar conclusions could be drawn from the "Conclusion" of the *History of the Communist Party of the Soviet Union*, also included among the rectification documents. And an extract from Stalin's " the Future and Bolshevization of the Communist Party of Germany," which appeared in *Pravda* on February 3, 1924, made similar pronouncements:

> When formulating any slogan or directive, the Party should not rely on memorized formulas or historical comparisons, but on the concrete conditions of the revolutionary movement.... In its work the Party must be successful in combining the strongest stand in principle ... with the greatest degree of alliance and contact with the masses.... 14

The other Soviet documents supplemented and supported the views of the Chinese-authored documents on Party members' organizational behavior.15

THE *CHENG-FENG* IDEAL

What emerged from the *cheng-feng* movement and its study documents was a picture of a "model" Chinese Communist—one who could show both obedience to the Party and individual initiative; steer a narrow course between "commandism" and "tailism"; reconcile particular problems with "universal" principles of Marxism-Leninism; relate the details of "investigation and research" to the general revolutionary goals of Chinese Communism; and show closeness to the masses yet place loyalty to the Chinese Communist movement above personal ties. This "ideal-typical" model of a revolutionary leader did not, of course, match any one person, but it became a standard for all Party members to emulate—and it remains so today. It was not expected that every leader working under the Chinese Communist Party would meet the ideal. The hope was that the result of many individuals striving towards these ends would upgrade the capability and solidarity of the Party as a whole. There were potential gains for the Chinese Communists' organizational power if each cadre set to improve himself or herself according to *cheng-feng* guidelines.

The *cheng-feng* movement also had far-reaching implications for the Chinese Communists' political claims to speak for all of China. It attempted to deal with one of the major problems of modern Chinese civilization, the question of finding values that could be shared both by modernizing elites and the society at large.

One factor in the political, economic, and cultural trials faced by China since the mid-nineteenth century was the "elite-mass gap"[16] produced by the forces of modernization. Education may be the handmaiden of modernity, but it often separates leaders in developing societies from their people. Modern scientific and technical education, as imported from the West, has been criticized for creating a Chinese elite divorced in orientation from most of the Chinese people, especially those in the countryside.[17] Reintegrating an elite that was highly Westernized and urban in outlook was one of the major problems of the National Government during its bid for the leadership of China.

Any political movement aspiring to reunite China had to come to grips with this issue. The Chinese Communist Party explicitly took on the challenge in its leadership policy and training institutions. Experiments in leadership training methods were part of an effort to devise an educational system that could promote modernization while furthering the integration of Party leaders and society at large. Glorification of physical labor, "mutual help and collective study," the "mass line" and cadre concept, as well as curricula tailored to local problems are among the features of Chinese Communist leadership education addressed to this issue.

One creation of the *cheng-feng* architects was a system of values that could be shared by the leaders and the led. Although the Chinese Communist movement had arisen in response to Chinese problems, it drew its ideological framework and operational guidelines from foreign sources. Its survival and eventual political success depended on its ability to apply Marxism-Leninism to a backward agrarian society. The "Sinification of Marxism" received a great boost from the *cheng-feng* movement and the *hsia-hsiang* movement initiated in July 1941.[18]

The concern with tailoring foreign revolutionary doctrine to indigenous concerns is an outstanding theme of the *cheng-feng* study materials. Many of the writings in the *cheng-feng* collection made forceful arguments for detailed studies of local conditions and Chinese history as the basis of revolutionary theory and practice. Foreign revolutionary models, applied uncritically in China, were assailed for promoting "dogmatism," sectarianism," and "formalism" in Party work. *Cheng-feng* materials defined "real leadership" as "correct and concrete understanding of the actual conditions of the various social classes of China."[19] The *cheng-feng* movement thus furnished guidelines to make Chinese Communism, as a political movement, "China-centered," and it spurred on the Chinese Communists' penetration of the countryside. It provided theory to legitimate Chinese Communist activities that integrated elites with society, and contributed substantially to the Communists' victory in 1949 and their subsequent achievements in national reunification.

The *cheng-feng* movement also functioned as a sifting process for Chinese Communist leadership education. It helped to determine the most effective study methods for producing Communist cadres and disseminated them throughout the Communist leadership structure. Cadre training programs at lower levels of the Chinese Communist Party had traditionally emulated practices at higher levels. However, before the early forties, only a small portion of the entire Chinese Communist Party membership had been exposed to study on a formal basis. The *cheng-feng* movement set forth a distinct educational program for all Chinese Communist Party members. (December 17, 1941) and "On the education of Cadres In-Service" Chinese Communist Party resolutions "On the Yenan Cadre Schools" and investigation of individual life histories and work performance.[21] (February 28, 1942) defined the role of cadre education in Party life and its contributions to *cheng-feng* objectives.[20] The *cheng-feng* study program itself involved a "basic rectification methodology" consisting of reading the standard study materials, note-taking, directed group discussions, "struggle" over major issues raised by the documents, criticism and self-criticism, and investigation of individual life histories and work performance.[21]

This rectification methodology was distilled from the educational practices at K'ang-ta and other high-level Chinese Communist cadre schools and had roots in Chinese Communist leadership training procedures developed before the Yenan period. The *cheng-feng* movement furnished Chinese Communist leaders with the opportunity to review their educational policy and determine the most effective practices for molding leadership cadres. These learning practices were infused into the lower levels of the Chinese Party and eventually became regular features of Chinese Communist Party life.

CHENG-FENG AT HIGH-LEVEL SCHOOLS

High-level Chinese Communist leadership training institutions were

major centers of rectification activity. The schools in Yenan were the
closest to the Party's policy-making organs and thus readily acces-
sible for the implementation of new programs. Chinese Communist
educational innovations usually started in high-level leadership
training programs and spread downward. The *cheng-feng* movement
was no exception. In addition, leadership training institutions in
Yenan, by providing periodic training to ranking cadres from all the
base areas, operated as transmission belts between central and local
levels of the Party.

While there were certain universal objectives in the *cheng-feng* movement, the procedures and outcome of rectification showed
considerable variation throughout the Chinese Communist Party. Results were dependent on the cadres' educational background, organizational experience, and work requirements. Among the high-level
leadership training institutions, rectification proceeded differentially,
according to the requirements of each type of leadership model.

The Central Party School in Yenan was the focal point of the *cheng-
feng* movement for the entire Chinese Communist Party.[22] Hundreds
of ranking Party cadres were transferred to Yenan for training as part
of the campaign for "crack troops and simple administration." Local
Party delegates had been summoned to Yenan for a scheduled
Seventh Party Congress. Both the delegates and transferred cadres
were concentrated at the Central Party School, swelling the enrollment to almost one thousand.[23] Because of its role in coordinating
cadre activities throughout the Chinese Communist Party structure,
the Central Party School found its rectification activity the object
of close scrutiny and recurrent criticism from the top Party leadership. *Cheng-feng* work there lasted three years and the school underwent two reorganizations.

In accord with the December 17, 1941, Central Committee "Resolution on the Yenan Cadre Schools," the Central Party School
began its first reorganization in January 1942. It formulated a new
study plan, to be in effect from January 17, 1942, to February 1,
1944. A committee of Political Bureau members, scholars in Yenan,
and student representatiaves staged an "opening ceremony" for
the reorganized school, attended by over one thousand students,
guests, and Central Committee members. School principal Teng Fa
reported on the progress of reorganization: the study methods in the
new educational plan included "conformity of theory with practice,
overcoming dogmatism and subjectivism in education, learning
through practice, and the method of applying theories." Mao Tse-
tung then outlined his principles for cadre education in a speech on
"Reform in Learning, the Party and Literature." The rally ended
with a speech by student representative Chang Ting-ch'eng.[24]

Later reports on the reforms at the Central Party School were quite critical, claiming that the school was "only paying lip service to Mao's instructions." The school leadership came under fire for promoting "study for the sake of study" and a dogmatic outlook that discouraged "understanding of the spirit and practice of Marxism-Leninism." According to P'eng Chen the entire Central Party School during its first reorganization embarked on a study of Western and ancient Chinese history, which he felt was entirely unsuited to the Party's needs. The result was another reshuffle of school leadership, with Mao Tse-tung taking over the post of principal. Lin Piao and P'eng Chen both served as vice-principals and P'eng assumed responsibility for the organizational and ideological aspects of rectification.[25]

P'eng-Chen reported that the Central Party School thereafter published a periodic "study report" edited by Lu Ting-i. Before a new educational plan was formulated the school authorities elicited students' opinions of the instructional program. Under the new plan the basic curriculum became the history of China since 1911 and the application of Marxist-Leninist analytical methods to problems of the Chinese revolution. Students investigated the political climate of revolutions in various historical periods, Party policies and construction, organizational problems, military problems, and philosophy. Pedagogically the Central Party School turned to the *ch'i-fa* method —"from old to new and from near to far."

The prescribed rectification documents were read superficially at first and later more carefully to analyze "Party style, study style and writing style" before final synthesis. Students took notes on significant points, combining independent study with group discussion. There were two types of group study meetings: (1) "opinion meetings," loosely organized groups of three to ten people, and (2) "discussion meetings" involving small groups or one or two Party branches.[26] After examining the rectification documents each person probed his own thinking, life history, and work style, furnishing occasion for intensive criticism and self-criticism.[27] From the investigation of individuals the students turned to the work of the Party divisions to which they belonged. They studied the history of the Chinese revolution in the various border regions to determine if the "concrete conditions of the Chinese revolution" tallied with the "general truths of Marxism-Leninism."[28]

During the *cheng-feng* movement the Central Research Institute came to the fore as the center of the Chinese Communist drive against intellectuals and left-wing writers, many of whom were on the staff of the Lu Hsün Academy of Arts and other training schools. There were two areas of controversy: the degree of Westernization tolerable in literature and the extent to which practitioners of "literary realism" could criticize the policies of the Chinese Communist Party. These issues were the backdrop for the famous Yenan Forum on Art and Literature in May 1942.[29]

The following month the Party launched an attack against critical writers. Its chief target was Wang Shih-wei, a member of the Central Research Institute. Wang had argued with ideologue Ch'en Po-ta over the use of "national" forms in literature. He also had criticized Ch'en and others for grabbing official positions. Beginning on May 27, 1942, the Central Research Institute sponsored sixteen days of "struggle" sessions against Wang. Among those present were institute students and staff,[30] Ho Nai-feng of the Central Committee, Chou Wen and Liu Shih, secretary-general and education director, respectively, of the border region government, and cadres from other organizations. The session on June 8 was attended by one thousand representatives of Party organs and schools in the Yenan area.

Participants in the sessions studied Wang's writings in conjunction with the *cheng-feng* documents. Wang was severely criticized and labelled a "Trotskyite"; in the face of such charges he refused to recant and asked to withdraw from the Party. At one session the renowned leftist writer Ting Ling submitted to self-criticism for her piece "Reflections on the March Eighth Women's Day," which had scored the Party's treatment of female cadres.[31]

Other struggle targets at the Central Research Institute included Po Ho-p'ing, Tzu Chih-jan, Wang Li, P'an Fang, and Sung Ching. The campaigns at the institute were used to set down the Chinese Communist Party's line on the role of intellectuals in the "dictatorship of the proletariat." On the whole, the *cheng-feng* campaign among intellectuals did not seek to eliminate potential political conspirators but rather encouraged their reform through reeducation.[32]

The issues raised at the Central Research Institute also dominated the *cheng-feng* campaign at the Lu Hsün Academy of Arts. One of the Chinese Communist Party's leading specialists on the question of the relationship of politics to art, Chou Yang, had been vice-principal of the academy and concurrently education director of the Shensi-Kansu-Ningsia border region. Chou took charge of the rectification movement at the academy and set in motion his views on revolutionary art. He felt that, instead of emulating Western models, artists should draw inspiration from indigenous sources as did the Chinese peasants in their folk songs. He therefore sent the Lu Hsün students to villages, factories, and front lines to establish an "organic relationship" with the common people.[33]

The *cheng-feng* movement may have been a factor in the merger of the Lu Hsün Academy with Yenan University in 1943 and Yenan University's growing interest in linking specialized studies to practical border region problems. From April to September 1942 the university studied its educational philosophy and the issue of Communist Party controls in a united front school as its principal rectification problems. University authorities criticized the school's pre-*cheng-feng* "educational line" as "theory divorced from practice." Discussions among students and faculty culminated in a two-week assembly of the entire school to "combat liberalism."

After September the *cheng-feng* movement at Yenan University turned towards an investigation of the life histories of individual cadres. With the publicized criticisms of alleged "Trotskyite" Wang Shih-wei before them, faculty and students participated in a "confession movement," or "sincerity campaign" (*t'an-pai yün-tung*), that lasted until the following July. Reports revealed that 440 of the 1,877 faculty members and students had voluntarily confessed and criticized their past wrongdoings.[34]. Stepped-up ideological and organizational controls at Yenan University and other united front schools during the *cheng-feng* movement tried to draw intellectuals further toward Chinese Communism.

Very little is known about the rectification movement at K'ang-ta. By early 1941 the main school had moved behind enemy lines and, along with its branches, became increasingly oriented toward the production of military cadres. These cadres' work—in contrast to that of the "intellectuals"—may have been too vital to allow the sacrifice of several months to rectification work. It may also be the case that K'ang-ta's early pioneering pedagogical work exempted the main school from the types of charges levelled at other leadership training institutions.

The main and branch schools of K'ang-ta were reported to have undertaken *cheng-feng* study through 1943. Some ground work was prepared in 1939, when the Central Military Council issued a "Directive Concerning the Question of Reforming K'ang-ta." Linked to the Chinese Communist Party's 1939-1940 study campaign that led up to the *cheng-feng* movement, the directive stipulated that K'ang-ta and all other military and political schools that trained students from "intellectual" backgrounds should place special emphasis on political education.[35]

An account of the *cheng-feng* movement at the Fifth, or Central China, branch of K'ang-ta headed by Ch'en I and Feng Ting, suggests rectification work at this type of leadership training school was conditioned by the quality and leadership functions of its trainees. No systematic rectification study took place until the Party's Central China Bureau issued a study plan for May and June 1942. Many students had a "low cultural level" and spent most of their time in remedial work. In-service cadres and students of relatively high "cultural level" were instructed to read the *cheng-feng* documents and discuss their contents two to three times per week. After examining problems of subjectivism, sectarianism, Party formalism, Party spirit, and investigation and research, the students were required to investigate themselves.

During the course of rectification, students at this K'ang-ta branch exhibited "incorrect attitudes" such as failure to take notes, reluctance to participate in criticism and self-criticism, and the subordination of *cheng-feng* study to either "theoretical" or "practical" work. The school then began publishing a daily mimeographed progress report, singling out tendencies to be corrected. By the end of the two-month study period students' understanding of the significance of rectification had improved. However, the school's organizational difficulties inhibited *cheng-feng* progress. Cadres from various units faced different work situations, which along with disparities in educational background, proved ill-suited to standardized study procedures. The school faced perennial shortages of materials and could only allot one set of rectification documents to each class.

In July the Central China Bureau issued another study plan for the months of July through September. In-service cadres and students able to finish reading the twenty-two rectification documents were instructed to read twenty supplementary pieces. Less literate students were encouraged to read three to ten of the original documents. The extended study period did sensitize all types of students to the issues of the *cheng-feng* campaign as related to their own attitudes and behavior. But even with great gains reported, the *cheng-feng* movement at this branch of K'ang-ta never produced earth-shaking results. Literacy problems and the demands of military training prevented the campaign from supplanting the regular curriculum. Altogether rectification activities lasted five months, with few changes in ongoing operations.[36]

During most of 1942 the *cheng-feng* campaign remained concentrated at the higher-level cadre schools and upper administrative organs of the Chinese Communist Party. Due to difficulties in clarifying the issues in rectification and finding suitable personnel to supervise study programs, the movement spread very slowly to the local level. It managed to pick up some momentum, however, from the policy of movement "to the countryside" (*hsia-hsiang*) and the downward transfer of ranking cadres. By 1943 special *cheng-feng* training classes were common at the district and subdistrict levels of the Party. Study methods were flexible and tried to serve local needs.[37]

The rectification movement trailed into 1944 with mixed results. It did not produce a monolithic Party or eliminate all of the differences among the Chinese Communist leaders. Few Party leaders were transformed into ideal Communists, and the Party's links to the local level in many areas remained quite tenuous. However, the rectification program did articulate a coherent set of goals and common basis of commitment for all Chinese Communists. Exposure to education and group struggle did bring closer together diverse elements in the Chinese Communist leadership structure and widely-scattered segments of the Party organization. The campaign did improve the Communists' communication system and chain of command. Along with the "cooperative," "production," "to the village," and "crack troops and simple administration" movements, *cheng-feng* helped to extend the Chinese Communist movement further into Chinese society. It fortified all levels of the Party for the future challenges of revolution and war throughout the forties.

The *cheng-feng* movement witnessed the crystallization of the Chinese Communists' key techniques for Party-political education, still in operation today. The preparation of Chinese Communist leaders at present continues to employ learning methods developed at the high-level training schools and systematized during the *cheng-feng* movement. As opposed to purges, trials, arrests, and physical expulsion from the Party, these procedures have become the Chinese Communists' principal means of maintaining organizational solidarity and curbing intra-elite tensions.[38] Since the *cheng-feng* movement, the Chinese Communists have applied their programs for intra-Party education to the non-Party population. In China today political education for both leaders and led is an outgrowth of leadership training before 1949.[39]

NOTES

[1]Chinese Communist Party leaders found increasing difficulties in maintaining some form of control over policies and operations as the Party experienced enormous geographic and organizational expansion during the Sino-Japanese War. Its communications system was challenged by the proliferation of widely-scattered and isolated base areas with autonomous local Party and military units. The various problems confronting the CCP during the Yenan period were aggravated by the new Nationalist and Japanese drives against the border regions in 1941. The Hundred Regiments Campaign drew the full might of Japanese forces in China upon the Communist areas. Population shrank from forty-four to twenty-five million, with the Eighth Route Army losing one-fourth of its men. After the New Fourth Army Incident the national government tightened its blockade of the border regions and cut off united front subsidies for the Eighth Route Army and border region administration. The CCP was thus forced to raise quotas of military conscription and double tax levies in its base areas—policies that threatened to alienate its popular base of support. On the setting of the *cheng-feng* movement, see Selden, pp. 141-147, 188-191.

[2]There were originally eighteen *cheng-feng* documents, but four were added later in 1942. Seybolt, p. 386.

[3]Liu Shao-ch'i, "Training of the Communist Party Member," August 7, 1939; idem., "On the Intra-Party Struggle," July 2, 1941. Both are reproduced in Compton, pp. 108-155, 188-238.

[4]Ch'en Yün, "How to Be a Communist Party Member, " May 30, 1939, reproduced in Compton, pp. 88-107.

[5]"Central Committee Resolution on the Unification of Leadership in the Anti-Japanese War Bases," September 1, 1942, and "Central Committee Resolution on Strengthening the Party Spirit," in Compton, pp. 156-162.

[6]See "Second Preface to 'Village Investigations'," Compton, p. 55.

[7]This document can be found in Compton, pp. 246-251. See also Mao's celebrated statement of "mass line" principles, "Resolution of the Central Committee of the Chinese Communist Party on Methods of Leadership," June 1, 1943, in Compton, pp. 176-183.

[8]"Central Committee Resolution on Investigation and Research," August 1, 1941, in Compton, pp. 71-72.

[9]These works included "Reform in Learning, the Party and Literature" (February 1, 1942); "In Opposition to Party Formalism" (February 8, 1942); "The Reconstruction of Our Studies" (May 5, 1941); "In Opposition to Liberalism" (September 7, 1937); and "In Opposition to Several Incorrect Tendencies within the Party" (December 1929). All are available in Compton.

[10]See Mao Tse-tung, "Reform in Learning, the Party and Literature," in Compton, pp. 9-32.

[11]Mao Tse-tung, "In Opposition to Party Formalism" and "The Reconstruction of Our Studies," in Compton, pp. 33-53, 59-68.

[12]The Political-Economic Theory Research Association, formed in the spring of 1939, was headed initially by Wang Ssu-hua. Participants from the Academy of Marxism-Leninism and the teaching staffs of K'ang-ta, the Central Party School, and Workers' University worked on *Das Kapital*. With the aid of Wu Liang-p'ing, Ch'en Shao-yü directed a Marxism-Leninism Research Association, founded in April 1939. Participants likewise came from the Academy of Marxism-Leninism, Yenan cadre schools, and high-level administrative personnel in the Yenan area. Lo Fu (Chang Wen-t'ien) headed the Chinese Problems Research Association but relinquished his position to Yang Sung. Along with Ch'en Yün, Lo Fu also served as director of the Party Building Research Association. Nearly one hundred participants drawn from teachers, administrators, and local Party cadres discussed Party rules, Party membership, organizational principles and structure, cadre policy, branch work methods of leadership, work with the masses, Party consolidation, intra-Party education, and public and secret work. With Ai Szu-ch'i, Lo Fu headed the Philosophy Research Association, involving over eighty participants and numerous auditors. Its discussions were based on Ai's works (*An Outline of the New Philosophy* and *Philosophy for the Masses*), as well as a volume of his translations and commentaries published in May 1939. Discussions revolved around questions of "What is Philosophy?" "On Substance, Time and Space in Dialectical Materialism," "The Principles of the Dialectic Method," and "Epistemology." Such concerns and those of the other research associations gave substance to Maoist charges that educational circles were preoccupied with problems and abstract theory divorced from the realities of the Chinese Revolution. A description of the research associations can be found in *Hsüeh-hsi sheng-huo*, pp. 15-20.

[13]See "Chi-mi-t'e-fu lun kan-pu cheng-ts'e yü kan-pu chiao-yü cheng-ts'e," in *Cheng-tun san-feng* [Rectify the Three Styles] (Hong Kong: Wen-feng ch'u-pan she, 1946), pp. 191-203. For an English translation, see Georgi Dimitrov, *Selected Works*, vol. 2 (Sofia: Sofia Press, 1972), pp. 107-116.

[14]See Compton, pp. 269-271.

[15]These documents were excerpts from Stalin's "Report to the Seventeenth Congress of the CPSU" of January 1934 and his "Report and Conclusions at the Enlarged Plenum of the Central Committee of the CPSU" of March 1937 entitled "Leadership and Inspection"; an excerpt from *Problems of Leninism* entitled "Equalitarianism" Stalins's "Report to the Fifteenth Congress of the CPSU" in 1927; and extracts from Lenin's "One Step Forward, Two Steps Backward" under the titles "Party Discipline and Party Democracy" and "Self-Criticism." All of the Soviet-authored articles except the piece on "Self-Criticism" can be

found in the collection of *cheng-feng* documents entitled *Cheng-feng wen-hsien* [Rectification Documents] , ed. Chieh-fang she (n.p., Chieh-fang she, June 1943), pp. 215-222.

[16]See James S. Coleman, ed., *Education and Political Development* (Princeton: Princeton University Press, 1965), pp. 355-357.

[17]The leading exponent of this point of view is Y.C. Wang. See especially his preface to *Chinese Intellectuals and the West 1872-1949* (Chapel Hill: University of North Carolina Press, 1966).

[18]This campaign involved the transfer of large numbers of outside activists to local areas.

[19]Mao Tse-tung, "Second Preface to 'Village Investigations'," Compton, p. 55.

[20]See Compton, pp. 74-87.

[21]On *cheng-feng* study procedures, see Seybolt, pp. 129-140; and Selden, pp. 190-191. There was some variation in rectification procedures to take into account cadres' literacy level and experience, with fewer of the basic documents required for study by low-level cadres.

[22]Chang Ting-ch'eng, "Cheng-feng tsai Yen-an chung-yang tang-hsiao" [Rectification at the Yenan Central Party School] , in *Hsing-huo liao-yüan* [A Single Spark Can Start a Prairie Fire] , vol. 6 (Peking: Jen-min wen-hsüeh ch'u-pan she, 1962), p. 15. See also Warren Kuo, *Analytical History*, vol. 4, p. 566.

[23]Warren Kuo, *Analytical History*, vol. 4, pp. 566, 575.

[24]Ibid., pp. 573-576. See also Kusano Fumio, p. 116; and "Hsin ti chiao-yü fang-chen ch'e-ti kai-tsu" [Thoroughly Reorganize a New Educational Line] , *Chieh-fang jih-pao,* January 28, 1942.

[25]Chang Ting-ch'eng, p. 7; "Chung-yang tang-hsiao tsai-tu kai-tsu kao-chün ch'üeh-ting hsin ti chiao-yü chi-hua" [Reorganization of the Central Party School Announces a Certified New Educational Plan] , *Chieh-fang jih-pao,* April 1, 1942, p. 1.

[26]See note 25, above. A translation of a portion of Chang Ting-ch'eng can be found in Warren Kuo, *Analytical History*, vol. 4, p. 576.

[27]In some cases the victims of "thought struggle" meetings were branded "traitors" and "subversives." See "Yen-an fang-chien ching-yen chieh-shao" [Introduction to the experience of Guarding against Traitors in Yenan] , in *Chung-kung tsui-chin tang-nei tou-cheng nei-mu* [Inside View of Recent Chinese Communist Intra-Party Struggles] (n.p., T'ung-i ch'u-pan she, n.d.), p. 77, Yushodo Microfilms, reel 12.

[28]Chang Ting-ch'eng, pp. 8-10, 15.

[29]Harrison, *March*, pp. 338-339.

[30]Including institute head Lo Mai, vice-principal Fan Wen-lan, Ch'en Po-ta, Ai Szu-ch'i, and Chang Yu-hsin.

[31]Merle Goldman, *Literary Dissent in Communist China* (Cambridge, Mass.: Harvard University Press, 1967), pp. 38-42; Warren Kuo, *Analytical History,* vol. 4, pp. 617-618.

[32]See "Yen-an fang-chien," p. 77.

[33]Goldman, p. 50.

[34]*Yen-an ta-hsüeh kai-k'uang*, p. 2.

[35]*K'ang-ta*, pp. 5-8.

[36]On the *cheng-feng* movement at the Central China K'ang-ta branch see Hsüeh Mu-ch'iao, "Cheng-feng hsüeh-hsi tsai K'ang-ta" *[Cheng-feng Study at K'ang-ta]* , *Cheng-feng,* no. 1 (September 1942), pp. 39-44, Yushodo Microfilms, reel 12.

[37]The extent to which the *cheng-feng* movement actually affected the lower levels of the Chinese Communist Party is unclear. James P. Harrison, citing Nationalist sources, estimated that about 30,000 of a total of about 750,000 Communist cadres participated actively in *cheng-feng*. It should also be pointed out that the latter phase of the *cheng-feng* movement

had some features of a purge. In 1943-1944 rectification focused on ferreting out "subversives" and the investigation of cadres' histories. See Harrison, *March*, pp. 337, 340-341. On *cheng-feng* at lower levels of the CCP, see Seybolt, pp. 129-135.

38See Frederick C. Teiwes, "Rectification Campaigns and Purges in Communist China, 1950-1961" (Ph.D. dissertation, Columbia University, 1971), p. 35.

39On the influences of Yenan education on public education in contemporary China see Peter J. Seybolt, *Revolutionary Education in China: Documents and Commentary* (White Plains, N.Y.: International Arts and Sciences Press, 1973).

10 Conclusion

What has been the contribution of leadership training to Chinese Communism? Both before and since 1949 the Chinese Communists have sharpened their "organizational weapon" by assiduously preparing their elites. Recruitment policy and daily exposure to "Party life" have also helped to shape China's vanguard, but formal training remains a vital agent of leadership formation.

Leadership training programs have been most useful in creating settings where the Chinese Communist Party could systematically clarify the relationship between organizational means and ends. They have pinpointed goals, defined standards for attitudes and conduct, and provided ideological justification for personal commitment and sacrifice. The programs combined training in specific work skills with procedures to develop discipline and loyalty. They furnished a common meeting ground for individuals of diverse backgrounds, divided by geography, work assignment, and outlook. The Chinese Communists were more able to deploy and control effectively their elites developed through education than were their political competitors. For the same reason their system of leadership training remains an important instrument of centralization in China today.

Of course, the Chinese Communists have had other options for enforcing compliance. Their leadership policy—in theory—could have placed more emphasis on material rewards or external coercive pressure such as the Soviet system of terror. However, the Chinese Communists did not take power through a rapid seizure of well-developed institutions. Nor did they have access to large material or manpower reserves. To meet the demands of over twenty years of revolution, war, and nation-building, they chose to maximize their organizational resources, strengthening the links within their own chain of command and their leverage over local society. For this type of setting education was probably the least expensive means of upgrading Party leaders' commitment and skills. It was also the most suitable way, in the absence of strong channels of communication and control, to keep in line elites scattered over an extensive area. Formal training programs were particularly helpful in imparting information, ideas, and attitudes to semiliterate peasant cadres moved more by the force of face-to-face interaction than the written word. One should also keep in mind that the Chinese Communists' mass mobilization work involved extensive people-to-people relationships and close contact between leadership elements and the general population. These activities highlighted the role of leadership as meriting special attention.

Leadership training programs did provide some personal reward for participants in the form of heightened status and responsibility within the Chinese Communist movement, and the programs were important mechanisms for elite recruitment and mobility. Their main thrust, however, was not material but in the area of moral commitment. The Chinese Communists were not a well-established social group recruiting adherents with wealth and prestige. They were for most of their history political underdogs striving not merely to seize power but to transform an entire civilization. A dynamic social movement with strong messianic claims cannot survive long unless its members are prepared to struggle and sacrifice. Education was perhaps the best means of imbuing Chinese Communists with the necessary qualities.[1] By deepening the Chinese Communist leaders' understanding of their actions and surroundings it also heightened their belief in the power of their own minds and bodies to bring change. This may be one reason why education is still widely used in China to offset the dampening effects of routinization and material gains.

Leadership training programs have been strong stimulants of Chinese Communist innovations in both organization and ideology. They have helped to define the ideological boundaries of Chinese Communism and have been transmission centers for both "pure" and "practical" ideology.[2] Throughout Chinese Communist history, programs for leadership education have been focal points for adjusting "theory" to organizational "practice." They have been sounding boards for the Chinese Communists' movement-building strategy. The "cadre" concept and "mass line," a distinct Chinese Communist work style to forge links with local society, developed through the Party's search for appropriate leadership forms.

In this capacity Chinese Communist leadership education has both influenced and been influenced by Marxism-Leninism in China. As a system of ideas Marxism-Leninism helped to focus the preparation of Chinese Communist leaders in the direction of highly practical endeavors. It defined a Communist as one whose primary orientation was toward action and the attainment of concrete goals. Its concept of theory, as realized through practice, was a powerful antidote to the ivory tower attitude of learning for learning's sake. Dialectical materialism also directed the education of Chinese Communists to real-life problems in economics, science, technology, and social relationships—the problems of modernization and nation-building. The Marxian stress on class conflict as the driving force of history encouraged Chinese Communists to direct their concern to class issues and to mobilize participation from the masses.

Democratic centralism, which saw organization in military terms, reinforced this activist outlook. However, the Leninist organizational model alone cannot account for the effectiveness of Chinese Communism. Ideology, as Franz Schurmann has pointed out, has been the "cement" of the Chinese Communist organization. In imparting ideology in meaningful terms to leadership cadres, Chinese Communist training programs helped to give organizational life its vitality and meaning.

Without an organic relationship between ideology and organization the Chinese Communists would have lost much of their political impact. The Kuomintang had also borrowed its model of a political party from Lenin. But without reinforcement from a coherent ideology, its Leninist forms atrophied and could no longer promote cohesion and compliance. Unlike the Nationalists, the Chinese Communists formed a political movement that found expression through action rather than words. The ideological boundaries of Chinese Communism were neither narrow nor rigid; they attempted to appeal to broad segments of Chinese society. They were firm enough, however, unlike those of the Kuomintang, to designate specific social and economic programs that were not obscured by lofty but vague statements of intention.[3] Leadership training programs were part of the Chinese Communists' effort to narrow the gap between words and deeds.

Leadership training programs have also generated the basic leadership models—commanders and commissars, mass movement cadres and bureaucrats, technical experts and theorists—for Chinese Communism. These divisions, based on outlook and work activity, have been a source of intraelite tension and have fed into the ongoing "red-expert" controversy. But the training schools do not appear to have nurtured leadership cleavages based on factionalism and personal ties. There is little evidence of *t'ung-hsüeh* behavior in the history of Chinese Communism. The strongest cases for "school tie" factionalism are those of the "Red Whampoa Faction" and the "Twenty-eight Bolsheviks." A group with some links to Lin Piao may have emerged from the first K'ang-ta class.

I would refrain from overdrawing distinctions between those Chinese

Communists trained at specific institutions and those not exposed to formal study. Likewise one cannot posit one personality type for graduates of each kind of leadership training program—or for Chinese Communists as a whole. Nevertheless, each type of leadership training program encouraged a certain outlook and set of concerns that were probably shared by many of its graduates.

Graduates of the Communist University of the Toilers of the East or Sun Yat-sen University, for example, could be expected to be concerned with intra-Party affairs and organizational activities. Alumni of the latter school were more preoccupied with the question of organizational controls than were those of the former. Graduates of both institutions would differ considerably from products of Shanghai University or the Peasant Movement Training Institute, whose students would place priority on person-to-person communications skills and the Party's identification with specific class issues. It is likely that alumni of the Peasant Movement Training Institute would view their work more in terms of local rural issues than of general organizational objectives.

Military-political cadres prepared at schools such as Whampoa, the Red Army School, and the Red Army Academy represent another leadership type. They would be prone to view revolutionary objectives as military objectives and to place priority on military activities. To varying degrees they could be expected to show some sensitivity to political issues and general revolutionary goals. Of course, those trained as commissars and political workers would be more concerned with political questions and the maintenance of political controls within the military than would be the purely military specialists. One should also keep in mind that the content of political education at Whampoa differed from that at pure Chinese Communist schools such as the Red Army School and Red Army Academy. At Whampoa socioeconomic and class issues were less prominent than were discussions of anti-imperialism and the National Revolution. The Red Army School and Red Army Academy placed more emphasis on class issues and distinctions between the Chinese Communist Party and Kuomintang. Besides attempting to develop loyalty to Chinese Communism, the Juichin schools treated the operations of political departments and political commissars more systematically than did Whampoa.

The Red Army School and Red Army Academy, in turn, differed somewhat in the level of the skills they stressed. Both the political class at the Red Army Academy and all classes at the Red Army School appear to have stressed political concerns more than did the high-level command class at the Red Army Academy. The latter focused almost exclusively on purely military skills.

In evaluating K'ang-ta alumni one must distinguish between military cadres and united front mobilization workers. Their social backgrounds and training experiences were quite different. Most military or military-political cadres prepared in the high-level K'ang-ta class or at K'ang-ta's branch schools would be similar in outlook to commander or commissar types from the Red Army Academy. K'ang-ta-trained mobilization workers, on the other hand, developed skills for mass work similar to those of graduates of the Peasant Movement Training Institute, though at K'ang-ta the mobilization objectives were presented in terms of united front and national resistance rather than local or class issues. At specialist schools during the Yenan period (such as the Natural Sciences Research Institute and Yenan University), technical skills had priority over ideological questions, even after successive reorganizations and political campaigns.

Similar divisions based on the skills and outlooks of specialized leadership types operate within the Chinese Communist leadership structure today. While leadership education has tried to minimize these differences through political indoctrination, temporary changes in work assignment, or physical labor, it has continued to serve specialized demands. Today, as modernization calls for even more differentiated leadership, the *cheng-feng* leadership model for all Chinese Communist cadres may be even more difficult to emulate.

Unfortunately, there is little concrete information with which to evaluate the effectiveness of Chinese Communist leadership training programs. Biographical material on most graduates is either scanty or nonexistent, and Communist sources have little to say on this question. Party schools have been considered relatively effective tools for molding Communist cadres because of the schools' isolation from external influences and the intensity of the training experience.[4] Yet it is likely that very few graduates of Chinese Communist study programs corresponded to Communist ideals. If Party leadership training programs tried to measure success in terms of a total transformation of their students, most would be judged failures.

Martin Whyte's recent study of political rituals in China has shown that the "malleability of human nature" depends on a web of factors, including organizational goals, role demands, and the strength of family and friendship group influence.[5] Even the most sophisticated Chinese Communist leadership training programs before 1949 faced too many pressures to create an ideal environment for political transformation. Before 1949 the training institutions had very short periods of matriculation, ranging from several months to two years. They were buffeted by daily crises and numerous, impossible-to-fill demands for qualified leaders. Too much study also threatened to isolate leadership elements from the real world, widening the gaps between theory and practice and between those with and without education.

Most Chinese Communist leadership training programs have aimed at instilling in their students a basic understanding of the goals of Chinese Communism, specialized work skills, discipline and commitment to the Party, and an appreciation of the importance of one's day-to-day tasks for the fate of the revolution. Changing conditions have affected the programs' impact on behavior and attitudes. One measure of their continuing effectiveness has been the fact that the Chinese Communist Party has extended programs for political education to wider segments of its leadership and to the general public.

Leadership training programs have become more systematic in application and scope than they were before 1949; yet one should not conclude that today they are more effective agents of resocialization. Chinese Communist leaders' daily activities have become more routinized since 1949. Leadership training procedures likewise have become regularized "rituals," diluting their capacity to jolt and stimulate. They have remained useful in raising levels of participation and compliance in Chinese Communist organizational life, but have diminishing value as agents of attitude transformation. It is likely that the programs produced more changes in behavior and outlook before 1949, when revolution and war demanded a very high level of commitment and sacrifice. The "steeling" effect of daily challenges reinforced the impact of the training experience. Beginning with the *cheng-feng* movement, the Chinese Communists have tried to offset the regularization of cadres through rectification work, mass campaigns, and physical labor. These activities in effect simulate the pre-1949 revolutionary environment, heightening the effectiveness of training programs and the power of nonmaterial incentives.

The Chinese Communists' concern with leadership training should not be explained only in terms of organizational effectiveness. Their approach to leadership issues has also been influenced by their traditional heritage. During the imperial period the quality of leadership helped offset the technological and organizational limitations of premodern institutions. The education of scholar-officials produced a centralization of culture that in turn supported political centralization. One should also keep in mind that education in traditional China had been the badge of distinction of the elite. The use of education to cultivate a new Communist elite contributed to the legitimation of Chinese Communism in its own eyes and in those of Chinese society at large.

Certain strands of traditional Chinese practices—the idealization of social harmony, hierarchical social relationships, and values from the past; the disdain for those who used their hands to work and fight and those who studied "practical" pursuits—came under fire in Chinese Communist leadership training. Yet Confucianism was not entirely at odds with Chinese Communism and furnished precedents for "investigation and research," "self-cultivation," and self-criticism. The Confucian stress on the responsibility of the elite to come close to those it served is echoed in the "mass line" concept. Traditional Chinese values have glorified "steeling and suffering" and "self-sacrifice" for molding strong character.[6] The Chinese Communists also drew on the antiestablishment heritage of military heroes, popular rebellions, and secret societies to support their struggle against the social order.

This traditional legacy has interacted with the modern sources of influence on Chinese Communism. Both Marxism-Leninism and Confucianism held up one set of beliefs as a form of universal truth which when mastered produces right conduct. Lenin's "vanguard" concept of the Party and the special role of trained leadership in political life could find support in the Confucian belief in societal guidance by the educated.

As with Chinese tradition, the Chinese Communists have treated Soviet models of leadership and organization selectively. The models themselves have changed with time, but have remained influential in Chinese Communist intra-Party life. Soviet influence was strong in the Chinese Communist leadership training system well into the forties, and a large portion of the major figures in the Chinese Communists' educational and propaganda apparatus were trained in Soviet Party schools.

Yet it was in these areas that Chinese Communism made some of its greatest departures from Soviet practices. The Chinese have relied more heavily on education (as opposed to purges or coercion) to mold their Party vanguard. The "cadre" and "mass line" concepts, emphasizing the formal and informal leadership role of cadres to link the Party with grass roots society, was stimulated by Soviet rhetoric but is essentially a Chinese innovation. The history of Chinese Communist leadership education suggests that Soviet models have affected Chinese Communism in complex ways.

The system for training leadership in the Chinese Communist Party before 1945 is the foundation of Party-political education in China today. Its basic features were systematized during the *cheng-feng* movement, synthesizing over twenty years of experimentation. Over time formal study has been extended to wider segments of the Chinese Communist leadership structure. Even low-ranking cadres today engage in *hsüeh-hsi* (study) as an integral part of Party life. Since 1949 many leadership training practices have been applied to political education for the general non-Party public.

Among all of the groups in Chinese society, Chinese Communist Party cadres still receive the most intensive forms of political education. "Political theory study" is part of all cadres' daily routine. Many Chinese Communist cadres also participate in periodic training classes to upgrade the specialized skills related to their work assignments. For higher-level cadres, especially those concerned with political work, the Party operates a system of schools. They range from the high-level cadre school in Peking to schools run by Party committees at the county or municipal level.

The current Chinese Communist system for training military-political cadres is more elaborate today than that of the pre-1949 period. The People's Liberation Army has become more modern and professional, requiring its leaders to develop more technologically sophisticated skills. There are still schools to train commissars and political workers, but most expansion in formal training institutions has occured in the purely military area. Overall, the institutions that prepare commanders and commissars have become more specialized.[7]

After 1949 the modernization of the People's Liberation Army resulted in the growing neglect of political work in the training of both officers and the rank and file. This trend was reversed during the Great Leap Forward; political education received increasing attention during the Socialist Education Campaign and the Cultural Revolution. The current system of political education and political controls in the People's Liberation Army retains the essential features of the political work system developed in the Red Army during the thirties.

Chinese universities and technical colleges are the contemporary equivalents of the schools that prepared the technical specialists of the Yenan period. Like the military schools they, too, have become more differentiated and specialized to fit the needs of a modern society. However, political study remains part of their curricula and can consume a large portion of study time during mass campaigns.

Such shifts in the orientation of leadership education reflect the changing problems confronting Chinese Communism. Before 1949 the Chinese Communists' main concern was building a unified political movement that could bring them to power. Since then it has moved towards modernization and economic development. Leadership training is still an important means of maintaining organizational cohesion and of integrating elites with Chinese society, but it, too, has shifted emphasis to bureaucratic and technical skills. Local Communist cadres, the modern counterpart of the peasant mobilizers, are still trained in communications skills associated with the "mass line." But these skills are no longer applied to guerrilla warfare and base-building but to economic development. The proportion of Chinese Communist cadres with a technical orientation has been on the increase since 1949 and will continue to rise. And in leadership training programs in general, the amount of time devoted to technical problems has increased.

Theoretical study still gives treatment to historical issues, but more and more emphasis is placed on current policy problems. More than before, "theoretical issues" deal with economic development and the relationship of politics to the economy. During the early years of the People's Republic cadre training schools continued to use many of the theoretical materials developed for leadership education before 1945—the *cheng-feng* documents, translations of Marx, Lenin, and Stalin, and the *Short History of the Communist Party of the Soviet Union*. However, since the Great Leap Forward most of the Soviet-authored materials have been replaced by works by Chinese Communist theorists. Other pieces, such as those by Liu Shao-ch'i, have fallen victim to political campaigns. Even the works of Mao Tse-tung continue to rise and fall in popularity.

One area of considerable continuity has been the learning methodology for formal leadership training programs and daily political study. The format for *hsiao-tsu* (small study groups) for both cadres and the general population is very much like that synthesized from leadership training programs during the Yenan period—small group discussions, criticism and self-criticism, livelihood self-examination meetings, note-taking, reports, study outlines, and the application of lessons and study experiences to daily work. Party leaders are still expected to learn from the masses and to participate in physical labor. The function of physical labor, however, has changed somewhat since 1949. During the revolution cadres participated in manual labor or were sent to the countryside primarily to forge ties with the local society. Physical labor still serves this purpose and teaches cadres how to relate to the masses, but it is also used to offset the bureaucratic routinization that has accompanied post-1949 stability and order.

Leadership training has not solved all of the Chinese Communists' problems nor will it make the Chinese Communist Party more monolithic in the future. It will continue to serve as a source of cohesion and commitment; its divisive effects will be contingent on the manner in which the Chinese Communists choose to deal with modernization and their "red-expert" controversy. The central role of leadership training in Chinese political life will continue throughout the forseeable future.

NOTES

[1]The most systematic analysis of the relationship between forms of compliance and organizational goals is Amitai Etzioni's *A Comparative Analysis of Complex Organizations* (New York: The Free Press, 1961).

[2]The distinction between "pure" and "practical" ideology is discussed in Franz Schurmann, *Ideology and Organization in Communist China* (Berkeley and Los Angeles: University of California Press, 1966), chapter 1.

[3]The relationship between the ideology of the National Government and its political effectiveness is discussed in Lary, especially pp. 202-213. See also Eastman, pp. 9-14, on the weak activist orientation of the National Government.

[4]For an evaluation of the role of Party schools in molding Communist Party members, see Meyer, *Molding*, pp. 162-164.

[5]Martin King Whyte, *Small Groups and Political Rituals in China* (Berkeley and Los Angeles: University of California Press, 1974), especially pp. 23-28, 54-55, 93-95, 213-214.

[6]Nivison, "Communist Ethics," pp. 58-61.

[7]For example, by 1962 there were at least seventy-seven military schools offering specialized training. They include institutions such as the General Staff and War College at Nanking, the Military Research Institute in Peking, the Academy of Military Sciences in Peking, the General Military Academy in Harbin, the Advanced Artillery School in Mukden, the Naval Academy, and numerous schools specializing in infantry work, engineering, air defense, armored forces, etc. See Joffe, pp. 21-22.

Bibliography

Almond, Gabriel. *The Appeals of Communism*. Princeton: Princeton University Press, 1954.

Andors, Phyllis. "K'ang-ta University." East Asian Institute Essay, Columbia University, 1972.

Ayers, William. *Chang Chih-tung and Educational Reform in China*. Cambridge, Mass.: Harvard University Press, 1971.

Barnett, A. Doak. *Cadres, Bureaucracy and Political Power in Communist China*. New York: Columbia University Press, 1967.

——————————, ed. *Chinese Communist Politics in Action*. Seattle: University of Washington Press, 1969.

Barrett, David D. *Dixie Mission: The United States Army Observer Group in Yenan, 1944*. Berkeley: Center for Chinese Studies, University of California, 1970.

Bauer, Raymond A. *The New Man in Soviet Psychology*. Cambridge, Mass.: Harvard University Press, 1952.

Beckmann, George M., and Genji, Okubo. *The Japanese Communist Party, 1922-1945*. Stanford, Calif.: Stanford University Press, 1969.

Bernstein, Thomas P. "Leadership and Mass Mobilization in the Soviet and Chinese Collectivisation Campaigns of 1929-30 and 1955-56: A Comparison." *China Quarterly*, no. 31 (July-September 1967), pp. 1-47.

Bialer, Seweryn. "Leninism and the Peasantry in the Russian Revolutions." Paper presented at SEADAG Rural Development Seminar, Savannah, Georgia, June 2-5, 1974.

Biggerstaff, Knight. *The Earliest Modern Government Schools in China*. Ithaca, N.Y.: Cornell University Press, 1961.

Bobrow, Davis Bernard. "Military in the Chinese Communist Movement," part 2, "Political and Economic Uses of the Military." Ph.D. dissertation, Massachusetts Institute of Technology, 1966.

——————————. "The Good Officer: Definition and Training." *China Quarterly*, no. 18 (April-June 1964), pp. 141-152.

199

Bottomore, T.B. *Elites and Society.* Harmondsworth, Middlesex, England: Penguin, 1966.

Brandt, Conrad. "The French Returned Elite in the Chinese Communist Party." In *Symposium on Economic and Social Problems of the Far East,* ed. E.F. Szczepanik. Hong Kong: Hong Kong University Press, 1962.

——————. *Stalin's Failure in China.* New York: W.W. Norton and Co., 1966.

Brandt, Conrad, Schwartz, Benjamin, and Fairbank, John K. *A Documentary History of Chinese Communism.* New York: Atheneum, 1966.

Brzezinksi, Zbigniew K. *Ideology and Power in Soviet Politics.* New York: Frederick A. Praeger, Publisher, 1962.

Bukharin, N. and Preobrazhensky, E. *The ABC of Communism,* ed. E.H. Carr. London: Penguin Books, 1969.

Carlson, Evans Fordyce. *Twin Stars of China.* New York: Dodd, Mead and Co., 1940.

Chang Ch'i-yün. *Tang shih kai-yao* [Outline of Party History]. 2 vols. Taipei: Chung-yang kai-tsao wei-yüan-hui wen-wu kung-ying she, 1951.

Chang Kuo-t'ao. *The Rise of the Chinese Communist Party, 1921-1927.* Lawrence: University Press of Kansas, 1971.

——————. *The Rise of the Chinese Communist Party, 1928-1938.* Lawrence: University Press of Kansas, 1972.

——————. "Wo ti hui-i" [My Recollections]. *Ming-pao,* nos. 5-31 (May 1966-July 1968).

Chang, T.C. *The Farmers Movement in Kwangtung,* trans. Committee on Christianizing Economic Relations. Shanghai: National Christian Council of China, 1928.

Chang Ting-ch'eng. "Cheng-feng tsai Yen-an chung-yang tang-hsiao" [Rectification in the Yenan Central Party School]. In *Hsing-huo liao-yüan* [A Single Spark Can Start a Prairie Fire], vol. 6. Peking: Jen-min wen-hsueh ch'u-pan she, 1962.

Chao Ch'ao-kou, ed. *Yen-an i yüeh* [One Month in Yenan]. Nanking: Hsin-min, 1946.

Ch'en, Jerome. *Mao and the Chinese Revolution.* London: Oxford University Press, 1965.

Ch'en Kung-po. *The Communist Movement in China,* ed. C. Martin Wilbur. New York: Columbia University East Asian Institute, 1960.

Ch'en Kuo-fu. "Chien-chün shih chih i-yeh" [One Page in the History of the Building of the Army]. In *Ko-ming wen-hsien* [Documents on the Revolution], vol. 10. Taipei: Tang shih-hui, 1955.

Ch'en Kuo-hsin. *So-wei pien ch'ü* [The So-called Border Region]. Chungking: Tu-li, 1939.

Ch'en Lien-hua. *K'ang-ta yü ch'ing-nien* [K'ang-ta and Youth]. Chungking, 1940.

Ch'en Shao-yü. "Chi-nien wo-men ti hui-tsu lieh-shih Ma Chün t'ung-chih" [Remembering Our Moslem Martyr Comrade Ma Chün]. In *Lieh-shih chuan* [Biographies of Martyrs], pp. 62-74. Moscow, 1936.

——————. "Tsai Yen-an Chung-kuo nü-tzu ta-hsüeh k'ai hsüeh tien-li ta-hui shang ti pao-kao" [Report on the Opening Ceremonies of Chinese Women's University in Yenan]. In *Kung-fei fan-tung wen-chien hui-pien* [Collection of Documents on the Reactionary Communist Bandits]. Yu-shodo Microfilms, reel 18.

Chen, Theodore Hsi-en. *The Maoist Educational Revolution.* New York: Praeger Publishers, 1974.

Ch'en Yi. "Ch'i-yüeh cheng-tun san-feng ti ch'u-pu tsung-chieh" [Preliminary Conclusion on Rectifying the Three Styles in July]. *Cheng-feng* [Rectification], no. 1 (September 1942), pp. 1-8.

Ch'eng Yüeh-ch'ang. "Nan-mang ti chiao-hui" [An Unforgettable Lesson]. In *Hsing-huo liao-yüan* [A Single Spark Can Start a Prairie Fire], vol. 6, pp. 19-25. Peking: Jen-min wen-hsüeh ch'u-pan she, 1962.

Cherepanov, Alexander Ivanovich. "The Northern Expedition of the National Revolutionary Army of China (Notes of a Military Adviser, 1926-1927), tr. Caroline Rogers and Lydia Holubnychy, ed. Lydia Holubnychy. Unpublished manuscript, East Asian Institute, Columbia University, 1970.

——————————. *Notes of a Military Adviser in China,* trans. Alexandra O. Smith, ed. Harry H. Collier. Taipei: Office of Military History, 1970.

Chesneaux, Jean. *Le Mouvement Ouvrier Chinois de 1919 à 1927.* Paris: Mouton and Co., 1962.

——————————. *Popular Movements and Secret Societies in China, 1840-1950.* Stanford, Calif.: Stanford University Press, 1972.

Chiang-hsi sheng Su-wei-ai cheng-fu hsün (ti-shih ch'u0. "Kuan-yü shih-hsing pao-kao chih-tu" [On Implementing the Report System], April 13, 1933. Shih-sou Collection, reel 10.

Chiang K'ang-hu. *Hsin O yu-chi* [Record of a Journey to New Russia]. 2nd ed. Shanghai: Shang-wu, 1923.

Chieh-fang she, ed. *Cheng-feng wen-hsien* [Rectification Documents]. n.p., Chieh-fang she, June 1943.

"Chien-ku cheng-chih wei-yüan chih-tu pao-kao ta-kang" [Outline of a Report on Strengthening the Political Commissar System], ed. Tsung cheng-chih pu, Kung-nung hung-chün ta-hsüeh hsün-lien pu, January 4, 1934. Shih-sou Collection, reel 8.

Ch'ien Ta-chün. "Huang-p'u chün-hsiao k'ai-ch'uang shih-ch'i chih tsu-chih" [The Organization of the Whampoa Military Academy at the Time of Its Founding. In *Ko-ming wen-hsien* [Documents on the Revolution], vol. 10. Taipei: Tang shih-hui, 1955.

Chōshinten kikanryō kōba kōbashi hensan iinkai, ed. *Chōshinten tetsudō monogatari* [The Story of the Ch'ang hsin-tien Railroad]. n.p., Shin Nippon shuppansha, 1963.

Chow Tse-tsung. *The May Fourth Movement.* Cambridge, Mass.: Harvard University Press, 1960.

Ch'ü Ch'iu-pai. *Ch'ih-tu hsin-shih* [Impressions of the Red Capital]. Shanghai: Shang-wu, 1924.

——————————. "O-hsiang chi-ch'eng" [Record of hungerland]. In *Ch'ü Ch'iu-pai wen-chi* [Collected Writings of Ch'ü Ch'iu-pai], vol. 1. Peking: Jen-min wen-hsüeh ch'u-pan she, 1953.

——————————. "To yü ti hua" [Superfluous Words]. *I-ching,* 3, nos. 25-27 (March 5-April 5, 1937).

Chung-kuo hsien-tai shih tzu-liao ts'ung-k'an. *Ti-i tz'u kuo-nei ko-ming chancheng shih-ch'i ti nung-min yün-tung* [The Peasant Movement in the First Revolutionary Civil War]. Peking: Jen-min ch'u-pan she, 1953.

Chung-kuo hsien-tai shih yen-chiu wei-yüan-hui, ed. *Chung-kuo hsien-tai ko-ming yün-tung shih* [History of the Modern Chinese Revolutionary Movement]. Hong Kong: Hsin min-chu ch'u-pan she, 1947.

Chung-kuo hsin min-chu chu-i ch'ing-nien t'uan, Hua-nan kung-tso wei-yüan-hui. *Hsüeh-hsi Jen Pi-shih t'ung-chih* [Study Comrade Jen Pi-shih]. Canton: Ch'ing-nien ch'u-pan she, 1950.

Chung-kuo jen-min ko-ming chün-shih po-wu-kuan, ed. *K'ang-ta.* Canton, 1966.

Chung-kuo kung-nung hung-chün tsung cheng-chih pu, ed. "Kung-ku hung-chün chung wu-ch'an chieh-chi ling-tao wen-t'i pao-kao ta-kang" [Outline of a Report on Strengthening Proletarian Leadership in the Red Army]. Reprinted by Hung-ta-hsüeh hsün-lien pu, January 4, 1934. Shih-sou Collection, reel 8.

"Chung-kuo Kuo-min-tang chiang-hsi-so k'ai-hsüeh chih" [Record of the Opening of the Chinese Kuomintang Institute]. *Chung-kuo Kuo-min-tang chou-k'an* [Chinese Kuomintang Weekly], no. 28 (June 29, 1924).

Chung-kuo Kuo-min-tang chung-yang chih-hsing wei-yüan-hui hsüan-ch'uan pu. "Chung-kuo Kuo-min-tang chiang-hsi-so t'ung-kao" [Announcement of the Chinese KMT Institute], July 2, 1924. Yokota Collection, Toyo Bunko, Tokyo.

—————————. "Chung-kuo Kuo-min-tang chiang-hsi-so yen-chuang shih-chien piao" [Chart of the Lecture Schedule of the Chinese KMT Institute]. Yokota Collection, Toyo Bunko, Tokyo.

Chung Wei-chien. "Tse-yang shih hung-ta chiao-yü shih-chi hua" [How to Practicalize Education at the Red Army Academy]. *Ko-ming yü chan-cheng* [Revolution and War], no. 2 (April 1934), pp. 36-43.

Chung-yang ko-ming chün-shih wei-yüan-hui t'iao-ling chiao-ts'un pien-chi wei-yüan-hui kei yü hung-chün ta-hsüeh-hsiao kuan-yü shih chan-shu ti fen-tsu shang-k'o ti chih-shih" [Instructions of the Editorial Committee for Prescribed Teaching Materials of the Revolutionary Military Council to the Red Army Academy-School concerning the Divided Group Class on the Implementation of Tactics]. *Ko-ming yü chan-cheng* [Revolution and War], no. 1, pp. 10-13.

Chung-yang kuan-yü kan-pu wen-t'i ti chüeh-i [Resolutions of the Central Committee on the Cadre Question], August 27, 1931. Reprinted in Hsiao Tso-liang, *Power Relations within the Chinese Communist Movement, 1930-1934*, vol. 2, pp. 378-382. Seattle: University of Washington Press, 1967.

"Chung-yang kung-hung chien-ch'a wei-yüan-hui pu-kao ti-i hao, Kuan-yü chien-ch'a wei-yüan-hui ch'uan-tse fan-wei" [On the Jurisdiction of the Inspection Committee], March 28, 1934. Shih-shou Collection, reel 10.

Chung-yang lu-chün chün-kuan hsüeh-hsiao, ed. *Chung-yang lu-chün chün-kuan hsüeh-hsiao shih-kao* [Draft History of the Central Military and Political Academy]. Hangchow, 1936.

"Chung-yang tang-hsiao tsai-tu kai-tsu kao-chün ch'üeh-ting hsin ti chiao-yü chi-hua" [Reorganization of the Central Party School Announces a New Certified Education Plan], *Chieh-fang jih-pao* [Liberation Daily], April 1, 1942, p. 1.

Chung-yang tang-hsiao shih shih-liao pien-tsuan wei-yüan hui, ed. *Huang-p'u chien-chün san-shih nien kai-shu* [General account of thirty years of Whampoa and Building the Army]. Taipei: Chung-yang wen-wu kung-ying she, 1954.

Coleman, James S., ed. *Education and Political Development.* Princeton: Princeton University Press, 1965.

Compton, Boyd. *Mao's China: Party Reform Documents, 1942-1944.* Seattle: University of Washington Press, 1966.

Coser, Lewis. *The Functions of Social Conflict.* New York: The Free Press of Glencoe, 1956.

Degras, Jane, ed. *The Communist International, 1919-1943: Documents.* 2 vols. London: Oxford University Press, 1960.

Deutscher, Isaac. *Stalin: A Political Biography.* New York: Vintage Books, 1960.

Dorrill, William F. "Party Reform and Structural Change under the Returned Student Leadership." Paper presented at Connecticut Symposium on the Chinese Communist Movement, 1921-1971, March 25-27, 1971.

Eastman, Lloyd. *The Abortive Revolution: China under Nationalist Rule 1927-1937.* Cambridge, Mass.: Harvard University Press, 1974.

Elwood, Ralph Carter. "Lenin and the Social Democratic Schools for Underground Party Workers, 1909-11." *Political Science Quarterly,* vol. 81, no. 3 (September 1966), pp. 370-391.

Epstein, Israel. *The Unfinished Revolution in China.* Boston: Little, Brown and Co., 1947.

Erickson, John. *The Soviet High Command: A Military-Political History 1918-1941.* London: Macmillan and Co., 1962.

Eto Shinkichi. "Hai-lu-feng—The First Chinese Soviet Government." *China Quarterly,* no. 8 (October-December 1961), pp. 161-183, and no. 9 (January-March 1962), pp. 149-181.

Etzioni, Amitai. *A Comparative Analysis of Complex Organizations.* New York: The Free Press, 1961.

Eudin, Xenia J. and North, Robert C. *Soviet Russia and the East: 1920-1927.* Stanford, Calif.: Stanford University Press, 1957.

"Fa-chan tang ho kai-tsao tang ti kung-tso ta-kang" [Outline of Work on Developing and Reforming the Party], Central Bureau of Soviet Areas, June 12, 1932. Reprinted in Hsiao Tso-liang, *Power Relations within the Chinese Communist Movement, 1930-1934,* vol. 2. Seattle: University of Washington Press, 1967.

Fainsod, Merle. *How Russia is Ruled.* Cambridge, Mass.: Harvard University Press, 1965.

Feng Ting. "Tang-hsiao cheng-feng" [*Cheng-feng* in the Party School], *Cheng-feng,* no. 1 (September 1942), pp. 25-38. Yushodo Microfilms, reel 12.

Fitzpatrick, Sheila. *The Commissariat of Enlightenment: Soviet Organization of Education and the Arts under Lunacharsky, October 1917-1921.* London: Cambridge University Press, 1970.

Forman, Harrison. *Report from Red China.* New York: Henry Holt and Co., 1945.

Fraser, Stewart. *Chinese Communist Education—Records of the First Decade.* Nashville: Vanderbilt University Press, 1965.

Garder, Michel. *A History of the Soviet Red Army.* London: Pall Mall Press, 1966.

Garthoff, Raymond L. *How Russia Makes War: Soviet Military Doctrine.* London: George Allen and Unwin, 1954.

Gasster, Michael. *Chinese Intellectuals and the Revolution of 1911.* Seattle: University of Washington Press, 1969.

Gelder, Stuart. *The Chinese Communists.* London: Victor Gollancz, 1946.

Gillin, Donald. *Warlord: Yen Hsi-shan in Shansi Province, 1911-1949.* Princeton: Princeton University Press, 1967.

Gitlow, Benjamin. *The Whole of Their Lives.* New York: Charles Scribner's Sons, 1948.

Gittings, John. *The Role of the Chinese Army.* New York: Oxford University Press, 1967.

Goldman, Merle. *Literary Dissent in Communist China.* Cambridge, Mass.: Harvard University Press, 1967.

Gourlay, Walter E. "The Chinese Communist Cadre: Key to Political Control." Harvard University Russian Research Center, February 1952.

Graham, Loren R. *Science and Philosophy in the Soviet Union.* New York: Alfred A. Knopf, 1972.

Gray, Jack, ed. *Modern China's Search for a Political Form.* London: Oxford University Press, 1969.

Griffith, Samuel B. *The Chinese People's Liberation Army.* New York: McGraw-Hill, 1967.

Guillermaz, Jacques. *A History of the Chinese Communist Party, 1921-1949,* trans. Anne Destenay. New York: Random House, 1972.

Hackett, Roger F. "Chinese Students in Japan, 1900-1910," in *Papers on China,* vol. 3. Cambridge, Mass.: Harvard University Committee on International and Regional Studies, 1949.

Haimson, Leopold H. *The Russian Marxists and the Origins of Bolshevism.* Boston: Beacon Press, 1955.

Hao-hsi-shih ta-hsüeh hsün-lien pu, ed. "Hung-chün ta-hsüeh shang-chi cheng-chih k'o cheng-chih kung-tso chiang-shou ta-kang" [Lecture Outline of Political Work for the High-level Political Class of the Red Army Academy], November 25, 1933. Shih-sou Collection, reel 8.

Harrell, Paula Sigrid. "The Years of the Young Radicals: The Chinese Students in Japan, 1900-1905." Ph.D. dissertation, Columbia University, 1970.

Harrison, James P. *The Communists and Chinese Peasant Rebellions.* New York: Atheneum, 1969.

——————. *The Long March to Power: A Political History of the Chinese Communist Party.* New York: Praeger Publishers, 1973.

Hatano Kenichi, ed. *Chūgoku kyōsantō shi* [History of the Chinese Communist Party]. 7 vols. Tokyo: Jiji Press, 1961.

——————. "Shū Onrai den" [Biography of Chou En-lai]. *Kaizō,* vol. 19, no. 7 (July 1937), pp. 86-91.

History of the Communist Party of the Soviet Union (Bolsheviks): Short Course ed. Commission of the Central Committee of the CPSU. New York: International Publishers, 1939.

Ho Ch'ang-kung. *Ch'in-kung chien-hsüeh sheng-huo hui-i* [Recollections of Diligent Work and Frugal Study Life]. Peking: Kung-jen ch'u-pan she, 1958.

Ho Kan-chih. *A History of the Modern Chinese Revolution.* Peking: Foreign Language Press, 1959.

Ho Ping-ti and Tang Tsou, ed. *China in Crisis.* 3 vols. Chicago: University of Chicago Press, 1968.

Hofheinz, Roy Mark, Jr. "The Peasant Movement and Rural Revolution: Chinese Communists in the Countryside (1923-1927)." Ph.D. dissertation, Harvard University, 1966.

Holubnychy, Vsevolod. "Mao Tse-tung's Materialistic Dialectics." *China Quarterly,* no. 19 (July-September 1964), pp. 3-37.

Hsi-men Chung-hua. "Chung-kuo liu-O hsüeh-sheng cheng-chih tou-cheng shih" [History of Political Struggles of the Chinese Students in Russia]. *Chung-kuo yü Su-O,* 1933, pp. 156-164.

Hsia, Tsi-an. *The Gate of Darkness.* Seattle: University of Washington Press, 1968.

Hsiao San. *Mao Tse-tung t'ung-chih ti ch'ing-shao-nien shih-tai* [The Childhood and Youth of Comrade Mao Tse-tung]. n.p., Hsin Hua shu-tien, 1949.

Hsiao Tso-liang. *The Land Revolution in China, 1930-1934.* Seattle: University of Washington Press, 1969.

——————————. *Power Relations within the Chinese Communist Movement, 1930-1934.* 2 vols. Seattle: University of Washington Press, 1961 and 1967.

Hsiao Tu. "Yü Yu-jen yü Shang-hai ta-hsüeh" [Yü Yu-jen and Shanghai University]. In *Hsien-tai shih-liao,* vol. 1, pp. 285-295. n.p., Hai-t'ien ch'u-pan she, 1933.

Hsieh Chien-ying. "Kao-chu Mao Tse-tung ssu-hsiang wei-ta hung-ch'i i K'ang-ta wei pang-yang pan K'ang-ta shih ti hsüeh-hsiao" [Raise High the Great Red Flag of Mao Tse-tung's Thought and Take K'ang-tal as an Example to Run K'ang-tal type Schools], July 1965. *Fei-ch'ing jih-pao* [Bandit Situation Daily], vol. 55.

Hsieh Chung-liang. "Tsai hung-hsiao hsüeh kung-ping" [Studying Engineering at the Red School]. In *Hsing-huo liao-yüan,* vol. 2, pp. 161-165. Peking: Jen-min wen-hsüeh ch'u-pan she, 1962.

"Hsin ti chiao-yü fang-chen hsia chung-yang tang-hsiao ch'e-ti kai-tsu" [Thoroughly Reorganize the Central Party School under a New Educational Line]. *Chieh-fang jih-pao,* January 28, 1942.

Hsiung, James Chieh. *Ideology and Practice.* New York: Praeger Publishers, 1970.

Hsü Kai-yu. *Chou En-lai: China's Gray Eminence.* Garden City, New York: Doubleday and Co., 1968.

Hsü Kwan-san. "Liu Shao-ch'i and Mao Tse-tung (1922-1947)," trans. Douglas G. Spelman. *Chinese Law and Government,* vol. 3, nos. 2-3 (Summer-Fall 1970), pp. 206-250.

Hsü Meng-ch'iu. "I-yüeh lai ti hung-chün ta-hsüeh" [The Past Month at the Red Army Academy]. *Ko-ming yü chan-cheng,* no. 2 (April 1934), pp. 28-35.

Hsü Shu-huai. *K'ang-ta kuei-lai* [Return from K'ang-ta]. Hankow: Ch'iu-shih ch'u-pan she, 1939.

Hsüeh, Chün-tu. *The Chinese Communist Movement, 1921-1937.* Stanford University: The Hoover Institution on War, Revolution and Peace, 1960.

——————————. *The Chinese Communist Movement, 1937-1949.* Stanford University: The Hoover Institution on War, Revolution and Peace, 1962.

——————————. *Revolutionary Leaders of Modern China.* New York: Oxford University Press, 1971.

Hsüeh Mu-ch'iao. "Cheng-feng hsüeh-hsi tsai K'ang-ta" [*Cheng-feng* Study at K'ang-ta], *Cheng-feng,* no. 1 (September 1942), pp. 39-44. Yushodo Microfilms, reel 12.

Hsüeh Mu-ch'iao. *Chung-kuo ko-ming chi-pen wen-t'i* [Basic Problems of the Chinese Revolution]. Hong Kong: Nan-hai ch'u-pan she, 1948.

Huang Chen-hsia. *Chung-kung chün-jen chih* [Records of Chinese Communist Officers].Hong Kong: Research Institute of Contemporary History, 1968.

"Hui-i Hung-ta, K'ang-ta yü Chün-ta" [Recollections of the Red Academy, K'ang-ta and the Military Academy]. *Kuang-ming jih-pao*, September 15-18, 1957.

Hu-nan sheng-chih pien-tsuan wei-yüan-hui, ed. *Hu-nan sheng-chih*:I: *Hu-nan chin-pai nien ta-shih shu* [Annals of Hunan Province:I: Account of Important Events in Hunan for the Last Hundred Years]. Changsha: Hu-nan jen-min ch'u-pan she, 1959.

"Hung-chün hsüeh-hsiao chih tsu-chih" [The Organization of the Red Army School], June 30, 1931. In *Ch'ih-fei chi-mi wen-chien hui-pien*, vol. 2. Shih sou Collection, reel 20.

Hung-hsiao tou-cheng [Struggle in the Red School], no. 5 (July 8, 1933), ed. Kung-nung hung-chün hsüeh-hsiao cheng-chih pu. Shih-sou Collection, reel 1.

Hung I. "Chia-chin kai-tsao Su-wei-ai ch'ü-yü nei wo-men tang ti tsu-chih" [Stepping up the Reorganization of Our Party in the Soviet Areas], March 8, 1931. Reprinted in Hsiao Tso-liang, vol. 2, pp. 349-351.

Huntington, Samuel P. *Political Order in Changing Societies*. New Haven: Yale University Press, 1968.

I Shih-fang. "Chung-kuo liu-O hsüeh-sheng cheng-chih tou-cheng chi" [Record of the Political Struggles of Chinese Students in Russia]. *Chung-kuo yü Su-O,* 1, no. 4 (April 10,1933).

"Instruction on How to Carry on Political Education of Officers," early 1926. British Foreign Office Public Records Office, Document Z 50 FO 8322/3241/40, Annex 3.

Isaacs, Harold. *The Tragedy of the Chinese Revolution*. 2nd rev. ed. New York: Atheneum, 1966.

Jackson, George D., Jr. *Comintern and Peasant in Eastern Europe, 1919-1930.* New York: Columbia University Press, 1966.

Joffe, Ellis. "China's Military Elites." *China Quarterly*, no. 62 (June 1975), pp. 310-317.

——————. *Party and Army: Professionalism and Political Control in the Chinese Officer Corps, 1949-1964.* Cambridge, Mass.: Harvard University East Asian Research Center, 1965.

Johnson, Chalmers, ed. *Ideology and Politics in Contemporary China.* Seattle: University of Washington Press, 1973.

——————. *Peasant Nationalism and Communist Power.* Stanford, Calif.: Stanford University Press, 1962.

——————. *Revolutionary Change.* Boston: Little, Brown and Co., 1966.

Kagan, Richard Clark. "The Chinese Trotskyist Movement and Ch'en Tu-hsiu: Culture, Revolution and Polity," Ph.D. dissertation, University of Pennsylvania, 1969.

"Kan-pu cheng-chih chiao-yü chi-hua" [Plan for Political Education of Cadres], 1932(?). Shih-sou Collection, reel 8.

"Kao-chu Mao Tse-tung ssu-hsiang wei-ta hung-ch'i" [Raise High the Great Red Flag of Mao Tse-tung's Thought]. *Kuang-ming jih-pao*, July 31, 1966.

Kao-pu-tse-po. "I nung-min yün-tung chiang-hsi-so ti hsüeh-hsi sheng-huo"

[Recollections of Study Life at the Peasant Movement Training Institute]. *Min-tsu t'uan-chieh,* no. 7 (July 1962), pp. 7-10.

Kao, Ying-mao, Chancellor, Paul M., Ginsburg, Philip E., and Perrolle, Pierre M. *The Political Work System of the Chinese Communist Military: Analysis and Documents.* Providence, R.I.: Brown University East Asia Language and Area Center, 1971.

Katz, Zev. "Party-Political Education in Soviet Russia." Ph.D. dissertation, University of London, 1957.

Kazama, Jokichi. *Mossukō kyōsan daigaku no omoide* [Recollections of Communist University in Moscow]. Tokyo: Sangen sha, 1949.

Kim, Ilpyong J. *The Politics of Chinese Communism: Kiangsi under the Soviets.* Berkeley and Los Angeles: University of California Press, 1973.

Klein, Donald W. and Clark, Anne B. *Biographic Dictionary of Chinese Communism, 1921-1965.* 2 vols. Cambridge, Mass.: Harvard University Press, 1971.

Kuhn, Philip. *Rebellion and Its Enemies in Late Imperial China.* Cambridge, Mass.: Harvard University Press, 1970.

Kung Ch'u. *Wo yü hung-chün* [I and the Red Army]. Hong Kong: Nan-feng ch'u-pan she, 1955.

"Kung-nung hung-chün hsüeh-hsiao ti-szu ch'i pi-ye hsüeh-sheng chung ch'uan-t'i tang-yüan chi lien i-chi i-shang kan-pu ti tang-yüan ta-hui chüeh-i" [Resolutions of the Enlarged Meeting of Party Members and Corps Members of the Fourth Graduating Class of the Worker-Peasant Red Army School and Cadres above the Company Level]. *Tou-cheng,* no. 3 (February 16, 1933).

Kung-nung hung-chün ta-hsüeh, ed. "Cheng-chih kung-tso chiang-i" [Lectures on Political Work], June 6, 1934. Shih-sou Collection, reel 8.

Kung-nung hung-chün ta-hsüeh cheng-chih ch'u, ed. "Chung-kuo ko-ming wen-t'i cheng-chih ch'ang-shih chiang-i" [Lectures on Political Common Knowledge of Problems of the Chinese Revolution], March 28, 1934. Shih-sou Collection, reel 8.

Kung-nung hung-chün ta-hsüeh hsün-lien pu, ed. "Chan-lüeh chiang-i" [Lectures on Strategy], January 16, 1934. Shih-sou Collection, reel 8.

Kuo, Warren. *Analytical History of the Chinese Communist Party.* 4 vols. Taipei: Institute of International Relations, 1968-1971.

_____. "The CCP Pledge of Allegiance to the Kuomintang." *Issues and Studies,* 4, no. 11 (August 1968), pp. 36-50, and no. 12 (September 1968), pp. 31-49.

_____. "The Zigzag Flight of Red Army Troops." *Issues and Studies,* 4, no. 10 (July 1968), pp. 36-56.

Kusano Fumio, *Shina henku no kenkyū* [Study of the Chinese Border Regions]. Tokyo: Kokumin sha, 1944.

Landis, Richard Brian. "Institutional Trends at the Whampoa Military School: 1924-1926," Ph.D. dissertation, University of Washington, 1969.

_____. "The Origins of Whampoa Graduates Who Served in the Northern Expedition." *Studies on Asia,* University of Washington Far Eastern and Russian Institute Modern Chinese History Project Reprint Series, no. 9 (1964).

Lary, Diana. *Region and Nation: The Kwangsi Clique in Chinese Politics, 1925-1937.* London: Cambridge University Press, 1974.

Lenin, V.I. *Selected Works.* Moscow: Progress Publishers, 1968.

Leonhard, Wolfgang. *Child of the Revolution,* trans. C.M. Woodhouse. Chicago: Henry Regnery Co., 1958.

Lerner, Warren. *Karl Radek: The Last Internationalist.* Stanford, Calif.: Stanford University Press, 1970.

Lewis, John Wilson. "Leader, Commissar and Bureaucrat: The Chinese Political System in the Last Days of the Revolution." In *China in Crisis,* ed. Ping-ti Ho and Tang Tsou, vol. 1, book 2. Chicago: University of Chicago Press, 1968.

──────────. *Leadership in Communist China.* Ithaca: Cornell University Press, 1963.

──────────. *Party Leadership and Revolutionary Power in China.* London: Cambridge University Press, 1970.

──────────. *Peasant Rebellion and Communist Revolution in Asia.* Stanford, Calif.: Stanford University Press, 1974.

Li Ang. *Hung-se wu-t'ai* [The Red Stage]. Hong Kong: Sheng-li ch'u-pan she, 1941.

Li, Bernadette Yu-ning. "A Biography of Ch'ü Ch'iu-pai: From Youth to Party Leadership (1898-1928)." Ph.D. dissertation, Columbia University, 1967.

──────────. *The Introduction of Socialism to China.* New York: Columbia University Press, 1971.

Li Jui, *Mao Tse-tung t'ung-chih ti ch'u-ch'i ko-ming huo-tung* [Comrade Mao Tse-tung's Early Revolutionary Activities]. Peking: Chung-kuo ch'ing-nien ch'u-pan she, 1957.

Li Li-san. "Chi-nien Ts'ai Ho-sen t'ung-chih" [Remembering Comrade Ts'ai Ho-sen]. In *Hung-ch'i p'iao-p'iao,* , vol. 1, pp. 46-50. Peking, 1957.

──────────. "I Hsiang Ching-yü t'ung-chih" [Recalling Comrade Hsiang Ching-yü]. In *Hung-ch'i p'iao-p'iao,* vol. 5. Peking, 1957.

Li Yün-han. *Tsung jung-kung tao ch'ing-tang* [From Admitting the Communists to the Purification of the Party]. 2 vols. Taipei, 1966.

Liao Yüan, ed. *Hua-nan ko-ming shih-chi* [Historical Records of the Revolution in South China]. Canton: Hua-nan jen-min ch'u-pan she, 1951.

Lieberthal, Kenneth Guy. "Reconstruction and Revolution in a Chinese City: The Case of Tientsin." Ph.D. dissertation, Columbia University, 1972.

Lifton, Robert Jay. *Thought Reform and the Psychology of Totalism.* New York: W.W. Norton and Co., 1963.

Lindbeck, John M.H., ed. *China: Management of a Revolutionary Society.* Seattle: University of Washington Press, 1971.

Lindsay, Michael. *Notes on Educational Problems in Communist China, 1941-1947.* New York: Institute of Pacific Relations, 1950.

Liu, Alan P.L. *Communications and National Integration in China.* Berkeley and Los Angeles: University of California Press, 1971.

Liu, F.F. *A Military History of Modern China, 1924-1949.* Princeton: Princeton University Press, 1956.

Liu Hsüeh-hai. *I-nien lai Shen-pei kung-tang chih tung-t'ai* [The Situation of the Communist Party for the Past Year in North Shensi]. n.p., 1942.

Liu Tao-sheng. "Sen-lin chung ti hung-chün ta-hsüeh [The Red Army Academy In the Forest]. *Hung-ch'i p'iao-p'iao,* vol. 3, pp. 45-50. Peking, 1957.

Lo Ch'i-yüan. "Pen pu i-nien lai kung-tso pao-kao kai-yao" [Outline of a Report on the Work of our Bureau during the Past Year], *Chung-kuo nung-min,* no. 2 (February 1, 1926), pp. 147-207.

Lo Fu. "Kuan-yü hsin ti ling-tao fang-shih" [On the New Method of Leadership]. *Tou-cheng,* no. 2 (February 4, 1933), no. 5 (March 15, 1933), no. 20 (August 5, 1933) and no. 28 (September 30, 1933).

——————————. "Lun ch'ing-nien ti hsiu-yang" [On the Cultivation of Youth], April 12, 1938. Yushodo Microfilms, reel 19.

Lo Jui-ch'ing. "Kuan-yü min-chu wen-t'i" [On the Question of Democracy], July 16, 1938. Yoshodo Microfilms, reel 19.

Lo Jui-ch'ing and Ch'eng Fang-wu, ed. *Shen-pei ti ch'ing-nien hsüeh-sheng sheng-huo* [Study Life of Young Students in North Shensi]. Shanghai: Chien-she ch'u-pan she, 1940.

Lo Mai. "Shen-pei kung-hsüeh fen-hsiao ti ch'eng-chiu" [Attainments of the Branch School of the North Shensi Public School]. *Chieh-fang,* no. 54 (October 15, 1938), pp. 16-20.

Lowe, Donald M. *The Function of "China" in Marx, Lenin, and Mao.* Berkeley and Los Angeles: University of California Press, 1966.

Lu P'ing, ed. *Sheng-huo tsai Yen-an* [Life in Yenan]. n.p., 1938.

"Lun hsün-lien kan-pu wen-t'i" [On the Problem of Cadre Training], *Hung-ch'i chou-pao,* no. 59 (August, 1933).

Ma Chi-ling. *Shen-pei niao-k'ao* [A Bird's Eye View of North Shensi]. Chengtu: Cheng-chih, 1941.

Ma-k'o-ssu kung-ch'an chu-i hsüeh-hsiao, ed. *Chung-kuo ko-ming chi-pen wen-t'i* [Basic Problems of the Chinese Revolution]. Sha-chou-pa, March 18, 1934. Shih-sou Collection, reel 10.

Ma Kuo-ch'ang. *Yen-an ch'iu hsüeh chi* [Record of Seeking Study in Yenan]. n.p., Hu-pei jen-min ch'u-pan she, 1959.

MacFarquhar, Roderick L. "The Whampoa Military Academy." In *Papers on China,* no. 9. Cambridge, Mass.: Harvard University East Asia Program of the Committee on Regional Studies, 1955.

Mao Szu-ch'eng. *Min-kuo shih-wu nien i-ch'ien ti Chiang chieh-shih hsien-sheng* [Mr. Chiang Kai-shek before 1926]. Hong Kong: Lung-men shu-tien, 1965.

Mao Tse-tung. *Selected Works of Mao Tse-tung.* 4 vols. Peking: Foreign Languages Press, 1965-67.

Mao Tse-tung chi [The Works of Mao Tse-tung], ed. Takenchi Minoru. Tokyo, 1970.

Marx, Karl and Engels, Friedrich. *Basic Writings on Politics and Philosophy,* ed. Louis Feuer. Garden City, New York: Doubleday Anchor Books, 1959.

Meisner, Maurice. "Leninism and Maoism: Some Populist Perspectives on Marxism-Leninism in China." *China Quarterly,* no. 45 (January-March 1971), pp. 2-36.

——————————. *Li Ta-chao and the Origins of Chinese Marxism.* Cambridge, Mass.: Harvard University Press, 1967.

Meyer, Alfred G. *Leninism.* Cambridge, Mass.: Harvard University Press, 1957.

——————————. *Marxism: The Unity of Theory and Practice.* Cambridge, Mass.: Harvard University Press, 1954.

Meyer, Frank S. *The Moulding of Communists: The Training of the Communist Cadre.* New York: Harcourt, Brace and Co., 1961.

Mickiewicz, Ellen Propper. *Soviet Political Schools.* New Haven: Yale University Press, 1967.

Mo Wen-hua. "Hung-chün ta-hsüeh sheng-huo jih-chi (1936)" [Diary of Life at the Red Army Academy, 1936]. In *Hsing-huo liao-yüan,* vol. 4, pp. 145-150. Peking: Jen-min wen-hsüeh ch'u-pan she, 1962.

"Mu-ch'ien tang tsu-chih shang ti chung-hsin kung-tso" [Central Work for the Present Party Organization]. *Tou-cheng,* no. 5 (March 15, 1933).

Niu K'o-lun. "The Smelting Furnace." (*Jen-min jih-pao,* August 23, 1965). Translated in *Current Background,* no. 777, (November 18, 1965), pp. 30-35.

Nivison, David. "Communist Ethics and Chinese Tradition." *Journal of Asian Studies,* vol. 16, no. 1 (November 1956), pp. 51-74.

Nollau, Gunther. *International Communism and World Revolution.* New York: Frederick A. Praeger, 1961.

North, Robert C. *Moscow and the Chinese Communists.* Stanford, Calif.: Stanford University Press, 1963.

North, Robert C. with Ithiel de Sola Pool. *Kuomintang and Chinese Communist Elites.* Stanford, Calif.: Stanford University Press, 1952.

"Nung-min yün-tung chiang-hsi-so tsu-chih chien-chang" [Simple Regulations for the Organization of the Peasant Movement Training Institute]. *Chung-kuo Kuo-min-tang chou-k'an,* no. 29 (June 30, 1924).

"Nung-min yün-tung ti-i pu shih-shih fang-an" [Plan for a First Step in the Peasant Movement]. *Chung-kuo Kuo-min-tang chou-k'an,* no. 29 (June 30, 1924).

Ozaki Hotsumi. "Shū Onrai no chii" [The Position of Chou En-lai], *Chūō kōron,* vol. 52, no. 12 (November 1937), pp. 97-105.

Pipes, Richard. *Social Democracy and the St. Petersburg Labor Movement, 1885-1897.* Cambridge, Mass.: Harvard University Press, 1963.

Po Ku. *Lien kung-tang shih yü Lieh-ning chu-i* [The History of the Communist Party of the Soviet Union and Leninism]. Ma-k'o-ssu kung-ch'an-chu-i chiao-yü ch'u, July 18, 1933. Reprinted by Kung-nung hung-chün hsüeh-hsiao, August 15, 1933. Shih-sou Collection, reel 12.

Po Ku and Lo Fu, ed. *Min-chung ko-ming yü min-chung cheng-ch'üan* [Mass Revolution and Mass Political Power]. n.p., Ch'u-pan wei-yüan-hui, 1932.

"Political Lessons for Enlisted Personnel," late 1925. British Foreign Office Public Records Office, Peking Raid Document Z 50 FO F8322/3241/10 Annex 2.

"Political Work in the National Revolutionary Army," March 15, 1926(?). British Foreign Office Public Records Office, Document Z 50 FO F8322/3241/10.

Powell, Ralph L. *The Rise of Chinese Military Power, 1895-1913.* Princeton: Princeton University Press, 1955.

"Pu-er-sai-wei-k'o ti kung-tso fang-fa" [Bolshevik Work Methods]. *Tou-cheng,* no. 4 (March 5, 1933).

Rankin, Mary Backus. *Early Chinese Revolutionaries: Radical Intellectuals in Shanghai and Chekiang, 1902-1911.* Cambridge, Mass.: Harvard University Press, 1971.

Rigby, T.H. *Communist Party Membership in the USSR, 1917-1967.* Princeton: Princeton University Press, 1968.

Rue, John E. *Mao Tse-tung in Opposition, 1927-1935.* Stanford, Calif.: Stanford University Press, 1966.

Scalapino, Robert A., ed. *Elites in the People's Republic of China.* Seattle: University of Washington Press, 1972.

—————————. *The Japanese Communist Movement, 1920-1966.* Berkeley and Los Angeles: University of California Press, 1967.

Scalapino, Robert A. and Yu, George T. *The Chinese Anarchist Movement.* Berkeley: University of California, Center for Chinese Studies, 1961.

Schapiro, Leonard. *The Communist Party of the Soviet Union.* New York: Vintage Books, 1960.

Schram, Stuart. *Mao Tse-tung.* Baltimore: Penguin Books, 1967.

—————————. *The Political Thought of Mao Tse-tung.* New York: Praeger Publishers, 1963.

Schram, Stuart and d'Encausse, Helene Carrere. *Marxism and Asia.* London: Allen Lane, 1969.

Schurmann, Franz. *Ideology and Organization in Communist China.* Berkeley and Los Angeles: University of California Press, 1966.

Schwartz, Benjamin I. *Chinese Communism and the Rise of Mao.* Cambridge, Mass.: Harvard University Press, 1951.

—————————. "The Legend of the 'Legend of Maosim'." *China Quarterly,* no. 2 (April-June 1960), pp. 35-42.

Selden, Mark. *The Yenan Way in Revolutionary China.* Cambridge, Mass.: Harvard University Press, 1971.

Selznick, Philip. *The Organizational Weapon: A Study of Bolshevik Strategy and Tactics.* New York: McGraw-Hill Book Co., 1952.

Seybolt, Peter J. *Revolutionary Education in China: Documents and Commentary.* White Plains, N.Y.: International Arts and Sciences Press, 1973.

—————————. "Yenan Education and the Chinese Revolution, 1937-1945." Ph.D. dissertation, Harvard University, 1969.

Shang K'un. "Chuan-pien wo-men ti hsüan-ch'uan ku-tung kung-tso" [Transform Our Propaganda and Agitation Work] *Tou-cheng,* no. 2 (February 4, 1933).

Shao Shih-p'ing. "Shen-pei kung-hsüeh shih-shih kuo-fang chiao-yü ti ching-yen yü chiao-hsün" [Experience and Lesson of North Shensi Public School Implementing National Defense Education]. *Chieh-fang,* no. 37 (May 6, 1938), pp. 11-14.

Sheng Yüeh. *Sun Yat-sen University in Moscow and the Chinese Revolution: A Personal Account.* Lawrence, Kansas: University of Kansas Center for East Asian Studies, 1971.

Siao Yu. *Mao Tse-tung and I Were Beggars.* Syracuse, New York: Syracuse University Press, 1959.

Smedley, Agnes. *Battle Hymn of China.* New York: Alfred A. Knopf, 1943.

—————————. *China's Red Army Marches.* London: Lawrence and Wishart, 1936.

—————————. *The Great Road: The Life and Times of Chu Teh.* New York: Monthly Review Press, 1956.

Smith, Henry DeWitt, II. *Japan's First Student Radicals.* Cambridge, Mass.: Harvard University Press, 1972.

Snow, Edgar. *Journey to the Beginning.* London: Victor Gollancz, 1960.
—————. *Random Notes on Red China (1936-1945).* Cambridge,
Mass.: Harvard University Press, 1957.
—————. *Red Star over China.* New York: Grove Press, 1961.
—————. *Scorched Earth.* 2 vols. London: Victor Gollancz, 1941.
Solomon, Richard H. *Mao's Revolution and the Chinese Political Culture.*
Berkeley and Los Angeles: University of California Press, 1971.
Ssu Ma-lu. Ch'ü Ch'iu-pai chuan [Biography of Ch'ü Ch'iu-pai]. Hong Kong:
Tzu-lien ch'u-pan she, 1962.
—————.*Tou-cheng shih-pa nien* [Struggle for Eighteen Years]. Hong
Kong: Ya-chou ch'u-pan she, 1952.
Stalin, Joseph. *Foundations of Leninism.* New York: International Publishers,
1939.
—————. *Problems of Leninism.* Moscow: Foreign Languages
Publishing House, 1953.
—————. *Works.* Moscow: Foreign Languages Publishing House, 1955.
Stein, Gunther. *The Challenge of Red China.* New York: Whittlesey House, 1945.
"Su-ch'ü tang ti-i tz'u tai-piao ta-hui t'ung-kuo tang ti chien-she wen-t'i chüeh-
i-an" [Resolution of the First Party Congress in the Soviet areas on the
Reconstruction of the Party], November 1931. Reprinted in Hsiao Tso-
liang, *Power Relations within the Chinese Communist Movement,
1930-1934,* vol. 2, pp. 397-404. Seattle: University of Washington Press,
1967.
Swarup, Shanti. *A Study of the Chinese Communist Movement.* London:
Oxford University Press, 1966.
Swearingen, Rodger and Langer, Paul. *Red Flag in Japan.* Cambridge, Mass.:
Harvard University Press, 1952.
Ta shih-tai ti yung-lu [Crucible of a Great Period]. n.p., Hua-tung chün-shih
cheng-chih ta-hsüeh cheng-chih pu, 1950.
Tan, Chester C. *Chinese Political Thought in the Twentieth Century.* Garden
City, New York: Doubleday Anchor Books, 1971.
"Tang-hsiao hung-chün pan cheng-chih kung-tso chiang-i" [Lectures on Political
Work for the Red Army Class of the Party School], 1931(?). Shih-sou
Collection, reel 8.
Tang-hsiao hung-chün pan chi hung-chün cheng-chih ying, ed. "Cheng-chih
kung-tso chiang-i" [Lectures on Political Work], Shih-sou Collection, reel 8.
Tang, Peter S.H. "The Training of Party Cadres in Communist China." Research
Institute on the Sino-Soviet Bloc, Washington, D.C., 1961.
"Tang ti chien-she chiang-shou t'i-kang" [Lecture Outline on the Reconstruction
of the Party], 1931. Shih-sou Collection, reel 2.
Teiwes, Frederick C. "Rectification Campaigns and Purges in Communist China,
1950-61," Ph.D. dissertation, Columbia University, 1971.
Teng Wen-i. *Huang-p'u ching-shen chi ch'i chiao-yü* [The Whampoa Spirit and Its
Education]. Chengtu: Chung-yang lu-chün chün-kuan hsüeh-hsiao, 1940.
—————. *Huang-p'u chün-hsiao chih chien-she* [The Construction of
the Whampoa Military Academy]. n.p., Chen-shih ch'u-pan she, 1943.
Teng Ying-ch'ao. "Hsin ti ling-tao fang-shih yü ch'e-ti chuan-pien" [The New
Method of Leadership and a Thorough Transformation]. *Tang ti chien-she,*
no. 1 (June 5, 1931). pp. 3-9.

"The Whampoa Military School: A Report Compiled from Soviet Documents." Modern Military Records Division, U.S. National Archive, File 2657-1-281/ 120 (A-44).

Thornton, Richard C. *The Comintern and the Chinese Communists, 1928-1931.* Seattle: University of Washington Press, 1969.

T'ien Chia-ku, ed. *K'ang-chan chiao-yü tsai Shen-pei* [Resistance War Education in North Shensi]. Hankow: Ming-jih ch'u-pan she, 1938.

Ting Shou-ho, Yin Hsü-i, and Chang Po-chao, ed. *Shih-yüeh ko-ming tui Chung-kuo ko-ming ti ying-hsiang* [The Influence of the October Revolution on the Chinese Revolution]. Peking: Jen-min ch'u-pan she, 1957.

Tōa Keizai chōsa kyoku. *Shina sobietō undō no kenkyū* [Research on the Chinese Soviet Movement]. Tokyo, 1934.

Totten, George Oakley, III. *The Social Democratic Movement in Prewar Japan.* New Haven: Yale University Press, 1966.

Townsend, James R. *Political Participation in Communist China.* Berkeley and Los Angeles: University of California Press, 1967.

Treadgold, Donald W., ed. *Soviet and Chinese Communism: Similarities and Differences.* Seattle: University of Washington Press, 1967.

Ts'ai Hsiao-kan. *Chiang-hsi Su-ch'ü hung-chün hsi-ts'uan hui-i* [Recollections of the Kiangsi Soviet Area, the Red Army and Sikang]. Hong Kong: Ta Chung-hua ch'u-pan she, 1970.

Ts'ao Ching-hua. "Tien-ti i Ch'iu-pai" [A Bit of Recollection about Ch'iu-pai]. *Wen-i pao,* no. 11 (June 15, 1955), pp. 47-48.

Ts'ao Po-i. *Chiang-hsi Su-wei-ai chih chien-she chi peng-kuei (1931-1934)* [The Establishment of the Kinagsi Soviet and its Collapse]. Taipei: Kuo-li cheng-chih ta-hsüeh tung-ya yen-chiu-so, 1969.

Ts'eng San. "Hung-se t'ung-hsin hsüeh-hsiao" [The Red Communications School]. In *Hsing-huo liao-yüan,* vol. 2. Peking: Jen-min wen-hsüeh ch'u-pan she, 1962.

Tsou Lu. *Chung-kuo Kuo-min-tang shih-kao* [Draft History of the Chinese Kuomintang]. 2 vols. Shanghai: Shang-wu yin-shu-kuan, 1945.

Tsung cheng-chih pu, ed. "Cheng-chih kung-tso chiang-i" [Lectures on Political work]. Shih-sou Collection, reel 8.

T'ung-i ch'u-pan she, ed. *Chung-kung chih chiao-yü* [Chinese Communist Education]. n.p., 1944.

Tung-yüan she. *K'ang-ta tung-t'ai.* [The Situation at K'ang-ta]. Hankow, 1939.

Ulam, Adam. *The Bolsheviks: The Intellectual and Political History of the Triumph of Communism in Russia.* New York: The Macmillan Co., 1965.

Van Slyke, Lyman P., ed. *The Chinese Communist Movement: A Report of the the United States War Department, July 1945.* Stanford, Calif.: Stanford University Press, 1968.

Vishnyakova-Akimova, Vera Vladimirovna. *Two Years in Revolutionary China 1925-1927,* trans. Steven I. Levine. Cambridge, Mass.: Harvard University East Asian Research Center, 1971.

Vogel, Ezra. *Canton under Communism.* New York: Harper Torchbooks, 1971.

——————. "From Revolutionary to Semi-Bureaucrat: The 'Regularisation' of Cadres." *China Quarterly,* no. 29 (January-March 1967), pp. 36-60.

Wakeman, Frederic, Jr. *History and Will: Philosphical Perspectives on Mao Tse-tung's Thought.* Berkeley: University of California Press, 1973.

Wales, Nym. *The Chinese Labor Movement.* New York: The John Day Co., 1945.

Wales, Nym. *Inside Red China.* New York: Doubleday, Doran and Co., 1939.
——————. *My Yenan Notebooks.* Madison, Conn.: Helen F. Snow, 1961.
——————. *Red Dust.* Stanford, Calif.: Stanford University Press, 1952.

Wang Chia-ch'iang. "Fan-tui tsu-chih shang ti chi-hui-chu-i, wei tang ti kai-tsao erh tou-cheng" [Oppose Organizational Opportunism, Struggle for the Reform of the Party], February 5, 1931. Reprinted in Hsiao Tso-liang, *Power Relations within the Chinese Communist Movement, 1930-1934,* vol. 2, pp. 331-334. Seattle: University of Washington Press, 1967.

Wang Chien-min. *Chung-kuo kung-ch'an-tang shih-kao* [Draft History of the Chinese Communist Party]. 3 vols. Taipei, 1965.

Wang Chüeh-yüan. *Liu-O hui-i lu* [Record of Recollections about Study in Russia]. Taipei: San-min shu-chü yu-hsien kung-szu, 1969.

Wang Hsüeh-wen. "Chinese Communists' Yenan Spirit and Educational Tradition." *Issues and Studies,* vol. 7, no. 5 (February 1971), pp. 50-63.

Wang Hung-hsün. "Wei-ta shih-yüeh ti hsi-li" [Baptism of Ten Great Years]. In *Hung-ch'i p'iao-p'iao,* vol. 4. Peking, 1957.

Wang I-chih. "I T'ai-lei" [Recalling T'ai-lei]. In *Hung-ch'i p'iao-p'iao,* vol. 5. Peking, 1957.

"Wang Jo-fei t'ung-chih ku-shih p'ien-tuan" [A Slice of the Story of Comrade Wang Jo-fei]. In *Hung-ch'i p'iao-p'iao,* vol. 5. Peking, 1957.

Wang Shou-tao. "The Peasant's Role in China's Revolution: A Memoir of the National Institute of the Peasant Movement." *China Reconstructs,* vol. 12, no. 10 (October 1963), pp. 24-28.

Wang, Y.C. *Chinese Intellectuals and the West, 1872-1949.* Chapel Hill: University of North Carolina Press, 1966.

Watt, John R. *The District Magistrate in Late Imperial China.* New York: Columbia University Press, 1972.

Wei Li. "Introduction to the Classical Works of Marxism-Leninism about the Time of the May 4 Movement." *Jen-min jih-pao,* May 5, 1959. Translated in *Survey of China Mainland Press,* no. 2021, pp. 7-9.

Wen Chi-tse. "Ch'ü Ch'iu-pai t'ung-chih chan-tou ti i-sheng" [Comrade Ch'ü Ch'iu-pai's Lifetime of Struggle]. *Hung-ch'i p'iao-p'iao,* vol. 5. Peking, 1957.

Wen-feng ch'u-pan she, ed. *Cheng-tun san-feng* [Rectify the Three Styles]. Hong Kong: Wen-feng ch'u-pan she, 1946.

Wen-hua chiao-yü yen-chiu hui, ed. *Hsüeh-hsi sheng-huo* [Study Life]. n.p., Wen-hua chiao-yü yen-chiu-hui, 1941.

White, D. Fedotoff. *The Growth of the Red Army.* Princeton: Princeton University Press, 1944.

Whiting, Allen S. *Soviet Policies in China, 1917-1924;* Stanford, Calif.: Stanford University Press, 1968.

Whitson, William, ed. *The Military and Political Power in China in the 1970's.* New York: Praeger Publishers, 1972.

Whitson, William W. with Chen-hsia Huang. *The Chinese High Command: A History of Communist Military Politics, 1927-71.* New York: Praeger Publishers, 1973.

Whyte, Martin King. *Small Groups and Political Rituals in China.* Berkeley and Los Angeles: University of California Press, 1974.

Wilbur, C. Martin and Lien-ying How, Julie, eds. *Documents on Communism, Nationalism and Soviet Advisers in China, 1918-1927.* New York: Columbia University Press, 1956.

Wilbur, C. Martin. "Forging the Weapons: Sun Yat-sen and the Kuomintang in Canton, 1924." Unpublished paper, Columbia University, February 19, 1966.

——————————. "The Influence of the Past: How the Early Years Helped to Shape the Future of the Chinese Communist Party." In *Party Leadership and Revolutionary Power in China,* ed. John Wilson Lewis. London: Cambridge University Press, 1970.

——————————. "The National Revolution in China, 1922-1928." Unpublished manuscript, Columbia University, April 24, 1969.

Wittfogel, Karl A. "The Legend of Maoism." *China Quarterly,* nos. 1 and 2 (January-March and April-June 1960).

Womack, Lynda Norene. "Anyuan: The Cradle of the Chinese Workers' Revolutionary Movement, 1921-1922." East Asian Institute Essay, Columbia University, 1970.

Wright, Mary Clabaugh, ed. *China in Revolution: The First Phase, 1900-1913.* New Haven: Yale University Press, 1968.

——————————. *The Last Stand of Chinese Conservatism.* New York: Atheneum, 1966.

Wu Tien-wei. "A Selected and Annotated Bibliography of the Ch'en Ch'eng Collection." Manuscript in preparation, Harvard University.

Wu Yü-chang. "Hui-i Po-ch'ü t'ung-chih" [Recalling Comrade Po-ch'ü]. *Chung-kuo ch'ing-nien,* no. 12 (June 16, 1960), pp. 13-15.

Yamamoto Katsunosuke and Arita Mitsuho. *Nihon kyōsan shugi undō shi* [History of the Japanese Communist Movement]. Tokyo, 1951.

Yang Chih-hua. "I Ch'iu-pai" [Recalling Ch'iu-pai]. In *Hung-ch'i p'iao-p'iao,* vol. 8, pp. 24-56. Peking, 1958.

Yang Yen-nan. *Chung-kung ti kan-pu chiao-yü* [Chinese Communist Cadre Education]. n.p. Yu-lien ch'u-pan she, 1945(?). Yushodo Microfilms, reel 4.

Yang Tzu-lieh. "Mo-ssu-k'o Chung-shan ta-hsüeh tou-cheng ti shih-k'uang" [The real situation of the struggles at Sun Yat-sen University in Moscow]. *Chan-wang,* no. 173 (April 16, 1969).

——————————. "Mo-ssu-k'o tung-fang ta-hsüeh" [Eastern University in Moscow]. *Chan-wang,* no. 169 (February 16, 1969).

"Yen-an fang-chien ching-yen chieh-shao" [Introduction to the Experience of Guarding against Traitors in Yenan]. In *Chung-kung tsui-chin tang-nei tou-cheng nei-mu,* ed. T'ung-i ch'u-pan she. n.p., n.d. Yushodo Microfilms, reel 12.

"Yen-an ta-hsüeh kai-k'uang" [General situation at Yenan University]. Mimeographed material, June 1944.

Yen-ta hsüeh wei-yüan-hui. "Yen-ta t'an-pai ta-hui yü san-t'ien t'u-chi kuei-ch'üan yün-tung ti ching-yen tsung-chieh" [Summary of the experience of the Yenan University Confession Meeting and Three Days Surprise Attack and Admonition Movement]. In *Chung-kung tsui-chin tang-nei tou-cheng nei-mu,* ed. T'ung-i ch'u-pan she. n.p., n.d. Yushodo Microfilms, reel 12.

Yu Che. *Hsin O hui-hsiang lu* [Reminiscences of New Russia]. Peking, 1925.

Yü Fei-p'eng. "Huang-p'u chün-hsiao k'ai-chuang chih hui-i" [Recollection of the Founding of the Whampoa Military Academy]. In *Ko-ming wen-hsien,* vol. 10. Taipei: Tang shih-hui, 1955.

"Yung-hu Su-wei-ai chiang-shou ho t'ao-lun ta-kang" [Lecture and Discussion Outline on Supporting the Soviets]. Su-wei-ti-fang wu-chang kan-pu hsüeh-hsiao cheng-chih k'o-pen chih erh, December 19,1932. Shih-sou Collection, reel 8.

Yung Ying-yue. "P'eng P'ai and the Kensetsushadomei: A Case Study of Sino-Japanese Relations among Left-wing Intellectuals in the Early Twentieth Century." Masters essay, Columbia University, 1971.

Index

Studies of the East Asian Institute

The Ladder of Success in Imperial China, by Ping-ti Ho. New York: Columbia University Press, 1962.

The Chinese Inflation, 1937-1949, by Shun-hsin Chou. New York: Columbia University Press, 1963.

Reformer in Modern China: Chang Chien, 1853-1926, by Samuel Chu. New York: Columbia University Press, 1965.

Research in Japanese Sources: A Guide, by Herschel Webb with the assistance of Marleigh Ryan. New York: Columbia University Press, 1965.

Society and Education in Japan, by Herbert Passin. New York: Bureau of Publications, Teachers College, Columbia University, 1965.

Agricultural Production and Economic Development in Japan, 1873-1922, by James I. Nakamura. Princeton: Princeton University Press, 1966.

Japan's First Modern Novel: Ukigumo of Futabatei Shimei, by Marleigh Ryan. New York: Columbia University Press, 1967.

The Korean Communist Movement, 1918-1948, by Dae-Sook Suh. Princeton: Princeton University Press, 1967.

The First Vietnam Crisis, by Melvin Gurtov. New York: Columbia University Press, 1967.

Cadres, Bureaucracy, and Political Power in Communist China, by A. Doak Barnett. New York: Columbia University Press, 1967.

The Japanese Imperial Institution in the Tokugawa Period, by Herschel Webb. New York: Columbia University Press, 1968.

Higher Education and Business Recruitment in Japan, by Koya Azumi. New York: Teachers College Press, Columbia University, 1969.

The Communists and Chinese Peasant Rebellions: A Study in the Rewriting of Chinese History, by James P. Harrison, Jr. New York: Atheneum, 1969.

How the Conservatives Rule Japan, by Nathaniel B. Thayer. Princeton: Princeton University Press, 1969.

Aspects of Chinese Education, edited by C. T. Hu. New York: Teachers College Press, Columbia University, 1970.

Documents of Korean Communism, 1918-1948, by Dae-Sook Suh. Princeton: Princeton University Press, 1970.

Japanese Education: A Bibliography of Materials in the English Language, by Herbert Passin. New York: Teachers College Press, Columbia University Press, 1970.

Economic Development and the Labor Market in Japan, by Koji Taira. New York: Columbia University Press, 1970.

The Japanese Oligarchy and the Russo-Japanese War, by Shumpei Okamoto. New York: Columbia University Press, 1970.

Imperial Restoration in Medieval Japan, by H. Paul Varley. New York: Columbia University Press, 1971.

Japan's Postwar Defense Policy, 1947-1968, by Martin E. Weinstein. New York: Columbia University Press, 1971.

Election Campaigning Japanese Style, by Gerald L. Curtis. New York: Columbia University Press, 1971.

China and Russia: The "Great Game," by O. Edmund Clubb. New York: Columbia University Press, 1971.

Money and Monetary Policy in Communist China, by Katharine Huang Hsiao. New York: Columbia University Press, 1971.

The District Magistrate in Late Imperial China, by John R. Watt. New York: Columbia University Press, 1972.

Law and Policy in China's Foreign Relations: A Study of Attitudes and Practice, by James C. Hsiung. New York: Columbia University Press, 1972.

Pearl Harbor as History: Japanese-American Relations, 1931-1941, edited by Dorothy Borg and Shumpei Okamoto, with the assistance of Dale K.A. Finlayson. New York: Columbia University Press, 1973.

Japanese Culture: A Short History, by H. Paul Varley. New York: Praeger, 1973.

Doctors in Politics: The Political Life of the Japan Medical Association, by William E. Steslicke. New York: Praeger, 1973.

Japan's Foreign Policy, 1868-1941: A Research Guide, edited by James William Morley. New York: Columbia Univerity Press, 1974.

The Japan Teachers Union: A Radical Interest Group in Japanese Politics, by Donald Ray Thurston. Princeton: Princeton University Press, 1973.

Palace and Politics in Prewar Japan, by David Anson Titus. New York: Columbia University Press, 1974.

The Idea of China: Essays in Geographic Myth and Theory, by Andrew March. Devon, England: David and Charles, 1974.

Origins of the Cultural Revolution, by Roderick MacFarquhar. New York: Columbia University Press, 1974.

Shiba Kōkan: Artist, Innovator, and Pioneer in the Westernization of Japan, by Calvin L. French. Tokyo: Weatherhill, 1974.

The Chinese Family in Taiwan, by Myron L. Cohen. New York: Columbia University Press, 1975.

Insei: Abdicated Sovereigns in the Politics of Late Heian Japan, by G. Cameron Hurst. New York: Columbia University Press, 1975.

Rebels and Bureaucrats: China's December 9ers, by John Israel and Donald W. Klein. Berkeley: University of California Press, 1955.

Neo-Confucianism and the Political Culture of Late Imperial China, by Thomas A. Metzger. New York: Columbia University Press, 1975.

Deterrent Diplomacy, edited by James William Morley. New York: Columbia University Press, 1975.

Embassy at War, by Harold Joyce Noble. Edited with an introduction by Frank Baldwin, Jr. Seattle: University of Washington Press, 1975.